The Late-Victorian Little Magazine

Edinburgh Critical Studies in Victorian Culture
Series Editor: Julian Wolfreys

Recent books in the series:

Rudyard Kipling's Fiction: Mapping Psychic Spaces
Lizzy Welby

The Decadent Image: The Poetry of Wilde, Symons and Dowson
Kostas Boyiopoulos

British India and Victorian Literary Culture
Máire ní Fhlathúin

Anthony Trollope's Late Style: Victorian Liberalism and Literary Form
Frederik Van Dam

Dark Paradise: Pacific Islands in the Nineteenth-Century British Imagination
Jenn Fuller

Twentieth-Century Victorian: Arthur Conan Doyle and the Strand Magazine, *1891–1930*
Jonathan Cranfield

The Lyric Poem and Aestheticism: Forms of Modernity
Marion Thain

Gender, Technology and the New Woman
Lena Wånggren

Self-Harm in New Woman Writing
Alexandra Gray

Suffragist Artists in Partnership: Gender, Word and Image
Lucy Ella Rose

Victorian Liberalism and Material Culture: Synergies of Thought and Place
Kevin A. Morrison

The Victorian Male Body
Joanne-Ella Parsons and Ruth Heholt

Nineteenth-Century Settler Emigration in British Literature and Art
Fariha Shaikh

The Pre-Raphaelites and Orientalism
Eleonora Sasso

The Late-Victorian Little Magazine
Koenraad Claes

Coastal Cultures of the Long Nineteenth Century
Matthew Ingleby and Matt P. M. Kerr

Dickens and Demolition: Literary Afterlives and Mid-Nineteenth-Century Urban Development
Joanna Hofer-Robinson

Artful Experiments: Ways of Knowing in Victorian Literature and Science
Philipp Erchinger

Victorian Poetry and the Poetics of the Literary Periodical
Caley Ehnes

The Victorian Actress in the Novel and on the Stage
Renata Kobetts Miller

Forthcoming volumes:

Her Father's Name: Gender, Theatricality and Spiritualism in Florence Marryat's Fiction
Tatiana Kontou

The Sculptural Body in Victorian Literature: Encrypted Sexualities
Patricia Pulham

Olive Schreiner and the Politics of Print Culture, 1883–1920
Clare Gill

Dickens's Clowns: Charles Dickens, Joseph Grimaldi and the Pantomime of Life
Johnathan Buckmaster

Victorian Auto/Biography: Problems in Genre and Subject
Amber Regis

Culture and Identity in Fin-de-Siècle Scotland: Romance, Decadence and the Celtic Revival
Michael Shaw

Gissing, Shakespeare and the Life of Writing
Thomas Ue

The Arabian Nights and Nineteenth Century British Culture
Melissa Dickson

The Aesthetics of Space in Nineteenth Century British Literature, 1851–1908
Giles Whiteley

For a complete list of titles published visit the Edinburgh Critical Studies in Victorian Culture web page at www.edinburghuniversitypress.com/series/ECVC

Also Available:
Victoriographies – A Journal of Nineteenth-Century Writing, 1790–1914, edited by Diane Piccitto and Patricia Pulham
ISSN: 2044–2416
www.eupjournals.com/vic

The Late-Victorian Little Magazine

Koenraad Claes

EDINBURGH
University Press

Edinburgh University Press is one of the leading university presses in the UK. We publish academic books and journals in our selected subject areas across the humanities and social sciences, combining cutting-edge scholarship with high editorial and production values to produce academic works of lasting importance. For more information visit our website: edinburghuniversitypress.com

Edinburgh University Press Ltd
The Tun – Holyrood Road,
12(2f) Jackson's Entry,
Edinburgh EH8 8PJ

First published in hardback by Edinburgh University Press 2018

Typeset in 11/13 Adobe Sabon by
IDSUK (DataConnection) Ltd

A CIP record for this book is available from the British Library

ISBN 978 1 4744 2621 3 (hardback)
ISBN 978 1 4744 2622 0 (paperback)
ISBN 978 1 4744 2623 7 (webready PDF)
ISBN 978 1 4744 2624 4 (epub)

Contents

Series Editor's Preface

'Victorian' is a term, at once indicative of a strongly determined concept and an often notoriously vague notion, emptied of all meaningful content by the many journalistic misconceptions that persist about the inhabitants and cultures of the British Isles and Victoria's Empire in the nineteenth century. As such, it has become a by-word for the assumption of various, often contradictory habits of thought, belief, behaviour and perceptions. Victorian studies and studies in nineteenth-century literature and culture have, from their institutional inception, questioned narrowness of presumption, pushed at the limits of the nominal definition, and have sought to question the very grounds on which the unreflective perception of the so-called Victorian has been built; and so they continue to do. Victorian and nineteenth-century studies of literature and culture maintain a breadth and diversity of interest, of focus and inquiry, in an interrogative and intellectually open-minded and challenging manner, which are equal to the exploration and inquisitiveness of its subjects. Many of the questions asked by scholars and researchers of the innumerable productions of nineteenth-century society actively put into suspension the clichés and stereotypes of 'Victorianism', whether the approach has been sustained by historical, scientific, philosophical, empirical, ideological or theoretical concerns; indeed, it would be incorrect to assume that each of these approaches to the idea of the Victorian has been, or has remained, in the main exclusive, sealed off from the interests and engagements of other approaches. A vital interdisciplinarity has been pursued and embraced, for the most part, even as there has been contest and debate amongst Victorianists, pursued with as much fervour as the affirmative exploration between different disciplines and differing epistemologies put to work in the service of reading the nineteenth century.

Edinburgh Critical Studies in Victorian Culture aims to take up both the debates and the inventive approaches and departures from convention that studies in the nineteenth century have witnessed for the last half century at least. Aiming to maintain a 'Victorian' (in the most positive sense of that motif) spirit of inquiry, the series' purpose is to continue and augment the cross-fertilisation of interdisciplinary approaches, and to offer, in addition, a number of timely and untimely revisions of Victorian literature, culture, history and identity. At the same time, the series will ask questions concerning what has been missed or improperly received, misread, or not read at all, in order to present a multi-faceted and heterogeneous kaleidoscope of representations. Drawing on the most provocative, thoughtful and original research, the series will seek to prod at the notion of the 'Victorian', and in so doing, principally through theoretically and epistemologically sophisticated close readings of the historicity of literature and culture in the nineteenth century, to offer the reader provocative insights into a world that is at once overly familiar, and irreducibly different, other and strange. Working from original sources, primary documents and recent interdisciplinary theoretical models, Edinburgh Critical Studies in Victorian Culture seeks not simply to push at the boundaries of research in the nineteenth century, but also to inaugurate the persistent erasure and provisional, strategic redrawing of those borders.

Julian Wolfreys

Acknowledgements

The author of this book has a lot to be thankful for. First of all I would like to thank the wonderful editors at Edinburgh University Press, Michelle Houston, James Dale, Adela Rauchova and Ersev Ersoy, for the smooth collaboration and their consistently positive attitude. Series editor Julian Wolfreys also could not have been more supportive. The majority of the images in this book were generously provided by the Mark Samuels Lasner Collection at the library of the University of Delaware. Modern-day Maecenas Mark Samuels Lasner and his research assistant Rebecca Olsen provide an invaluable service to the scholarly community in making available such important and often rare material, especially for those of us who do not live close to research libraries specialising in the British Fin de Siècle. Early versions of sections of this book were published in the journals *English Studies*, *Victorian Periodicals Review* and *Scottish Literary Review*, and in the *Dictionary of Nineteenth-Century Journalism*. I am grateful to the editors and peer reviewers of these esteemed publications for their feedback. It was tremendously helpful to be able to check the digitised holdings of several little magazines on the ever-growing webpage *Yellow Nineties Online*, edited by Dennis Denisoff and Lorraine Janzen Kooistra. I recommend all readers interested in avant-garde periodical media of the British Fin de Siècle to start their explorations there.

Much of the research for this book was undertaken during my doctoral fellowship at Ghent University (2007–11), which was funded by the Research Foundation Flanders (FWO). I am very grateful to my then supervisor Marysa Demoor for taking a gamble on an unknown student who had little to recommend himself except for his enthusiasm. Besides Marysa, the following people have also commented on material that has found its way into this book, or have selflessly provided me with research notes and typescripts of forthcoming publications:

Kostas Boyiopoulos, Laurel Brake, Leah Budke, Yoonjoung Choi, Yuri Cowan, Jolein De Ridder, Helena Gurfinkel, Marius Hentea, Andrew King, Frederick King, Lorraine Janzen Kooistra, Geert Lernout, Kate Macdonald, Rebecca N. Mitchell, Frederick Morel, Linda Peterson, Sarah Posman, Jasper Schelstraete, Michael Shallcross, Michael Shaw, Birgit Van Pumbroeck and Marianne Van Remoortel.

I have also benefited greatly from discussions with undergraduates who were brave enough to undertake dissertations on advanced issues in late-Victorian literature and on little magazines: Chloë Carrette, Esther De Baecke, Marlies Dekimpe, Eva De Ridder, Karen Desloover, Eline Hendrickx, Thomas Hoebeke, Jelke Lauwaet, Elien Uyttendaele and Jessica Vandevoorde. The 2016 class of the MA in English & American Lit at the Paris campus of the University of Kent kindly allowed me to test out some approaches. I hope that they are none the worse for it.

As Aestheticism always does, this work has oozed into the Real World, where ideally only 'peace comes dropping slow'. It has inflicted itself on my family, my friends, and other patient people of whom I could have been more appreciative than I have been. Thank you all.

Thy soul I know not from thy body, nor
Thee from myself, neither our love from God.

D. G. Rossetti, 'Heart's Hope'

Introduction

'*Cedo junioribus*.' In the introspective month of December of the year 1896, not even two years after making his debut, the essayist and caricaturist Max Beerbohm announced that he would 'withdraw in favour of the younger' and retire from the literary scene. With the rising publisher John Lane at the Bodley Head, he published his *Works of Max Beerbohm*, consisting of seven essays that had originally appeared in artistic-literary periodicals such as the *Yellow Book* and the *Savoy*, that are categorised in the academic discipline of periodical studies as 'little magazines' for their small-scale production and limited audience. The epilogue to this valedictory collection was a short piece entitled 'Diminuendo' that appeared simultaneously in the annual *Pageant* under the title 'Be It Cosiness'. Now that 'the tumult of [his] disillusioning was past', having reached the ripe age of twenty-three, the author felt that he should look back upon his aesthetic education. With a grand gesture he yielded the stage (for a few months anyway) to 'younger men, with months of activity before them, with fresher schemes and notions, with newer enthusiasm'.[1] The illusion that he had given up was the possibility of an integration of medium and message, form and content, ethics and aesthetics, that would be necessary to produce what has come to be known as the 'Total Work of Art'. This book tells the story of how during the Fin de Siècle this ideal shaped the British avant-garde journals that are the first examples of the still thriving genre of the little magazine, and why understanding the motivations behind it is key to grasping the often puzzling diversity of the schools and movements that are nowadays grouped together as Aestheticism.

In his abdication speech, Beerbohm reminisces about his arrival as a student in Oxford in the autumn of 1890, eager to attend the lectures of the legendary Walter Pater, but being laughed at by his assigned tutor when he declared the wish. The keen fresher soon understood the cause for this hilarity when he ran into the Aesthete don in the local Ryman's, consuming in his 'gem-like flame' a portfolio of prints:

> a small, thick, rock-faced man, whose top-hat and gloves of bright dog-skin struck one of the many discords in that little city of learning or laughter. The serried bristles of his mustachio made for him a false-military air. I think I nearly went down when they told me that this was Pater.[2]

This was but 'one of the many discords', as he found plenty to be disappointed about. Oxford itself had already looked less romantic than he had imagined it, and both town and gown were very dull. 'Could it be that there was at length no beautiful environment wherein a man might sound the harmonies of his soul?'[3] He made occasional escapes to London to seek refuge in Aestheticist safe spaces that like-minded seekers had set up, some of which took the form of allegedly uncompromising print publications from which all mundane corruptions seemed to have been barred. Having tried 'writing a little for a yellow quarterly' (of course the *Yellow Book*) and thereby achieving only 'that *succès de fiasco* which is always given to a young writer of talent',[4] he decided to call it quits. He concludes that he would rather retreat into a small suburban villa, devote himself to the pleasures of a well-stocked library, and cultivate his mind undisturbed.

Like all of Beerbohm's essays, this mock-memoir is more than a string of witty anecdotes. It is in fact a critique of an ideal that was prevalent among artists and authors of the late nineteenth century, and an apt commentary on how theory relates to practice in art and literature. Like other young men at the time, Beerbohm had come to the university hoping to find there the inspiring atmosphere that had nurtured a revered preceding generation of artists and writers, from the followers of John Ruskin and of the Pre-Raphaelites such as William Morris and A. C. Swinburne, to former acolytes of Pater, such as Oscar Wilde. His explanation why the place did not meet his expectations is revealing. He refers to the faults he finds in Oxford as 'discords': instances of a lack of harmonious correspondence between notes in music, or, metaphorically, between constituent parts in any other situation that is evaluated on its internal coherence. The university town would not have fulfilled its purpose as a site for self-development because, with its many jarring notes, it would not furnish the appropriate context. Quite remarkably, Beerbohm loses his faith in Pater after meeting the man in person: 'I suppose it was when at length I saw him that I first knew him to be fallible.'[5] Pater as failed representative of his own message comes to embody the lack of correspondence between form and content that is characteristic of Oxford as a whole, and for that matter the entire world.

Beerbohm's high demands fit in with what Jonathan Freedman has pointed out as the major common theme of British Aestheticism: 'the exploration of cultural contradictions – but without abandoning the option of contradicting contradiction itself, without the loss of the nostalgia for a lost unity and the desire to project such a unity into the vision of a future consummation'.[6] A previous generation had felt this problem as keenly, and the correction of such 'discords' may well be termed the fundamental concern shared across the diverse perspectives that have come to be jointly known as Aestheticism. For all their diversity, the politicised aesthetics of Ruskin, the interior decoration of Edward Godwin, the meticulously planned exhibitions of James Whistler, the cooperative enterprises of the Arts and Crafts Movement, up to the dandies taking after Wilde, all questioned the conventional demarcations of art by bourgeois society. Ignoring the conventional wisdom that sought to keep art in its proper place where it could not encroach upon established – though increasingly questioned – moral, religious and social duties, these movements sought to expand the notion of what constituted art, involving contextual elements into their multimedial artistic projects that were thereby 'aestheticised', or assessed by principles analogous to those that before had only pertained to the abstracted, quarantined artwork.

Aestheticism thereby entails an acute awareness of what Derrida has called the 'parergon'; a conceptual frame around the work that is '*au bord, à bord*', an untranslatable pun rendered by his translators as 'on the border, on board'.[7] The realm of the aesthetic is affirmed by bordering non-artistic phenomena that are seen as setting off its limits, but that by their alterity challenged many late-nineteenth-century artists and authors to further expand their operations in the hope that these imperfect surroundings could somehow be integrated into the aesthetic project as well. This is a work-in-progress that can be temporarily halted along the way, but never finished, and the advancing avant-garde is bound to be faced with resistance from an antagonised outside world or 'mainstream' unwilling to be converted.

Beerbohm's satirical account of Aestheticist pedantry tells us what this might lead to. He is superbly acting out the 'dangers' into which 'weaker minds' would be led, according to one early detractor, by the seminal conclusion to Pater's *Studies in the History of the Renaissance* (1873).[8] After being lost to all causes but the pursuit of Beauty, Beerbohm claims to have become convinced that he was to shun all that is of no aesthetic value, which pushed to its most extreme interpretation effectively means alienating oneself from everyday reality. The only possible solution was to try to stimulate change through superb examples of what could be. This is what Beerbohm attempted to do in London among the artistic and literary avant-garde, who were issuing a specific kind of journal known as 'little magazines' to publicise their ideals and promote their work. His articles in the *Yellow Book*, the genre's most famous exponent, had caused a big stir when they first came out, and were one of the main targets for attacks by self-proclaimed anti-Decadent critics. The first issue of that magazine (April 1894) featured his well-known essay 'A Defence of Cosmetics', in which he defended the view that England in the 1890s was so dreary that thorough artistic interventions would be needed to create initially superficial beauty for society to live up to, a cliché of this period that for instance also pops up throughout the writings and histrionic lectures of Wilde, and not unlikely an impish perversion of the politicised aesthetics of socially engaged activists such as William Morris.[9]

His 'Cosmetics' essay, said in the following issue to have been dismissed by one (probably fictitious) critic as 'the most nauseous thing in all literature',[10] was taken as representative of the *Yellow Book* in early contemporary reviews. Its editor Henry Harland and initial art director Aubrey Beardsley sought out such sensational contributions, but also made their magazine an attractive and well-made object that would assure the reader from a simple glance at the bindings that the literature and pictorial art contained therein was as remote as possible from the disposable content of the also materially disposable mainstream magazines. According to Murray Pittock, for the British avant-garde of the Fin de Siècle, 'the magazine, both in its contents and method of production, was to act as a complete statement of its own alternativeness: its aesthetic unity symbolised its aesthetic integrity, its commitment to art over bourgeois society'.[11] Periodicals like the *Yellow Book* stood out through the conspicuous involvement into their aesthetic project of what Gérard Genette calls the 'paratext', easiest understood as the above-mentioned parergic 'frame' specific to printed texts. Genette places under this heading all the manifold elements that turn the ideal work into a material object: for example, cover and endpapers designs, typesetting and choice of typeface, typographical or engraved ornaments, and the properties of the used materials, like inks, bindings and paper. The paratext is

> a zone between text and off-text, a zone not only of transition but also of transaction: a privileged place of a pragmatics and a strategy, of an influence on the public, an influence that – whether well or poorly understood and achieved – is at the service of a better reception for the text and a more pertinent reading of it.[12]

Genette metaphorically calls the paratext '*un seuil*', and this 'threshold' may be said to be crossed by the Aestheticist little magazines. Next to their innovative content, this attention to design as well as production and distribution processes was what set these little magazines apart from the periodicals of the perceived mainstream against which they opposed themselves in order to affirm their own avant-garde position. Not only were their contributors unified through common goals and did they frequently present their work as cross-medial collaborations; by seizing strictly material features as an opportunity for artistic expression, and taking control of how they were being published and distributed, the little magazine approaches the status of a Total Work of Art.

This present study aims to provide the first history of the ways in which the most important little magazines of the Victorian age sought to present themselves as thoroughly conceptualised aesthetic projects, which, given the centrality of this endeavour to these journals, simultaneously makes it a history of this periodical genre in its earliest, still often disregarded stages. This book can be read in several ways depending on the specific interests and time constraints of the reader. Read front-to-back (or back-to-front if you are approaching the subject from the subsequent modernist era), it delivers a historical narrative of the development of the little magazine genre in the Victorian era. This will help readers gain an overview of the diversity in these early little magazines, and of how their avant-garde producers interacted between themselves in their pages, and engaged with the uninitiated outside when targeting readerships or antagonising a mainstream press that was not always that different from themselves. Each chapter can however also be read on its own, as each will deal with one proposed category of little magazine, whereby the extensive discussion of specific publications is introduced by means of contextual sections providing art- and literary-historical background.

Chapter 1 opens with a general definition of the little magazine genre, and then illustrates its early history by looking at two titles that have been suggested as its starting point: the Pre-Raphaelite journal *The Germ* (1850), and the closely affiliated *Oxford and Cambridge Magazine* (1856) that anticipates the Arts and Crafts Movement. The emphasis of Aestheticist journals on the formal and material aspects of the printed text stems from Pre-Raphaelite book design and the contemporaneous mid- to late-Victorian 'Revival of Fine Printing', which I argue developed alongside the little magazine genre. All through the second half of the nineteenth century, the British avant-garde consisted of various intermingling groups, all of which had prominent members dedicated to applied arts, the various book arts being a particular favourite. These groups propagated their ideals through usually short-lived little magazines that were platforms for their views as well as portfolios of their increasingly diverse work in illustration and book design. This means that these magazines communicated their manifestly heterodox message not only verbally in critical articles and through literature, and they were not merely portable exhibition spaces for the reproduced pictorial art either. By meticulous attention to how their content was presented, these journals now also signalled paratextually that they did not adhere to the artistic views and production methods of the mainstream. Marshall McLuhan's creed 'the medium is the message' may sound to us like a hackneyed phrase of the 1960s,[13] but the idea would already have made perfect sense to some late-Victorian designers of books and periodicals. Whereas these two early little magazines do not show the same degree of conceptual integration as later titles, both feature preliminary experiments that will be elaborated on later, and they contain the first publications of some of the later most respected leading practitioners and theorists of Aestheticism in Britain.

Chapter 2 is dedicated to a later pioneering little magazine, the *Hobby Horse* (1884/6–94) initially issued by the early Arts and Crafts organisation the Century Guild, which considered the paratext as much as its actual contents a zone for artistic production, out of an ideologically motivated aesthetic artisanship. Each issue of the magazine is thereby suggested to have a lasting relevance beyond the next number, and it commands for its applied artist producers the same respect that is usually reserved for artists working within the category of 'Fine Art'. This was timely, as the formerly greater prestige of the latter was then increasingly being questioned. After the demise of the Guild in 1893, this periodical was temporarily revived by the enterprising publishers Elkin Mathews and John Lane at the Bodley Head to boost that firm's Print-Revivalist credentials as an asset in the literary market. As we shall see, the *Hobby Horse* thereby not only played a vital role in the Arts and Crafts Movement and the promotion of the Revival of Fine Printing, it is also an early example of how originally avant-garde principles are sometimes difficult to distinguish from plainly commercial strategies.

This is true even for the seemingly most uncompromising and thereby littlest little magazines, as Chapter 3 explains. The critical success of the *Hobby Horse* encouraged the foundation of the *Dial* (1889–97) by Charles Ricketts and Charles Shannon, struggling artists who chose to circulate their splendid work in periodical form in order to draw more public attention to themselves and a coterie of select friends. The single issue of the *Pagan Review* (1892), written entirely by William Sharp under various pseudonyms, contains no pictorial art but has interesting typographical designs, and can be read as a writerly portfolio in which the author experimented with different voices and tested their appeal for potential future writing projects. The *Page* (1898–1901) of Edward Gordon Craig, who would gain prominence as a poster artist and a leading stage designer of the modernist era, was almost entirely filled by its editor, who used the magazine to advertise his services as a designer of bookplates and personalised dinner menus. Like the *Hobby Horse* and to a lesser extent *The Germ*, the *Dial*, the *Pagan Review* and the *Page* were thereby in large part publicity schemes for the publishers, artists and authors involved.

Chapter 4 discusses at length the two best-publicised little magazines of the 1890s, whose relationship reveals much about the reception of their conceptual integration of form and content in wider late-Victorian print culture. The slyly marketed *Yellow Book* (1894–7) is probably the most notorious yet also the most ingeniously commercialist little magazine of all time, and it styled itself a 'book' for good reason. By emulating the appearance of a book, its editors and publisher hoped to safeguard their publication against the ephemerality and relative lack of prestige of periodical texts. For a while they certainly succeeded, and the magazine drew a number of large advertisers and sold remarkably well until it was implicated in the Wilde trial in 1895. Fascinatingly, its look had at that point become so recognisable that the magazine, as well as its rivals at the *Savoy* (1896) founded by the *Yellow Book*'s ousted alleged 'Decadent' ringleaders Arthur Symons and Aubrey Beardsley, felt that they needed to rethink their design aesthetic. Clearly, some material characteristics associated with the little magazine had become iconic and associated with their supposedly corrupted and corrupting content. The strategy behind both magazines' 'marketed notoriety', to borrow a phrase from Laurel Brake, would soon peak, and the literal disintegration of the form occurs at the same time as the waning of critical interest in the aesthetics and poetics promoted by these magazines.[14]

Whereas the previously discussed little magazines were all published from London, Chapter 5 demonstrates that some relevant journals were also produced in other places in Britain. These journals were often the organs of localised organisations that wanted to engage with the local communities in which they operated. The *Quest* (1894–6), issued by the Birmingham Guild of Handicraft, with the Arts and Craft Movement's major theorists Ruskin and Morris 'resisted any structural differentiation between the worlds of production and consumption, preferring the unified ideal of a community of producers meeting common needs through mutual cooperation'.[15] Outside of England, writers of the budding Celtic Revival wrote for several little magazines, but no artistic and literary journals of ambitions comparable to the aforementioned were set up before the early twentieth century. One notable exception was the Edinburgh-based *Evergreen* (1895–6), a splendid example of a conceptually integrated periodical, this time not only inspired by a local variant of the collaborative spirit characterising the Arts and Crafts journals, but also meant to exemplify an advocated 'organic' unity for the city where its producers lived and worked, and from there for Scotland and 'North Britain' at large.

The British Fin-de-Siècle avant-garde peaked in productivity and public attention around the middle of the 1890s, but even afterwards, its integrated design aesthetic continued to exert an explicit influence. Significantly, it can be discerned in periodicals that feature very similar content and many of the same contributors as the little magazines, but that had given up on the avant-garde position that these little magazines had so insistently claimed. Chapter 6 shows how the *Dial* coterie moved on to publications such as the *Pageant* (1896–7) and the children's gift book *Parade* (1897) that imported into the Aestheticist format features from the decidedly mainstream gift book genre, or the *Dome* (1897–1900) that presented itself as an insider's alternative to the most commercially successful art magazines of its period. All three journals in this chapter relativised the former vanguardist strategy of their producers through their contents as well as through their presentation, and even questioned the validity of the purist doctrines that only a few years before were deemed essential, including that of the Total Work of Art.

The Little Magazine as Total Work of Art

The conceptual unity of form and content that is conspicuous in several little magazines of the mid- to late-Victorian period could fulfil different functions, the predominance of which varied from one magazine to another, and was subject to changes in the context and the literary marketplace. For instance, it functioned as an organising principle that brought cohesion to the contents, as a demonstration of the collaboration between different contributors and producers, or as palpable proof of the feasibility of advocated design and production canons by means of the portable and relatively affordable medium of a printed text. As we shall see, this aim has obvious parallels with the so-called 'Book Beautiful' or 'Ideal Book' of the same period theorised by influential designers of the contemporaneous Revival of Fine Printing such as William Morris and T. J. Cobden-Sanderson, for whom all material aspects of the book (bindings, typography, page layout, ornaments, illustration) would be painstakingly coordinated, and also, as often was the case, collectively undertaken by several artist-craftsmen.[16] Magazines have to overcome the additional challenge of being less stable texts than books: periodicals need to establish continuity throughout their run, and to interact continuously with an envisaged readership. According to Ian Fletcher, the conceptual unity of Aestheticist little magazines reflects a desire for a stabilisation of the magazine format that must be considered

> part of the Romantic programme that had always been for 'a progressive universal poetry' that transcended the genres. [The little magazines] had aspirations towards becoming the venue of total art; in the last two decades of the century, magazines in England, Germany, France, Austria and the United States aspired to reach full fusion of type, paper, illustration, letterpress.[17]

The most famous application of this 'Romantic programme' is no doubt Wagner's *Gesamtkunstwerk*. In his most acclaimed music dramas, the German composer sought to achieve a balance between the different 'sister arts' of acting, music and poetry that would elevate each individual component art to a higher level. As he states in his essay *The Artwork of the Future* (1849), 'the solitary unit is unfree'.[18] By the lavish stage decorations and above all the construction of the Bayreuth *Festspielhaus* specifically for performances of his work, he introduced yet more component arts into his expansive artistic projects. Wagner had high hopes for his *Gesamtkunstwerk* that went far beyond successful performances of his music dramas, envisioning that they permeate through society and become the catalyst for a much needed social reunification process throughout Europe, which during the second half of the nineteenth century was plagued by revolutionary tensions over social inequality and stalling democratic reform. Both his artistic and his theoretical work exerted an inestimable influence all over Europe, especially during the 1880s and 1890s, when specialist journals were dedicated to his thought, such as the Parisian *Revue Wagnérienne* (1885–8) and the London-based *Meister* (1888–95), and he is a regular reference in the little magazines under scrutiny in this book. There he is invariably praised for the example that he set in harmonising art forms to achieve a sublime aesthetic experience.[19] The common term 'Total Work of Art' that was used before as a categorical term for sites of cross-medial art and literary periodicals in particular, is a popular translation of Wagner's term *Gesamtkunstwerk*, which in critical literature has come to have a far wider coverage than the operatic legacy of the celebrated composer. It is invoked regularly in assessments of other kinds of artworks, and even of political events that bear no obvious relationship to art at all.

In his tellingly entitled critical history of *The Total Work of Art: From Bayreuth to Cyberspace* (2007), Matthew Smith assures us that

> [i]t takes form in literature, in music, in opera, in painting, in dance, in theatre, in drama, in film, in politics. Baudelaire, Mallarmé, Marinetti, Mann; Wagner, Strauss, Schönberg, Böcklin, Kandinsky, Moholy-Nagy; Diaghilev, Schlemmer, Duncan; Maeterlinck, Meyerhold, Appia, Craig; Gropius, Corbusier, Van der Rohe; Eisenstein, Riefenstahl, Disney. Mussolini, Hitler, Stalin.[20]

Because the term 'Total Work of Art' has been applied to so many vastly different phenomena, and surfaces in widely dissimilar historical and national contexts, definitions have to focus on the methodology by which such works are constituted rather than on an essential common meaning or function. It will, however, take us a long way if we understand it as an artistic project whereby several art forms are joined to strive for a combined effect that could not be achieved separately, the whole greater than the sum of its parts. As David Roberts has noted, where such an endeavour is found, it is invariably undertaken according to a theory of the unity of the arts (explicit or implicit) in the service of a more or less concrete worldview that it is meant to illustrate and exemplify.[21] The Total Work of Art is an organising principle for the construction and perception of the material work rather than a concrete object in itself, into which the audience has to be invited to participate. The unity of Total Works of Art is realised through the aesthetic experience of the artist(s) themselves and of a receptive audience, existing, as art historian Harald Szeemann states, 'only as fictional greatness, as articulated thought constructions of a Wholeness'. It can therefore only be properly grasped in its 'relationship as thought construct to actual practice'.[22] When we study the workings of Total Art, we are therefore looking for the means by which a cross-medial work would signal its cohesion and the rationale behind it to its audience. Nothing is or is not Total Art; it is made so through a compact of producer(s) and consumers.

When the work in question is a printed text, like with a little magazine, the arrangement of paratextual elements, which Jerome McGann refers to as the text's 'bibliographic code',[23] will have to facilitate a reading that ties each element of the material text together. Roberts, discussing Mallarmé's thirty-year thought experiment of *Le Livre* (see Chapter 3), a mystic book that was to capture the whole of reality, reminds us that this 'can offer no more than an ideal representation, to be accomplished through the reading of the Book'.[24] The artist/author must through a combination of verbal, visual and material hints entice the audience to participate in the realisation of the ideal unity of the artwork. Poet, critic and tireless contributor to little magazines Arthur Symons remarked of his two greatest idols: '[c]arry the theories of Mallarmé to a practical conclusion, and you have Wagner. It is his failure not to be Wagner. [. . .] It was "the work" that he dreamed of, the new art, the new religion, whose precise form in the world he was never quite able to settle.'[25]

Wagner's 'practical conclusion' of bringing his ideal Total Art into the light of day, however, led to another kind of disappointment. According to Symons's contemporary G. B. Shaw, Wagner's vision was contaminated by the commercialism that threatens every mass spectacle, and the *Meister* died thoroughly disillusioned about the feasibility of his great life's work.[26] The inevitable, continually deferred realisation of the Total Work of Art is caused by the utopian nature of all such endeavours, that concerns both the inward aspect of the formal organisation and the outward aspect of how the work is introduced to its public through means of publication, performance or unveiling. As has been stated before, the avant-garde little magazine as a site of Total Art is an expansive medium, and this places it in a paradoxical situation. It needs to involve an audience to concretise the unity of its components, but at the same time it needs to posit itself against the outside world. Or, as Smith puts it:

> The *Gesamtkunstwerk* suffers from two principal neuroses: a fear of absorption from without and a fear of contamination from within. The former [. . .] generally takes the form of a fear of absorption into the larger totality of mass spectacle. The latter [. . .] generally takes either the form of a fear of contamination by corrupt bodies of the (racial, sexual, ethnic, class-based) Other.[27]

In order to function in the outside world, the Total Work of Art is forced to engage with the socio-economic context from which it would set itself apart. Out of sheer financial necessity, little magazines often needed to accept into their integrated projects certain foreign bodies that they could not do without. The threat of 'contamination' posed by these to the integrity of the artwork magazine would then need to be neutralised by either banishing them demonstratively to a parergic margin, or in some way aestheticising them so as to make them seem integrated into the artwork. We cannot allow ourselves to be taken in by these ruses, clever as they often are, and will investigate them for every magazine that is discussed. For instance, we will look at the advertisements that were present in some form in most little magazines, often banished to various kinds of supplemental sections which could be easily ignored and have proven more ephemeral than the journals they came with. Sometimes higher-quality prints were inserted loosely or tipped in to be collected by readers in albums and commonplace books, or framed and hung on the wall. In light of the hypothesis of the Total Work of Art, the ambiguous nature of such very particular paratextual addenda is highly problematic, as they simultaneously are and are not part of the periodical they are supplementing. It is revealing to see how editors dealt with the problems of contamination, and how these strategies relate to their editorial policy in aesthetic as well as commercial matters. An informed reading of such items thereby offers a rare chance to call into question the traditional separation of aesthetics and commercial positioning. The relationship between the avant-garde and the mainstream is always more ambiguous than it may seem, because even a periodical on the periphery of the market is still conditioned by the workings of its centre. Whether dismissing perceived inadequacies or emulating successful features of their rivals, little magazines are characterised by distinct marketing practices that were determined by the choices they made in bringing their periodical to the market.

The threat of 'absorption' entails that the outside world towards which the artistic project seeks to expand manages to turn this challenge to its own advantage. It is this threat that Wagner, according to Shaw, had succumbed to. His vision would have failed because his work was appropriated by the alienated plutocratic reality which it sought to oppose. There is, of course, no such thing as a pure aesthetic. As Regenia Gagnier has noted, 'taste, understood as evaluative distinction, has had everything to do with property and individualism, whether in the sphere of practical or philosophical aesthetics'.[28] Aestheticism in particular has often been accused of whitewashing, wittingly or unwittingly, the very kind of commercialism that it claimed to oppose. Adorno in *Aesthetic Theory* (1970) repeatedly referred to the paradoxical influence of *Jugendstil*, specifically a term for German and Austrian currents of Art Nouveau but including for him too British Aestheticist authors such as Wilde, which

> with its ideology of the reintroduction of art into life [. . .] served as preludes to the culture industry. Progressive subjective differentiation, the heightening and expansion of the sphere of aesthetic stimuli, made these stimuli manipulable; they were able to be produced for the cultural marketplace.[29]

Adorno observes that the beautiful 'interiors of a chic aestheticism' that form the setting of texts like Wilde's *Dorian Gray* 'resemble smart antiques shops and auction halls and thus the commercial world that Wilde ostensibly disdained'.[30] As critics such as Margaret Stetz have observed, books and magazines of the period in a similar way cultivated in their readership a form of lucrative bibliophilia.[31] Every collector and connoisseur, inevitably, is also a consumer.

During the 1890s, various socio-ideological profiles may be discerned in the British avant-garde that present different, sometimes competing visions. Militant artistic craftsmen aiming at greater social equality might price themselves out of the competition and appeal solely to a small elite, while artists and authors with no interest in politics may suddenly find themselves minor celebrities and ironically address a larger public. Every periodical, be it defiantly heterodox or complacently orthodox, aims at its own particular ideal readership. Especially in the context of a turbulent class politics like that of the late-Victorian age, the commercial interests of a periodical cannot be situated in a spectrum as an absolute opposite to the aesthetic, but both aspects need to be studied together to learn to what purpose and for whom these magazines were published. Whereas some little magazine editors were happiest catering for a small and exclusive audience, others did not scruple to seek wider public attention.

Adorno had already reflected on this topic in *Dialectic of Enlightenment* (1944), specifically addressing the complex relationship of the Total Work of Art ideal to mass media. This polemical study is famous for its critique of the above-mentioned Culture Industry. As of the twentieth century, media such as '[f]ilms, radio and magazines make up a system which is uniform as a whole and in every part', 'derisively fulfilling the Wagnerian dream of the *Gesamtkunstwerk*'.[32] Adorno and Horkheimer find that it had become exceedingly difficult to evade capitalist recuperation, as the protean Culture Industry is able to absorb its challengers. Whenever we perform culture (in a broad sense including but not restricted to the practice and appreciation of the arts), we are compelled to follow the laws of the market, and its logic permeates our lives to such an extent that it determines what we come into contact with and can aspire to produce ourselves. The cynical result is that even when we think we are making a difference, we are usually at best suggesting to the Culture Industry that it adapt itself in order to accommodate a shift in consumer expectations:

> Realistic dissidence is the trademark of anyone who has a new idea in business. In the public voice of modern society accusations are seldom audible; if they are, the perceptive can already detect signs that the dissident will soon be reconciled.[33]

The avant-garde, inevitably starting off in the position of challenger, can all too easily be absorbed into the mainstream.

From the earliest examples to the present day, little magazines are inevitably part of the market and need to position themselves intelligently in relation to the rest of the market if they want to achieve their aims. Their integrated and expansionist artistic projects may have been intended to repel the influences of an outside world which they wanted to save from corruption, but to what extent were they themselves 'contaminated' or even 'absorbed'? Compromises will have to be made concerning what a publication is known for, and how it relates to what may be found elsewhere, but: to what extent are little magazines then a sustainable alternative to a perceived mainstream that they attack as limiting and even oppressive? There are serious conundrums behind the comical crisis of the Incomparable Max.

Notes

1. Beerbohm, 'Be It Cosiness', p. 235.
2. Ibid., p. 230.
3. Ibid., p. 231.
4. Ibid., p. 235. Emphasis original.
5. Ibid., p. 230.
6. Freedman, *Professions of Taste*, pp. 8–9.
7. Derrida, *Truth in Painting*, p. 54.
8. Wordsworth, 'John Wordsworth on Pater's Philosophy', p. 62.
9. Beerbohm, 'Defence of Cosmetics', p. 71.
10. Beerbohm, 'Letter to the Editor', p. 281.

11. Pittock, *Spectrums of Decadence*, p. 163.
12. Genette, *Paratexts*, p. 2.
13. McLuhan, *Understanding Media*, p. 9.
14. See Brake, 'Marketing Notoriety', *passim*.
15. Adamson, *Embattled Avant-Gardes*, p. 51.
16. While the majority of the participants in the movement were obviously male, as is reflected in the choice for the male pronoun throughout this book, an increasing number of women were involved with the Arts and Crafts Movement, and these should of course not be forgotten.
17. Fletcher, 'Decadence and the Little Magazines', p. 173.
18. Wagner, 'Artwork of the Future', p. 96.
19. See Sutton, *Aubrey Beardsley and British Wagnerism in the 1890s*, *passim*.
20. Smith, *Total Work of Art*, p. 8.
21. Roberts, *Total Work of Art in European Modernism*, pp. 7–10.
22. 'Gesamtkunstwerke existieren also nur als fiktive Größe, als zur Sprache gebrachte gedankliche Konstruktionen eines Ganzen'; 'das Verhältnis von Gedankenkonstruktion zu faktischem Handeln' (Szeemann, *Hang zum Gesamtkunstwerk*, p. v).
23. McGann, *Textual Condition*, pp. 56–8.
24. Roberts, *Total Work of Art in European Modernism*, p. 133.
25. Symons, 'Mallarmé', p. 180.
26. Shaw, *Perfect Wagnerite*, p. 161.
27. Smith, *Total Work of Art*, p. 115.
28. Gagnier, *Insatiability of Human Wants*, p. 12.
29. Adorno, *Aesthetic Theory*, p. 312.
30. Ibid., p. 21.
31. See Stetz, 'Sex, Lies, and Printed Cloth', *passim*.
32. Adorno and Horkheimer, *Dialectic of Enlightenment*, pp. 120, 124.
33. Ibid., p. 132.

Chapter 1

The Germs of a Genre: *The Germ* and the *Oxford and Cambridge Magazine*

What is a little magazine?

There are few terms pertaining to print culture that are used more absent-mindedly than 'magazine'. In everyday situations, we use it as a self-evident alternative for 'journal', 'review' or any number of generic names we give to a periodical publication that is not a newspaper. Each of these terms, however, has its own historical connotations. The metaphor is lost in contemporary English, but 'magazine' (from Italian: *magazzino*) originally referred to 'a storehouse'. A periodical that styles itself 'a magazine' thereby suggests that the publishers wish the text to be considered a storehouse of information. This is a popular conceptual metaphor in the nineteenth-century press, and several variants occurred. Some preferred the confidential-sounding 'repository', for example the *Ladies' Repository* (1841–76) and the theological *Monthly Repository* (1806–37), while others favoured the more presumptuous 'museum', as in the *Lady's Museum* (1798–1832), and there even was a successful monthly *Ladies' Treasury* (1857–95). These names are all linked by a shared metaphorical background, but the neutral and therefore perhaps most productive 'magazine' has proved the most enduring. Over the course of the eighteenth and nineteenth centuries, a 'magazine' came to be understood as a periodical publication that accommodated a variety of authorial voices, unlike the largely single-authored essay periodicals of the eighteenth century such as *The Spectator* (1711–12/15) by Addison and Steele or Dr Johnson's *Rambler* (1750–2). Magazines would also contain a variety of textual genres, unlike review periodicals such as the *Edinburgh Review* (1802–1929). Magazines would predominantly contain original material (unlike periodical miscellanies of which few clear-cut examples existed in the Victorian age), and did not specialise in coverage of current events (unlike newspapers). Some publications did not pigeonhole themselves neatly in the categories that we place them in now, and the deceptive appropriation of titles or formal features suggested with more prestigious periodical genres for marketing purposes was rife. For instance, as we shall see, some of the magazines under scrutiny in this book appropriated characteristics then associated with review periodicals to increase their prestige.

The qualified term 'little magazine' is if anything more problematic, as this was only applied in hindsight to publications which clearly share several important features, but which the proprietors may not have thought of as 'little'. It was not current in the nineteenth century, being likely only coined by the French critic Remy de Gourmont in *Les Petites Revues: Essai de bibliographie* (1900), an overview of the Francophone counterparts to what we now consider little magazines from Britain, of the period 1885–95, although the earliest examples that are cited in the preface go as far back as the 1860s.[1] Naturally, de Gourmont, himself a contributor to some of the periodicals that he documented, did not mean to belittle the quality of these *revues* (confusingly French for 'magazine') by labelling them 'petite'. Their littleness referred strictly to their targeting a readership that is small in comparison with the broad public of mainstream publications, because their purpose was to publish the work of contributors who considered themselves to constitute an avant-garde, delivering not mindless reading fodder but the 'littérature d'art' (whatever that means) of the Symbolist movement.[2] The English translation 'little magazine' only became the generally accepted term for this genre after the publication of the influential study by Hoffman, Allen and Ulrich, *The Little Magazine: A History and a Bibliography*, in 1947. Looking for a historically attested name for this particular type of small-scale literary and artistic periodical, the authors opted for 'little magazine' as a catch-all term over other current terminology such as 'small magazine' and 'little review'. In their recent study of *Modernism in the Magazines* (2010), Scholes and Wulfman speculate about the eventual victory of the option 'little magazine', and propose the answer that 'the *lit* in *little* suggests literariness in the context of magazines, and the notion of a "little magazine" connotes cuteness as well. In the world of periodicals, little magazines were perceived as handsome little Davids confronting big ugly Goliaths.'[3]

Helpfully, the 1947 *History and Bibliography* does sum up a few broad requirements for a periodical to qualify as a 'little magazine', which are quite non-committal, but which continue to be the starting point of scholarship today. The bottom line is that '[a] little magazine is a magazine designed to print artistic work which for reasons of commercial expediency is not acceptable to the money-minded periodicals or presses.'[4] Little magazines operate in what the French sociologist Pierre Bourdieu called the field of restricted production, in which authors and artists primarily produce for 'other producers'.[5] This does not have to mean that they only aim to secure the support of literary and artistic practitioners or publishers, although these are a small but important demographic, but at least that potential readers who wish to understand their content will have to acquire specific new 'codes' in the form of aesthetic systems and poetic theories. In France, according to de Gourmont, speaking of the major French *Symboliste* authors of the Fin de Siècle, 'at no moment in their careers, did Villiers [Auguste Villiers de l'Isle-Adam], Verlaine, Mallarmé, or Laforgue ever publish their work elsewhere than in *revues* of which some were so "*petites*" that their name has become a mystery'.[6] In Britain too, little magazines were the preferred platform for the ambitious youths associated with currents within Aestheticism, contemporaries and often admires of these French writers.

Many contributors who later found their way into the canon started in such 'advance guard' publications, being taken up by the 'rear guard' of the mainstream press after their work was deemed to show sufficient commercial potential.[7] A breakthrough for one individual contributor could in its wake bring about rising prominence for other contributors and the initially heterodox aesthetic modes or political stances that they collectively represented, and therefore little magazines play an important role as catalysts in literary history. Little magazines tend to be founded to provide a forum for authors and artists sharing an interest in particular niche themes or styles, who are seen as belonging together through this common heterodoxy. As such, little magazines have been founded in support of regional literatures and identity politics, as for instance the Celtic Revival in Britain or the Southern Agrarians in the United States, politicised aesthetics and poetics such as Arts and Crafts or Marxist Social Realism, or simply as a common platform for coteries of young artists and writers seeking camaraderie, to raise their voices in unison and so be better heard. By studying the interactions within and between little magazines of a specific period, and the polemics these waged against media institutions that they viewed as ideologically or aesthetically orthodox and mainstream, we gain first-hand insights into the ways of thinking of that generation and the next. Some of the rebels of today will be the rulers of tomorrow.

Because of a general disregard for Victorian art and literature which lasted at least until the 1960s, the first British little magazines that received any academic scrutiny did not go back further than the modernist era, as was for instance the case for the pioneering study of Hoffman, Allen and Ulrich in 1947. Since then, countless studies have proven indisputably that there is no good reason to exclude from this genre category a number of periodicals that appeared in the second half of the nineteenth century.

The roots of the little magazine genre reach further back than the Fin de Siècle. As with every cultural phenomenon, the emergence of the little magazine is linked to events in social history. It stands to reason that ever since the first 'courants' and 'gazettes' ran off the presses in the seventeenth century, some periodicals have enjoyed a wider circulation than others. There have also always been titles that were originally founded to boost certain causes or bring down others deemed undesirable. The characteristic 'littleness' of the little magazines, however, has recently been theorised to have been the result of a specific, ambiguous position in the publishing market that arguably only became available around the middle of the nineteenth century. As Hadjiafxendi and Plunkett tell us, '[l]ittle magazines occupy a contradictory position in that, while they provided an alternative, usually avant-garde, publishing space, they were nonetheless influenced by dominant trends in periodical production.'[8] In the eighteenth century, for instance, the development of the magazine trade had first allowed for politically partisan publications to become viable, and soon titles specifically catering for female readers started to appear, as well as publications with a regional focus. Another wave of market fragmentation occurred in the early Victorian period, when the periodical press was again significantly influenced by a gradual increase in the total number of readers across society, although technological advances of course played a role as well. Successive educational reforms had brought about a rise in literacy rates, opening up a large potential readership with a social diversity that was greater than ever before. Before, the specific genre of review periodicals had catered for a small, educated elite interested in philosophical and political developments, but the great majority of newspapers, magazines and miscellanies aimed to appeal to a broad readership. Now, so-called 'class publications' would be marketed towards niche reader categories.[9] Although the term might suggest otherwise, these categories could not only correspond to a specific social stratum, but also to certain vocational and ideological affiliations.

To attract the readers to whom they wished to sell, then as now, publishers needed to consider both price and content. Cheaper periodicals would appeal to the large, less affluent readership with usually a lower educational background, and, conversely, more expensive publications provided content that was generally perceived as more complex. This diversification of the press would help establish a distinction between 'high' and 'low' culture that had never been as pronounced before, bringing about the juxtaposition of 'popular fiction' to 'literature' that is still maintained in many bookshops today. Penny magazines such as the *London Journal* (1845–1928) would furnish content appreciated by a great many readers who lacked the money to buy expensive periodicals and the educational level to enjoy sophisticated content, that was conversely deemed of low moral and artistic standards by more elitist readers whose distaste for periodicals that were accessible to the lower classes was a defining feature of their social habitus.[10] Such demanding and well-off readers turned to publications such as *Blackwood's Edinburgh Magazine* (1817–1980) or the *New Monthly Magazine* (1814–84), which purposely positioned themselves on the other end of the spectrum. 'Low' and 'high' thereby became separate submarkets for periodicals to compete in, a condition famously lamented by humanist critics like Matthew Arnold (see Chapter 2) who predicted in the 1860s that this would result in the abandonment of less-educated readers to the whims of the amoral mechanisms of supply-and-demand.

This two-tier Culture Industry, naturally, did not accommodate literary and artistic innovators who felt no affinity with either the low expectations of the newly literate masses, or the closed-mindedness of the highbrow reaction. The typical position of avant-garde little magazines as the odd-one-out in the market is a defining feature which is often disregarded. It is crucial, however, because it forced them to act in opposition to periodicals associated with established authorities, as well as formulate their own creeds that were remote from what the average reader was used to. The small editions and exigent design aesthetic of little magazines would often also make them unattractively expensive for lower- and lower-middle-class consumers. As little magazines thereby dictated their own rules and preferences, what Bourdieu calls 'a systematic inversion of the fundamental principles of all ordinary economics' would ensue, because financial profitability, accessibility to a wide public, and the endorsement of institutions such as art and literature academies are to varying extents deemed incompatible with the uniqueness of these enterprises.[11] Whatever their political agenda, little magazines would always to some extent have to be exclusive, or at least perceived as such. Small wonder, then, that in Britain the earliest days of this genre overlap with the formative years of Aestheticism, a set of creeds responding to the same circumstances as the little magazine.

Two early little magazines: *The Germ* and the *Oxford and Cambridge Magazine*

In 1881 a new operetta by Gilbert and Sullivan appeared on the London stage, that in itself was not any more avant-garde than other catchy masterpieces such as *H.M.S. Pinafore* (1878), but that is relevant to our purpose because its narrative was based on popular caricatures of the budding Aesthetic Movement, published in comical papers like *Punch* (1841–2002). This *Patience* was largely prompted by the recent rise to fame of provocative late-Victorian celebrities such as the poet A. C. Swinburne, the painter J. M. Whistler and the professional self-promotor Oscar Wilde. It preceded many important events now associated with Aestheticism, but by inflating the mannerisms of these spoofed celebrities at this early juncture, it did much to cement from the outset numerous salient clichés. Never does it do so more effectively than in its most famous musical number, known by the opening line 'Am I alone and unobserved?', which has the Aesthete caricature Reginald Bunthorne (a Frankensteinian hybrid of the aforementioned worthies) admit to the fourth wall that he is an 'aesthetic sham', offering guidance to those 'anxious for to shine in the high aesthetic line'. One of Bunthorne's less obvious recommendations is to 'get up all the germs of the transcendental terms / and plant them ev'rywhere'. The reference here is to *The Germ* (1850), the short-lived house journal of the Pre-Raphaelite Brotherhood that only lasted for four issues, but that constituted an important event in the history of British art, literature and print culture.

The Germ and its arguable successor the *Oxford and Cambridge Magazine* (1856), have been argued to be the earliest British little magazines. In 1970, R. S. Hosmon published an edition entitled *The Germ: A Pre-Raphaelite Little Magazine*, likely the first time that the term 'little magazine' was applied to a publication of the Victorian era. As Marysa Demoor has argued, the label suits the *Oxford and Cambridge Magazine* equally well because

> [b]oth of these magazines share the enthusiasm and the confidence of the 'little magazines' of the early decades of the twentieth century. It was their founders' intention to improve upon a previous generation, or to be the mouthpiece of an artistic group that wanted to do something different, something 'new'. They established their publication despite their impecuniousness and used it [. . .] as an immediate outlet for their best writings.[12]

The Germ is also immediately representative of the genre in the sense that it was, as one contributor later assessed the situation, from a commercial point of view 'a most decided failure'.[13] Yet, because of its association with the Pre-Raphaelites, it became one of the most romanticised periodicals of the nineteenth century, and, although it appeared over thirty years before the little magazine would come into its own, it would eventually function as a type for the entire genre.

The Germ recruited all of its contributors from the Pre-Raphaelite Brotherhood (PRB) or among close friends sympathetic to its principles. The PRB was more restricted than one would believe from the scores of artists and writers who were influenced by them and confusingly too designated as 'Pre-Raphaelite'. It was founded by William Holman Hunt, John Everett Millais, Dante Gabriel Rossetti and Thomas Woolner, and shortly after joined by William Michael Rossetti, James Collinson and Frederic Stephens. W. M. Rossetti, according to his own record considered the most administratively apt and journalistic of the seven Brethren, served as editorial *primus inter pares*.[14] Except for Millais, all members contributed critical articles, literary pieces or pictorial artwork, as did a few external temporary associates who never enjoyed the prerogative of signing their art with the hallowed 'PRB', a defiant nod to the titles 'ARA' and 'RA' that were the privilege of respectively associates and members of the Royal Academy. The magazine was published for the owners by Aylott & Jones, a small firm that had published the *Poems* (1846) of the Brontë sisters but specialised in non-fiction and above all religious tracts with a Methodist slant, and printed by George Frederick Tupper and Co., the business of the namesake lithographer and a connection of the PRB through their friend and external contributor John Lucas Tupper, son of the founder and brother of the then owner George Tupper Jr. *The Germ* ran for four monthly issues from January to April 1850 and, despite this short existence, under two different titles. The first two numbers bore the more familiar title *The Germ: Thoughts towards Nature in Poetry, Literature and Art*, and the last two were entitled *Art and Poetry: Being Thoughts towards Nature*, though all four issues are conventionally considered together as one single magazine. The initial title was abandoned after the proprietorship of the insolvent magazine had officially passed over to the printer. Sales figures differ somewhat, but it is generally believed that W. M. Rossetti's own estimate of the magazine never selling more than a hundred copies is reliable.[15] Printer George Tupper sympathised with the young artists, and after the second issue had proven an even greater financial disappointment than the first, he hoped to bring more professionalism into the venture by taking the business side into his own hands. This was unfortunately of no avail as there simply was not yet a sufficiently large audience for the content that *The Germ* offered, and the magazine folded but four months after it had started.

When comparing the two titles, it becomes clear that the new name urged by the new proprietors was meant to suggest at least some general relevance to a less specialised audience, and make the magazine appear of broader interest than the proceedings of a young clique of artists and theorists, being 'germinal', as in having ambitions still to come to fruition. It is clear that the group behind the magazine perceived itself as an avant-garde group bent on challenging a mainstream hostile to its beliefs. The first issue did not list the names of the contributors because of a 'general feeling that to appear publicly [. . .] as writers opposing the ordinary current of opinions on fine art would damage their professional position, which already involved uphill work more than enough'.[16] Although a notice in the first issue welcomed unsolicited manuscripts of 'unpublished poems, essays or other articles appearing to coincide with the views in which this periodical is established', the contributions in all four numbers came from within the Brotherhood or its direct environment.

The new name, while avoiding the sectarian connotations of the older title, did respect the original character of the magazine as envisioned by its founders. *Thoughts towards Nature*, present in the subtitle of both versions, had in fact been the working title for *The Germ* until just before the release of the first number. W. M. Rossetti recollects that this was

> a phrase which, though somewhat extra-peculiar, indicated accurately enough the predominant conception of the Præ-Raphaelite [sic] Brotherhood, that an artist, whether painter or writer, ought to be bent upon defining and expressing his own personal thoughts, and that these ought to be based upon a direct study of Nature, and harmonised with her manifestations.[17]

The periodical was and remained above all else a medium for poetry and criticism which would demonstrate and explain this often debated principle. Every issue also contained one etching, of which the magazine's mission statement also says that it was meant to 'illustrate this aim practically'.[18] Although the quality of most of the included poetry and even the execution of the etchings is below the heights to which some of the contributors would later soar, a few of these contributions have entered the canon of Victorian literature.

Although this is rather unfair to the other contributors, including an already promising young Christina Rossetti (under the pseudonym 'Ellen Alleyn') and precocious sixteen-year-old Coventry Patmore, *The Germ* is today mostly referenced as the place to find the first published versions of 'Hand and Soul' (No. 1), D. G. Rossetti's short story that doubles as a Pre-Raphaelite manifesto, and the much-anthologised poem 'The Blessed Damozel' (No. 2).

The ambitious contents of this early little magazine were also presented by means of a concept which in several ways looks ahead to the coming vogue for integrated book design and cross-medial art. The bibliographical code of *The Germ* was adapted both to be elegant and to accentuate the magazine's message. Unlike the standard layout of cheaper Victorian magazines, where often several columns of dense type clog the page, the text is allowed more room, with only one column of text and wide margins, as was customary in the more prestigious review periodicals. Although the page layout of *The Germ* was surely above average for its time, the typography, for one, did not yet reach the high standards of later little magazines (Figures 1 and 3). We still find here the typical mid-Victorian clutter of widely different typefaces on the same page. The titles are set in a poorly legible novelty font that is obviously meant to indicate the Renaissance and late-medieval inspirations of the group, but this stands in contrast to the body of the text with its modern roman typeface, and all textual ornaments come from the printer's stock instead of being especially designed as in some future little magazines that claimed inspiration from *The Germ*. These were early days yet. However, its typesetting is very noticeably neat, with items usually starting on a fresh page, and even shorter pieces such as sonnets are never tucked away wherever the editors found a few inches of room. An important consequence of this is that all contributions are presented as being of equal worth, a design statement that invites the PRB's desired reception of the magazine as the output of a cohesive group of equals. It is furthermore an apt choice for a periodical in which all contributions are presented as belonging to the same polemical strategy because they all apply or demonstrate the principles declared in the magazine's critical essays and in the mission statement on the back cover. There it is said that

> this work will contain such original Tales (in prose or verse), Poems, Essays, and the like, as may seem conceived in the spirit, or with the intent, of exhibiting a pure and unaffected style, to which purpose analytical Reviews of current Literature – especially Poetry – will be introduced; as also illustrative Etchings.

A programmatic journal like *The Germ* teaches not primarily by means of theory, as through its 'Essays' and 'analytical Reviews', but also by example, and each literary and pictorial contribution should therefore be viewed as a best-practice demonstration of its poetic and artistic beliefs.

Because of its still quite conventional typography, the main visual interest of this periodical lies in the etchings, consecutively by William Holman Hunt, James Collinson, Ford Madox Brown and Walter Deverell, that in each number are used as frontispieces that illustrate the poems always opening the issue. While D. G. Rossetti, who saw his vocation as a pictorial artist as complementary to his ambitions as a poet, painted numerous pictures to accompany his own verse, he did not contribute any pictorial work to *The Germ*. As the second title of the magazine indicates, it is equally invested in 'Art' *and* 'Poetry'. Unlike in most other periodicals of the time, its pictorial contributions should therefore not be seen as subservient to the poems, but as a commentary on and an elaboration of these, which Lorraine Janzen Kooistra has identified as a major breakthrough in Victorian book art.[19] The etchings function as illustrations when viewed in context with the adjacent poems, but the poem could just as well be said to elucidate the etching, and either can do without the other. The etching done by Collinson for the second issue accompanies a poem which is also by this artist's hand, joining the two as components of what in scholarship on the Pre-Raphaelites is often called a 'Double Work', but otherwise the illustrated poem is written by someone other than the illustrating artist. Hunt thereby joins his skill to that of Thomas Woolner, Brown to W. M. Rossetti, and Deverell to John Tupper. None of the etchings is particularly impressive, and in their distinctly un-Pre-Raphaelite lack of detail they seem closer to studies than to finished work. While the etchings do the Brotherhood little justice, for instance in the odd proportions of Deverell's Viola-as-Cesario from *Twelfth Night* (No. 4) (Figure 3), the artistic collaboration is effective from a conceptual point of view, as it again reinforces the coherence of *The Germ* as the common effort of a close-knit group and a venue for cross-medial artistic collaboration.[20] The magazine is not only the venue in which the contributors make a collective public appearance; its collaborations make it the medium through which the Brotherhood is consolidated as a collective entity. This was already noticed at the time, the reviewer for the *Guardian* (1821–) praising *The Germ* because 'English artists have hitherto worked each one by himself, with too little of common purpose, too little of distinct and steadily pursued intellectual object'.[21] This remark, not coincidentally coming from a newspaper of a political reformist tendency, would soon prove prophetic, as the Pre-Raphaelite legacy would play a major role in the coming Arts and Crafts Movement (see Chapter 2).

The Germ sold at 1 shilling, or one twentieth of a pre-decimal old pound. This may seem cheap, but assessing its dearness is not unproblematic because this magazine, for all the reasons stated above, was the first of its kind. Several genres of periodical would have to be used as reference points. As discussed above, little magazines will always hold an ambiguous position in the market. In the same year, several new penny magazines and Dickens's hit weekly *Household Words* (1850–9) at tuppence sought to be accessible to the widest possible readership, but, if only due to its demanding contents, *The Germ* never could have appealed to the same broad audience. For its publication frequency it could be compared to other monthly magazines, the more prestigious ones like *Blackwood's Edinburgh Magazine* or *Fraser's Magazine* selling for as much as 2s. 6d around this time, while some of *The Germ*'s design features, its sense of purpose and its strong editorial line were more reminiscent of (usually quarterly) review periodicals, that could be twice as expensive as that. *The Germ* could also be grouped with the above-mentioned specialist 'class publications' and magazines sponsored by professional bodies or religious and political pressure groups, which too had less commercial incentive behind them and were focused on either service to the profession or to propaganda, and often went for less than the highbrow cultural monthlies. Even so, few were as cheap as this Pre-Raphaelite journal.

While *The Germ* never made any profit and even was published at a loss, its price seems above all else to have been calculated to yield just enough for the magazine to pay its own way without scaring off potential readers. Its rudimentary financial strategy to cover the expenses actually went further than this. A fact curiously omitted in scholarship about *The Germ* is that two issues of this periodical carried a page-length advertisement for the insurance company the Provident Life Office. A financial institution like this is surely a surprising choice for a magazine of such lofty aims, but it already occurs in the first number, when hopes must have been at their highest, and the Brotherhood themselves were still the proprietors and unquestioned editors of the magazine. As the company itself cannot have had much to gain from the association with a periodical that was never going to sell widely, its advertisement was most likely a way of administering philanthropic support for the arts. The Provident Life Office had been founded in 1806 by the former professional painter Barber

Beaumont, who until his death in 1841 was known for patronising artistic and social welfare causes. Most likely this company tradition was kept alive by his son, J. A. Beaumont, who was the manager at the time of *The Germ*. The advertisement, printed on the recto of the back cover, is present again at the same place in the third number, being the first under the title of *Art & Poetry*. Its placement there did deviate from the standard practice in mid-Victorian magazines, where either the body text would be spliced with advertisements throughout, or a demarcated advertising section would precede and follow the body text of every issue. Restricting the adverts to one, and placing it on the paratextual verge of the covers, is therefore in itself a clear statement against a literally pervasive commercialism of the mainstream press. At the time, this restricted advertising practice was usually only found in deliberately elitist periodical genres such as quarterly reviews, whose high price allowed them to get all their revenue strictly from their subscribers. It remains remarkable, however, that in this early example of the little magazine genre we should find such a very worldly advertiser as an insurance company. As we shall see, little magazines published during the 1880s and 1890s, which were inspired by *The Germ* and its successors, usually only admitted advertisements by publishers, booksellers, artistic reproduction companies, vendors of art supplies, or other such aesthetically correct enterprises, or again in the words of Bourdieu quoted above, the 'other producers' of art and literature.

Some initially underappreciated little magazines find their way towards an appreciative readership, even if this can be a while in the making. Five years after its original publication, a copy of an unspecified number of *The Germ* reached a group of undergraduates at Oxford and Cambridge, who were among the earliest admirers of the Pre-Raphaelites, whose exhibition pieces had in the meantime proven more effective than their journal in attracting critical attention, along with a fair bit of controversy from all the right people – establishment figures whose reproach served as a negative endorsement. These enthusiastic students were united in their support of the Pre-Raphaelites and their fellow travellers, and the very existence of a magazine like *The Germ*, even if commercially unsuccessful, suggested the feasibility of a similar literary organ for their own group. The *Oxford and Cambridge Magazine*, henceforth *OCM*, was the result. With twelve issues, running from January to December 1856, this magazine enjoyed relative success in comparison with *The Germ*, and it too was priced at 1 shilling. Although its student proprietors were not professionals of the press any more than the PRB had been, the *OCM* from the beginning was a more professionally managed affair. It was published by the large firm of Bell & Daldy in London and printed by the already renowned Chiswick Press, the pinnacle of typography in mid-Victorian England. William Morris acted as editor for the first issue, but thereafter passed on this responsibility to William Fulford, a since forgotten poet of some fame during his lifetime.

The core members of this 'Set' – who also referred to themselves derivatively as 'the Brotherhood' and, half in jest, half in unfeigned infatuation with Tennysonian Arthurian chivalry, as 'the Order of Sir Galahad' – were Morris and Edward Burne-Jones.[22] Other members and *OCM* contributors included Morris's later associate Charles Faulkner, who became a decorator, and the now forgotten poet Richard Watson Dixon, who was later to be Swinburne's favourite candidate for the office of Poet Laureate after the death of Tennyson.[23] Because few of the members of the Set were artistic practitioners or published authors before the founding of the *OCM*, they could not present themselves as a defined school as the PRB had attempted to do, and none of the people involved had as yet distinguished themselves in the manner of their role models. However, they did share an interest in medieval(ist) literature and a distaste for Victorian academic art, and their efforts were given cohesion through their collective elaboration on the example of the Pre-Raphaelites.

Already in the first issue, Edward Burne-Jones goes out of his way to slip high praise for *The Germ* into what was supposed to be a review of Thackeray's novel *The Newcomes* (1855). Disapproving of Richard Doyle's illustrations for this novel, he remarks that 'engravings have of late become a very essential feature in book-making' and that reviewers should give them more attention and 'learn to read a picture as we would a poem'.[24]

> Some few years ago a monthly periodical was published upon the subject of art and poetry; it appears to have ceased after a few numbers, not without having spoken something that will live in echoes yet. As the frontispiece of one number was an etching by Holman Hunt, an illustration indeed to a poem, but the latter having so little reference to it, that it may well stand for an independent picture; truly a song without words, and yet not wholly speechless, for out of its golden silence came voices for all who would hearken, telling a tale of love.[25]

The Pre-Raphaelite principle of the Double Work and its equal partnership between illustrator and author is hereby specifically commended, and with startling critical foresight presented as the future of British illustration. Burne-Jones goes on to call an illustration of D. G. Rossetti's for William Allingham's *Day and Night Songs* (1854) 'the most beautiful drawing for an illustration I have ever seen', and asks why 'the author of the Blessed Damozel, and the story of Chiaro [i.e. 'Hand and Soul'] [is] so seldom on the lips of men'.[26] The latter two works had at the time only been published in *The Germ*, and this statement is therefore indirect praise for that earlier periodical as well. It should be noted that at this point no member of the Set had actually met or even corresponded with the Pre-Raphaelites. That only happened after the publication of this first issue, when a flattered Rossetti struck up an acquaintance with Burne-Jones and Morris that soon developed into a lifelong friendship. He contributed three poems to the new magazine, and the younger men must have been especially pleased to receive a revised version of the 'Damozel' for their November issue. Besides Burne-Jones, other contributors purposefully continued the line of *The Germ* as well. To give but a few examples, Morris adopts their brand of Tennysonian medievalism for his poetry and tales throughout the series, Fulford gives his own interpretations of Shakespeare (Nos. 2, 7 and 10) as Patmore had done in the third number of *The Germ / Art & Poetry*, and Vernon Lushington appraises exhibited paintings by D. G. Rossetti and F. Madox Brown (No. 8).

These are meaningful thematic links, but there were differences between the two periodicals as well. For instance, the *OCM* was less strictly committed to a uniform aesthetic programme than its predecessor, and it was also more political. Critical essays predominate, followed by a few 'tales' (prose narratives), and every issue has at least one poem. In the bound collected edition that appeared after the final number, the contents are listed in categories, showing that the editors distinguished 'Essays' (mostly but not always discussing literature) from 'Notices of Books'. Both usually feature a review of a recent literary publication, but whereas the 'Notices' are restricted to the critic's self-effacing evaluation of the merits of another's work, the 'Essays' (such as Burne-Jones's quoted above) are of the type that the Victorian critic Walter Bagehot called 'review-like essay and the essay-like review' typical of review periodicals, in which personal opinions were developed out of an often disproportionately concise assessment of the publication under scrutiny. The *OCM*'s non-literary essays for their Ruskinian rhetoric are already interesting glances ahead to the later politicised art activism of some contributors, and often still make use of literary references and analogies. These treat subjects such as 'Unhealthy Employments' (in No. 5 by Faulkner and Price) of industrial labour, and 'Woman, her Duties, Education, and Position'

(No. 8), for which Fulford considers Tennyson's *The Princess* (1847) an invaluable guide. By conceiving of aesthetic and social issues as intricately linked, the *OCM* played a formative role in the elaboration and propagation of a dialectics of art and society that would culminate in the Arts and Crafts Movement, for which several contributors would become leading representatives.

The *OCM*'s politicised aesthetic takes its cue from the Pre-Raphaelites' emphasis on artistic veracity, but with the added wish to put this principle of 'truth to nature' to the service of society. An unsigned 'Essay' in No. 6 (June) defends Ruskin's *Modern Painters* against a damning review by an anonymous Elizabeth Eastlake, a rival art critic as well as personal enemy of Ruskin's through her friendship with his ex-wife Effie Gray, which had appeared in the March issue of the conservative *Quarterly Review*:

> Judiciously has the reviewer of modern painters [sic] in the Quarterly put in the forefront of his [sic] battle the assertion, that the function of art is not to express thought, but to make pretty things; for herein lies the whole quarrel between Ruskin and the pedants in literature or art who have opposed him.[27]

The author of this vindication is speculated to have been Burne-Jones, with some help from Morris, which is likely as the opinion expressed here chimes with that in the above-mentioned review of *Newcomes*, where Ruskin is also cited approvingly, and the importance for good illustration to be intellectually on the same level as poetry is highlighted.[28] Against Eastlake's objections to Ruskin's historical and political readings of paintings, the *OCM* essayist approvingly quotes Ruskin's teaching that criticism had the duty to bring out the inherent social truths in the artwork, because 'no man ever yet who could speak melodiously wanted thoughts to speak; that was why his melody was given him, that he might think towards his fellows'.[29]

Georgiana Burne-Jones claims to have heard D. G. Rossetti exclaim of the *OCM* that 'it might easily be bound in the same volume as *The Germ*', meaning no doubt that the periodicals held similar content, but also that they looked similar.[30] A second important difference from *The Germ*, however, does lie in their visual aspects. The *OCM* is not illustrated, although the Set had a few already skilled draughtsmen on board, including Morris and Burne-Jones who would become one of the most internationally celebrated British book illustrators of the late nineteenth century. There are understated decorative elements in the form of decorated initials beginning every item, and an engraved design above opening articles (Figure 2). These were most probably not produced by a member of the Set but by the Chiswick Press's house engraver Mary Byfield, one of the many shamefully forgotten female artists of the Victorian era.[31] Impressive as these are, the magazine's limited budget makes it doubtful that they were designed specifically for the *OCM*. The typographical restraint characteristic of the Chiswick Press is, however, obvious throughout; a fitting partner because in the mid-nineteenth century it already resisted the age's major fault of crammed setting and excessive use of novelty typefaces, which as we have seen still hampered *The Germ*. The letterpress is set in flawless Caslon, a functional old-style font that would in the common decades become the font of choice for artistic printing, and the covers have the title in a black-letter that is more sober than that of *The Germ*. The return to two columns of text on the page and lack of margin, common in magazines at the time but not present in *The Germ* or the review periodicals with which the *OCM* in its essays shares a belligerent partisanship and declamatory tone, will have helped to keep printing costs down.

The few modest ornamental devices decorating the text are not there for ostentation alone. While it was not illustrated, the *OCM* did share *The Germ*'s evident concern that the material medium of the text be treated with the care befitting the artistic, and now also political purposes that it was meant to serve. This anticipation of Total Art is not explicitly theorised in the *OCM* as it would be in later little magazines, but it is arguably developed allegorically in a notable contribution to the first issue. In 'The Story of the Unknown Church', William Morris's first ever published short story, a ghostly narrator looks back across six centuries to recount how he once toiled for years on a monument for his deceased best friend and sister. The ornamental tomb was not only a material expression of the idea that the departed represented for him, but also a means for the artist to work through his grief: 'I painted it too as fair as I could, and carved it all about with many flowers and histories, and in them I carved the faces of those I had known on earth (for I was not as one on earth now, but seemed quite away out of the world).' Upon completing his work, the self-proclaimed 'master-mason' dies, 'my chisel in my hand, underneath the last lily of the tomb'.[32] This echoes the Pre-Raphaelite obsession with the possibility of art as a transcendental device, that is a prominent theme in both of D. G. Rossetti's contributions to *The Germ* praised in the OCM's '*Newcomes*' essay. Through the artwork, the 'master-mason' externalises a deeply personal message, and is able to detach from the outside world in the same way as Rossetti's pre-Renaissance painter Chiaro dell'Erma manages to zone out the bloody town feuds in 'Hand and Soul'. Rossetti's story ends with the anecdote of Chiaro's masterpiece being mocked for its primitiveness when it is finally exhibited centuries later, and the monument of the 'master-mason' does not survive, but this was never the point. The artwork is the material manifestation or what Rossetti's narrator calls the 'visible embodiment' of a spiritual truth, which will endure beyond it.[33] For artists, the redemptive power of the artwork is achieved through the dedication they apply to completing it in full fidelity to their personal vision. In the context of the little magazine, as much as an aesthetic philosophy, this is a rhetorical commonplace for avant-garde artists to defend themselves against an anticipated unfavourable reception.

The unanimity of the contributors throughout the run indicates that, like *The Germ* initially, they felt that their opinions would be controversial. Despite its title, there was no institutional support for the magazine from the two universities, and the young men invested a lot of money in its upkeep, above all Morris who is said to have put one third of his yearly income into the magazine.[34] Some of the publishing costs must have been covered by means of the regular advertisements, which again have been consistently overlooked by earlier commentators. Victorian advertising is a complex issue and it is likely that the interest of the advertisers in this magazine was passive, in the sense that they may have had contracts with its publisher Bell & Daldy for other periodicals issued by them and simply did not object to being in the *OCM* instead of actively seeking it out. However, that the proprietors of the magazine themselves approved of the sheer diversity of advertisements is intriguing. Whereas *The Germ* only has one recurring advert printed on the inside of the back cover, the *OCM* has a variety of advertisers. In all but one issue (No. 4), these are restricted to a single, unnumbered page, on the verso of the front cover. The most loyal advertiser is the magazine's own publisher, Bell & Daldy, presenting a list of publications on theology and language study, and occasionally canonical literary titles like the works of Shakespeare (as mentioned above, also regularly referenced within the magazine). A few advertisers are decidedly unscholarly as well as unliterary: James Carter & Co. twice get a full-page advert for their 'Dutch and Cape flowering bulbs' (Nos. 7 and 8), tea and coffee sellers Philips & Co. advertise in No. 4, and we find several adverts for different financial institutions over several numbers. Advertising publishers usually follow the example set by Bell & Daldy, and offer titles which could be of interest to an academic audience: for example, Deighton, Bell & Co. focusing on philosophy and ancient history (No. 2), and Richard Griffin & Co. publicising 'new works on the Middle Ages' (No. 10). Although its political and aesthetic allegiances were outspoken, the magazine presented itself conspicuously as a university publication. The subtitle was consistently 'Conducted by members of the two universities', even though not all of the contributors were students or faculty. The fact that they emphasised their academic connections by choosing the eventual title over the earlier alternative *The Brotherhood*[35] implies that they anticipated that this choice would procure them a wider audience.

The fourth number is the only one where a larger adverts section appears under the heading 'Advertisements', implying that the editors experimented here with such advertising practices which, as mentioned above, were a common feature in periodicals at the time. Puzzlingly, amongst the advertisements we find 'A sketch of the political history of the past three years in connection with the Press Newspaper and the part it has taken on the leading questions of the time'. This thirteen-page chronicle, without page numbering and preceding the listed contents of the *Press* (1853–66), appears to be meant to draw readers to this weekly newspaper 'of home and foreign politics, general news, [and] criticism', which, however, was a small player that would eventually merge with the more successful *St. James Chronicle* (1801–66).

In some instances there are links between topics discussed within the magazine and its advertisements. The above-mentioned Shakespeare edition by Bell & Daldy and the essay series by Fulford in the *OCM* could have been a coincidence. There is, however, also a five-part essay by Lushington on Carlyle in Nos. 4, 5, 6, 11 and 12, with a small slip of paper inserted in No. 4 offering at 1 shilling 'A photographic portrait of Thomas Carlyle, from a medallion by T[homas] Woolner, mounted so as to bind with the *Oxford & Cambridge Magazine*', available from the publishers. A few years later, the then still only 26-year-old Lushington would play a significant role in editing and annotating Carlyle's first *Collected Works*, published by Chapman & Hall in 1857–8.[36] The *OCM* No. 12, closing the Carlyle series, furthermore has an advertisement for 'Cheap editions of Carlyle's works' published by John Murray. We similarly find a three-part study of Tennyson in Nos. 1, 2 and 3, and a slip inserted in No. 11 subsequently offering, besides the earlier Carlyle portrait, a portrait of Tennyson again by the Pre-Raphaelite artist

Woolner at the same price of 1 shilling, to be similarly bound in. Loose paratextual items such as these slips leave no trace when taken out, and enabled the magazine to discreetly pursue commercial policies. Limiting the advertisements to a separate section has a similar effect, as hereby the contents of the magazine proper are suggested to be untainted by these financial necessities.

These and other inventive ways of zoning off commercial necessities in a gesture of dissociation would become very common in little magazines in the following decades, where they functioned as a suggested means of symbolic protection of the ever-precarious Total Work of Art against the threat of contamination.

Notes

1. de Gourmont, *Petites Revues*, p. 2.
2. Ibid., p. 3.
3. Scholes and Wulfman, *Modernism in the Magazines*, p. 56.
4. Hoffman et al., *Little Magazine*, p. 2.
5. Bourdieu, *Field of Cultural Production*, p. 120.
6. de Gourmont, *Petites Revues*, p. 2.
7. Hoffman et al., *Little Magazine*, p. 3. This is obviously a translation of the more usual 'avant-garde'.
8. Hadjiafxendi and Plunkett, 'Pre-history of the "Little Magazine"', p. 38.
9. Ibid., p. 42.
10. King, *London Journal*, pp. 34–8.
11. Bourdieu, *Field of Cultural Production*, p. 39.
12. Demoor, 'In the Beginning, There Was *The Germ*', p. 65.
13. Rossetti, 'Introduction', p. 11.
14. Ibid., p. 9.
15. Demoor, 'In the Beginning, There Was *The Germ*', p. 57.
16. Rossetti, 'Introduction', p. 10.
17. Ibid., pp. 9–10.
18. *The Germ*, notice on back cover recurring for No. 1 (January 1850) and No. 2 (February 1850).
19. Kooistra, *Artist as Critic*, p. 2.
20. See Spinozzi and Bizzotto, *The Germ*, *passim*.
21. 'Art and Poetry', p. 623.
22. Burne-Jones, *Memorials of Edward Burne-Jones*, p. 77.
23. Sambrook, 'Dixon, Richard Watson (1833–1900)'.
24. [Burne-Jones], 'Essay on *The Newcomes*', p. 59.
25. Ibid., p. 60.
26. Ibid., p. 60.
27. [Burne-Jones and Morris?], 'Ruskin and the Quarterly', p. 353.

28. LeMire, 'Introduction', p. xviii.
29. [Burne-Jones and Morris?], 'Ruskin and the Quarterly', p. 353.
30. Quoted in Marsh, *Dante Gabriel Rossetti*, p. 154.
31. Fleming, 'Oxford and Cambridge Magazine'.
32. [Morris], 'Story of the Unknown Church', p. 33.
33. [Rossetti], 'Hand and Soul', p. 23.
34. Boos, "'A Holy Warfare against the Age'", p. 346.
35. Fleming, 'Oxford and Cambridge Magazine'.
36. Tarr, 'Editions', p. 140.

Chapter 2

Mounting the *(Century Guild) Hobby Horse*

Arts and Crafts in/of the *Century Guild Hobby Horse*

The Germ and the *OCM* were trailblazers in both the little magazine genre and in British Aestheticism, and appeared too early to be able to fall back on a subculture from which to draw the contributors, patrons and even readers to make their enterprise an unmitigated success. The publication of their few issues was, however, a pivotal event in the formation of such a community. Whereas *The Germ*, though largely unnoticed at the time, had caught the attention of the younger generation of Morris and Burne-Jones and supplied them with themes and aesthetic concepts without which their talents might well have died in the bud, these core members of the *OCM* Set later in turn assumed as important a role by introducing their own younger followers to a coherent belief system that insisted on an unseverable link between politics and aesthetics. While an interesting but failed attempt to institutionalise Aestheticist art and literature was made through the more inclusively marketed magazine the *Dark Blue* (1871–3) (see Chapter 6), the remarkable earliness of these two pioneering little magazines is best appreciated if one considers that it took nearly three decades for them to receive a genuine successor, that like them was conceived as the periodical platform of an avant-garde group. The magazines under scrutiny in this chapter, the *Century Guild Hobby Horse* (1884/6–92) and its successor the *Hobby Horse* (1893–4), served to consolidate across the literary and artistic fields the notion of a diverse but interconnected Aestheticist avant-garde, and went much further than the little magazines of the 1850s in working out alternatives to common practices of the contemporaneous periodical market through aestheticising their own production methods. Thereby they turned the end product of the printed text into a never-before-seen integrated Total Art project, which would stimulate a whole new fashion in artistic book design and provide the blueprint for Aestheticist little magazines of the genre's coming first heyday in the 1890s.

To understand where these endeavours came from we need to return briefly to the background of the journals discussed in Chapter 1. As Linda Dowling put it, '[f]or Victorians at mid-century the belief that art could transform society had a name, and that name was John Ruskin'.[1] For this Victorian Sage, art history was inseparable from social history, and art criticism from social polemic. In his many writings, he advocated a new kind of social reform, similar to earlier British proto-socialist movements such as Chartism for its goal of empowering the working class within the production process, but unique in the sense that its critique of industrial capitalism was profoundly aesthetic. For Ruskin and his followers, who as we have seen included the Set that published the *OCM*, the utilitarianism of the Industrial Revolution had replaced the time-honoured dignity of collaborating but emancipated craftsmen with the drudgery of mechanised wage slavery, and the results of this are amongst others visible in the arts. Together with likeminded thinkers such as Thomas Carlyle and especially Augustus Pugin, Ruskin instigated a popular interest in the culture of the Middle Ages and Renaissance, when crafts organisations known as 'guilds' would have furnished a context for income protection and the development of skills, allowing even the most modest participant in the production process to leave the mark of their personal touch in the end product, as opposed to nineteenth-century labourers who were exploited by faceless corporations and turned into cogs in the industrial machinery. He therefore promoted the architecture of the period when this so-called 'Gothic' (as in late-medieval) element would have been at its height, and found analogues in other forms of applied art from that period. The fine art of the late medieval age and early Renaissance was for him exemplary as well, because of its joint emphasis on moral edification and truthful representation. This made him an early champion of the Pre-Raphaelites, whose principle of 'truth to nature' (see Chapter 1) he was one of the first critics to appreciate. Ruskin came to play a vital part in their early careers, for instance by publicly endorsing the early PRB pictorial output and by hiring D. G. Rossetti as a teacher for the Working Man's College in London, thereby first putting the essentially apolitical Pre-Raphaelite notions of art to work in a politicised environment.[2] It was also he who arranged for Rossetti, Morris and Burne-Jones to paint together the Oxford Union murals (1857–9), one of the latter two's first public projects and a hugely important early collaboration between members of the PRB and of the *OCM* Set. Without Ruskin, not only the philosophy of art of the Victorian age, but also its artistic practice, would have been unrecognisably different.

True to the little magazine's purpose of showcasing its producers to the right people, it was the *OCM* that brought the Set to Ruskin's attention. Robert Hosmon informs us that Ruskin sent an appreciative note to an 'ecstatic' Burne-Jones after having received from the latter a complimentary copy, writing to a friend: 'I am not Ted any longer, I'm not E. C. B. Jones now, I've dropped my personality – I'm a correspondent with RUSKIN, and my future title is "the man who wrote to Ruskin and got an answer".'[3] As we have seen, the *OCM* advocated putting art to the service of society, and this continued to be a major concern for its contributors after the magazine had folded. This was most famously the case for William Morris, who throughout his career pursued this mission in ideological essays as well as artistic practice, and was involved in political activism and social education programmes. Morris, and with him several other former contributors to the *OCM*, would from the 1880s be active in the burgeoning Arts and Crafts Movement, named by later critics for the Arts and Crafts Exhibition Society that was founded by Walter Crane in 1887 to promote the applied arts. They did this in the conviction that the design and artisanal production of furniture, decorative objects or books had the same potential for creativity and demonstration of skill as the fine arts. There were many such societies across Britain from the 1880s to the Second World War. Although the activities of many of these made them more closely resemble business networks than actual professional bodies, such societies often claimed inspiration from medieval and early-modern craft associations or guilds. The old guilds were collectivist enterprises that provided training, upheld standards of quality, and extended professional security to their members, all found lacking in Victorian labour regulations. Ruskin himself had set up an organisation that is still extant today, christened St. George's Company in 1870 but renamed the Guild of St. George in 1878. In the Ruskinian views adopted by the Arts and Crafts Movement, the ancient guilds were a counterforce to the monopoly formation of rising capitalism, which was increasingly perceived as the source of the major social ills of the nineteenth century. It would have had aesthetic implications as well: industrialisation had split production into shoddily produced goods for the masses and unnecessarily ostentatious goods with 'finish' for the wealthy, whereas in the age of artisan production everybody would be served with decent workmanship.

The Arts and Crafts Exhibition Society gave its name to the movement, but it was not the first of its kind. For a full five years before, there had been the Century Guild of Artists, founded in 1882 by the architect and designer Arthur Mackmurdo and his then apprentice Herbert Horne. The Century Guild functioned as a catalyst for the budding Arts and Crafts Movement, and may have provided its first manifesto:

> The aim of the Century Guild is to render all branches of Art the sphere, no longer of the tradesman, but of the artist. It would restore building, decoration, glass-painting, pottery, wood-carving, and metalwork to their rightful place besides painting and sculpture. By so placing them they would be once more regarded as legitimate and honourable expressions of the artistic spirit, and would stand in their true relation not only to sculpture and painting but to the drama, to music, and to literature. In other words, the Century Guild seeks to emphasise the Unity of Art; and by thus dignifying Art in all its forms, it hopes to make it living, a thing of our own century, and of the people.[4]

The Century Guild soon came to proclaim its Gospel through a periodical mouthpiece of its own, the *Century Guild Hobby Horse* (henceforth *CGHH*). Work by Century Guild members and associates may be viewed in some of the leading design museums across the globe, and books designed by them now fetch high prices, but it is indicative of the importance of the periodical press at this time that this little magazine was without a doubt the most famous work produced under the Guild's auspices. It is one of the most influential periodicals of the British Fin de Siècle, and although it does not come up in scholarship as often as later little magazines such as the *Yellow Book* and the *Savoy* (see Chapter 4), these journals of the 1890s would never have been founded without its example.

The *CGHH* has a confusing publication history. After a false start with one number in April 1884, seven annual volumes (priced at 10 shillings) of four quarterly numbers (2s. 6d each) appeared from January 1886 to 1892. This was followed by a short-lived 'New Series' of three numbers (1893–4) that, as we shall see, occupied a different position in the market and are best considered separately from the numbers under the old name. The editorial position went back and forth between the two founders. The single 1884 issue was edited by Mackmurdo alone, whereas the 1886 numbers were produced by both, with Horne taking on full editorial duties from 1887, to be superseded again briefly by Mackmurdo for the last numbers of January to October 1892. The 'New Series' under the new name, ultimately, would once more be edited singly by Horne.

The *CGHH* made a point of 'the spirit of independence' that would characterise the magazine. The extraneous 1884 number was said to have been published privately, 'no publisher making a chilling third' between the Guild and the reader.[5] However, strictly speaking this is not true. As the title page attests, the magazine at this time was published at least in association with George Allen, who at Sunnyside Villa in the Kentish village of Orpington (nowadays – as if to prove Ruskin's point – a suburb in Greater London) maintained a publishing business that sought to avoid the trappings of the late-Victorian literary market by delivering well-printed edifying or educational books at prices within reach of a wide demographic.[6] Not only had Allen been a close collaborator of Ruskin – who enjoyed regulating those whom he patronised, and had put him up in business and published with him exclusively in exchange for the prerogative to interfere assiduously in the policies of the firm – but he was also close to Rossetti and Morris, and these links must have been a valuable asset to the Century Guild. Although, as Brian Maidment has shown, Allen managed to exert a beneficial influence on publishing in the late-Victorian period through his example of sound workmanship and fair bookselling practices, he was also in much the same plight as his intentionally avant-garde business partners. Allen had to deal with regular conflicts between 'Ruskin's publicly argued and ferociously defended views on commercial practice' and 'the commercial and practical needs' of a viable publishing concern, and therefore he would also have made a suitable adviser for an organisation such as the Century Guild.[7]

The future issues in the first series would be published 'for the proprietors' by Kegan Paul. Again, it was not officially part of this publisher's roster, but the distinction is subtle. Though not by far as radical in his production and distribution methods as Allen, Charles Kegan Paul too had a sound reputation as a publisher of well-designed books, and had championed 'English Parnassian' poets with understated Aestheticist credentials such as Andrew Lang and Austin Dobson (the latter also a *CGHH* contributor).[8] A regular contributor on theological issues to periodicals like the *Fortnightly Review*, Kegan Paul had enough of a literary inclination to contribute two poems (June 1888 and April 1892), an article on Shakespeare (October 1889), and the script of a lecture on 'English prose style' (January 1889) to the *CGHH*. None of these are particularly memorable for their merits or insights, and it is not improbable that the Guild mainly fawned over this experienced and commercially successful publisher because he was valuable for his connections, and because he could offer guidance when the magazine faced dwindling sales figures at the end of the 1880s.[9]

The little magazine, while inevitably an exclusive genre, is not a vanity publication for the contributors; it is published to be noticed, even if only by readers who can make a difference in the careers of its producers. The contents of the magazine confirm this ambiguity. As much as a propaganda tool for its principles, the *CGHH*, like *The Germ* before it, was a demonstration of the practical application thereof. It was therefore secondarily a portfolio for the writers who delivered the copy, for the pictorial artists whose work was reproduced, and for the applied artists who worked on its design and material presentation. For the proprietors, who were applied art practitioners themselves, this must have been a major incentive, as the revenue coming directly from the sales of the magazine could hardly justify the work put into it. Mackmurdo states in a letter that the *CGHH* never had more than 500 subscribers, which added to an unspecified (and therefore likely negligible) number of loose copies sold in bookshops meant that it was not the smallest of the little magazines. Nevertheless, surviving ledger notes on Nos. 9–13 (April 1887–January 1888) indicate that these sold on average about 285 copies, and due to the high production costs the profits per issue in that period will have amounted to only a few pounds per issue.[10]

From the first number onwards, each number closes with a section called 'The Century Guild Work', which to all intents and purposes contains advertisements, albeit of a very particular kind. It is a list of endorsed artists/artisans with annotations on the services these provide. The overwhelming majority of these are not directly affiliated with the Century Guild, which, for all its ambitions, was never a large organisation. There do not appear to have been any official membership registers, but then it never was the intention of the Guild's founder to subsume the united artists into one monolithic entity. In an obvious tribute to the Pre-Raphaelite Brotherhood, Mackmurdo and Horne occasionally signed their work with 'MCG' – 'Member of the Century Guild' – for instance, for programmatic contributions in the 1884 number, but they were the only ones to do so, and besides them the artistic polymath and poet Selwyn Image was probably the only constant member. In contrast to later self-styled 'guilds' such as C. R. Ashbee's Guild and School of Handicraft, the Century Guild did not operate from one joint workshop, but rather viewed itself as a rallying point for applied artists, bringing independent artists together for collaborations. In many cases the parties listed in the *CGHH* were associates contracted by Mackmurdo and Horne when they had obtained architectural and interior design commissions.[11] As the first 'Work' section attests, '[b]y means of the co-operation of artists associated through the "Century Guild," it is possible to maintain some sort of alliance between the arts when conjointly employed'.[12]

It is unlikely that this publicity was paid for, but the Century Guild will have been amply compensated by the goodwill it generated. Through this section, they could imply that the Guild was a hub for the avant-garde, and the Guild's endorsement of the listed applied artists would be construed as reciprocal by its readership. Amongst others we find here William De Morgan ('painted pottery'), William Morris's firm Messrs. Morris and Co. ('Carpets, Silks, Velvets, Chintzes and Wall Papers, and Painted Glass') and William Michael Rossetti ('reproductions of Pictures by D. G. Rossetti'). Keeping such illustrious company helped the reputations of the Guild members, as well as those of the many humbler, now forgotten applied artists listed in this section. Besides these mercenary commercial advantages, the Century Guild also created for the first time the perception of an Aestheticist artistic scene sharing the same standards and principles, by bringing their collaborators together within the pages of this section. The newness of the little magazine as such a publicity scheme for a pre-selected clique can be gauged by early press notices on the magazine. Critics for the newspaper the *Edinburgh Evening News* (1873–) and the *Pall Mall Gazette* (1865–1923) already dismissed the Century Guild on the basis of its 1884 prospectus, respectively as a 'mutual admiration society' and 'a small but fervent set of mutual admirers', recalling du Maurier's *Punch* spoofs in which gatherings of Aesthetes are described in the same terms.[13] Although the 'Century Guild Work' section appears at the end of each number, there is something to be said for the cynical idea that the rest of the magazine served as bait to draw attention to it. As Chapter 3 shows, the potential function of the little magazine as a portfolio would be the predominant motivation behind several journals of the 1890s. The contents of the *CGHH*, however, are certainly interesting in their own right too, and belie all allegations of sectarianism. As Rebecca Mitchell has demonstrated, Mackmurdo and Horne were gifted networkers, which is evident from the list of contributors to the magazine.[14] Besides young talent such as Arthur Symons, Ernest Dowson and Lionel Johnson, they managed to persuade famous authors such as Ruskin, Matthew Arnold, Christina Rossetti and William Bell Scott to contribute. Established figures from the preceding generation who were already respected for their critical standards were thereby implied to approve of the ambitious debutants. Even if these greats delivered mostly informal essays or occasional verse that might never have been published without their names attached, these – once more – at least helped draw attention to the surrounding contributions by the younger generation.

Unlike later Arts and Crafts guilds for which the two aims were indivisible, for the Century Guild the artistic and professional activities dominated, and politics came decidedly second. In the early twentieth century, Mackmurdo did write a series of pamphlets advocating social and economic reform entitled the 'Hobby Horse Series', but in the *CGHH* itself he is more evasive about political issues than would soon become customary in the Arts and Crafts Movement, noting at the start of the magazine that 'large social questions' will be avoided. He goes so far as to call out Morris as '[a]n instance of an artist entering the circle of social politics, consequently advocating what we believe to be dangerously narrow-sighted remedies of existent evils'.[15] As stated above, the *CGHH* calls into question the distinction between fine and applied art, but within the early Arts and Crafts Movement, the views of Morris and his socialist comrades on the cancellation of the bourgeois juxtaposition of art and utility were much more radical than those of Mackmurdo and Horne. The primary interest that the *CGHH* shows for the world outside of the commonly defined artistic sphere concerns the question of how the appreciation of 'Beauty' can be introduced into everyday life.

The magazine nevertheless manages to avoid the cliché of Aesthete escapism by its minor educational agenda. While it does, like other little magazines, address its readers as implied connoisseurs, few of its critical articles are bogged down by esoteric jargon. This was no doubt a compromise intended to bring in converts as well as please Bourdieu's 'other producers', but on occasion it goes further than this. In the very first number, the script of a lecture by Selwyn Image appears, in which he exhorts his audience to 'continue to popularise art', and he certainly is not (only) talking about that of Century Guild artists.[16] To this end, an article by Mackmurdo follows straight after, introducing in very basic terms and with generous background information the earliest Italian painters in the National Gallery, explicitly written as an incentive for the reader to go and see this 'collection finer than any in the world'.[17] This piece of course did not address readers who were already well versed in art history. Typical of the bathos characteristic of the *CGHH*'s 1884 opening number, this piece is entitled 'Forenoon Echoes of Love's Evensong'. The article does not explain this cryptic title, but if it is decoded by means of D. G. Rossetti's sonnet 'St. Luke the Painter' from the programmatic 'Old Art and New' triptych in *House of Life*, it suggests that this article was meant to propagate a circular, Pre-Raphaelite take on art history. The 'noon' would then be the watershed painting of Raphael and his contemporaries after which art had started to decline (see Rossetti ll. 9–11: 'past noon, her toil began to irk, / And she sought talismans, and turned in vain / To soulless self-reflections of man's skill'), and the 'evensong' is the return to the sound principles from before this decline that as 'echoes' were registered by the Victorian Pre-Raphaelite painters (see Rossetti ll. 12–13: 'Yet now, in this the twilight, she might still / kneel in the latter grass to pray again').[18] The series is continued for two more instalments after the two-year interval between the abortive single number of 1884 and the fresh start in 1886, under the more sober title 'Notes on the National Gallery'. Finally, yet again in the first issue, Mackmurdo praises the Art for Schools Association for its efforts to promote arts education for children.[19]

All this suggests a concern for the common weal that goes beyond aesthetic hedonism or dignified commercialism. Arthur Galton, a regular contributor close to the editors, does not surprise when, two years after the death of Matthew Arnold, he notes smugly that the author of *Culture and Anarchy* (1869) was 'always interested in the fortunes of the "Hobby Horse"'.[20] In its emphasis on the correction of the uninformed reader's tastes, combined with its price that put it within reach of a wide audience, the *CGHH* does recall Arnold's mission to salvage the expanding British middle classes from philistinism. A laudable cause, but one that suggests that the editors initially misjudged their readership, given that it is not likely that the *CGHH* was actually read outside of the small segment of the population that was already in the know.

According to Image in the aforementioned lecture, two things were needed for the popularisation of art to succeed: 'the first is to cultivate a catholic spirit – and the other is to be sincere'.[21] Like *The Germ*'s insistence on 'a pure and unaffected style' or, more mischievously, Wilde's later satirical use of the adjective 'earnest', that second qualification could mean anything or nothing, but the first was certainly fulfilled by what Fletcher has called the 'disciplined eclecticism' of the magazine.[22] The *CGHH* features a wide array of voices in its essays and literary contributions, and as wide a range of styles in its illustrations. This too is a defining feature of this magazine, the very name of which was explained by Horne in a write-up on the Guild for the *Art Journal* as follows: '"De gustibus non disputandum," that is, as we find it translated in "Tristram Shandy," there is no disputing about Hobby Horses.'[23] The contents of the magazine span the whole spectrum of what is now known as Aestheticism, from the Pre-Raphaelite-inspired illustrations and Arts and Crafts ideological treatises of its beginnings, to the French Symbolist influence and the confrontational literary Naturalism that became trendy in the 1890s. It is a flexible publication that features authors as widely different as Wilde (making this one of the very rare appearances in Aestheticist little magazines of the self-crowned prince of the Aesthetes) in July 1886, and Ruskin in April 1887. Despite Mackmurdo's earlier negative comments, Morris allowed the magazine to print in its January 1892 number a lecture on 'The influence of building materials upon architecture' that he had given to the Art Workers' Guild, a similar organisation.[24]

In another lecture script printed in the magazine, Horne states that

> [a]s there is but one proper study of mankind, which is man; so is there but one art; the art of a fine and various expression of the human spirit; multipartia sed indivisibilis; of many forms, no doubt, but never possible to divide.[25]

At first glance, the diversity of its contents would argue against the supposed 'Unity of Art' declared here and elsewhere in the magazine. However, Hosmon confirms that, at least during Horne's tenure,

> [a]lthough the diverse contributors to the magazine were obviously free to pursue their personal convictions, no essay, poem, or illustration contradicted Horne's editorial policy. Unity in art meant unity in the magazine, and the magazine was the device [. . .] to promote that policy.[26]

For the *CGHH*, the magazine is not just a vessel for the magazine's content; through its design and material properties it brings cohesion between the individual input of all the different people who together create it: by editing, writing, illustrating, or literally crafting the material object. This is in line with Arts and Crafts ideology, and goes back to the views of Ruskin as developed in his vastly influential essay 'The Nature of Gothic', originally in the second volume of *The Stones of Venice* (1853), praised by Morris as 'one of the very few necessary and inevitable utterances of the century'.[27] There, Ruskin argues that 'the principle admirableness' of Gothic architecture was that 'out of fragments full of imperfection' it would 'indulgently raise up a stately and unaccusable whole'.[28] His point is that in a truly collective enterprise, such as the construction of a medieval cathedral, everybody involved, down to the most modest workman, would be allowed not only to contribute his labour but also to add the expression of his personal creativity. Or, in the words of Mackmurdo and transferred to the collective enterprise that the *CGHH* aspired to be:

> Each [contributor] stands alone responsible for the literary or pictorial form in which his spirit becomes incarnated. But as a body, we are responsible, and responsible only, for the tone and temper that will characterise this periodical; just as individually, for the local colouring that each writer may give to his subject.[29]

The Arts and Crafts Movement developed alongside the British labour movement, and their critique of industrial society was if anything more radical than that of most contemporaneous socialist schools of thought. Yet, unlike the early communists and trade unionists, it continuously emphasised the fact that society, though a collective entity, was an aggregate of individuals (see Chapter 5). When Mackmurdo in the same manifesto declares that 'class character like individual character acts automatically according to its bulk of higher human elements', this is not only an Arnoldian argument in support of the *CGHH*'s aforementioned educational mission, but also a reflection of how he would organise the movement for the rejuvenation of art, and the magazine which was to be at its centre.[30] The *CGHH* itself was to unite its producers and thereby exemplify the unity of apparently disparate manifestations of an ideal art, writ large: a Total Work of Art.

This approach was new, and, as with other aspects of the magazine, some commentators found it peculiar. A critic in the *Bibliographer* (1882–94), likely Grant Allen, does not 'know exactly how to notice this book', suspecting 'that the members [of the Guild] are very young men' (Mackmurdo was thirty-four at the time), and most of this lukewarm review of the first issue is dedicated to the *CGHH*'s attempt at conceptual unity.[31] The reviewer quotes Mackmurdo's wish that the magazine would

> provide a part song in which many voices may show their fullest harmony, and make that harmony as complete as enchanting, by the firmness with which each insists on his individual part, and thus bring out his most valued and self-distinguishing qualities of voice.[32]

Similar synaesthetic metaphors had occurred in both the theoretical works of Wagner (at that point not yet widespread in Britain) and also in the criticism of Walter Pater, a likelier source given the emulation of a Paterian prose style in the magazine's prospectus and its 1884 issue, and the frequent references to him in later issues.[33]

Still, it is no wonder that reviewers would not know exactly what to make of such statements. *The Germ* and the *OCM* had declared their conceptual unity only through thematic coherence and by reflecting in their editorial policies the artistic and ideological rapport between contributors. For the editors of the *CGHH*, situated against a developing Arts and Crafts background, the paratext and the modes of production of the magazine became a concern as well, in order to preserve 'the delicate balance between the matter to be expressed and the manner of expressing it',[34] and 'the Artistic character of the Periodical by maintaining Originality of Thought and by making Thorough all workmanship involved in its production'.[35] The union of the arts was for the Century Guild not merely desirable for the artistic potential of cross-medial collaboration, it also heralded a valorisation of aspects of the printing trade that up until then were hardly acknowledged. This fits in with the *CGHH*'s general campaign for emancipating the applied arts. Selwyn Image in January 1887 clarifies that 'when [. . .] we are talking about Art, let it be understood that we are going to use Art with a meaning which embraces more things than popularly it has the credit of embracing'.[36] Returning to the magazine's central idea, he explains that

> when we talk about the Unity of Art, we mean that all kinds of invented Form, and Tone, and Colour are alike true and honourable aspects of Art, whatever the material or purpose may be which employs them. We mean that the man, who is engaged in this invention, is an Artist.[37]

Painting or sculpture are not slighted, but there are also many articles in the magazine on architecture, glass-painting, woodcarving and metalwork, all artistic crafts in which the Guild and its associates excelled. What is even more important, is that the *CGHH* reads as an intensely self-aware periodical for its regular discussions of topics relevant to the production of the magazine itself. Quality printing and an elegant page layout had already been valued to some extent in earlier periodicals, including the two earliest little magazines previously discussed. Here, for the first time, the skills and knowledge behind the physical production of the magazine came to the forefront and were presented as of equal importance to those of the contributing writers and pictorial artists. Unlike those of *The Germ* and the *OCM* whose acceptance of typographical conventions and use of stock ornaments imply that they deferred to their printers, the editors of the *CGHH* assumed full control of the setting and all other aspects of the periodical's design. Through this the magazine played a role of importance in the so-called Revival of Fine Printing, a prominent tendency in British print culture of the second half of the nineteenth century that, in the concise description of Robert Seiler, 'rejected the commercialism that governed book production, and in doing so [. . .] inaugurated a new era in book design, its goal being to bring all the elements of the book into some kind of harmony'.[38] Mackmurdo and Horne's typographical practice and assertions of artistic as well as commercial independence were an inspiration to the much older William Morris when founding the Kelmscott Press, and certainly also for Charles Ricketts (see Chapters 3 and 6) when he set up his own press in the London Vale.

During the 1880s, a trend arose for amateurs to invest in such 'private presses', as they are often called, of which we find a considerable number in Britain. Before the Revival caught on in the book trade, its principles were often advocated by such curious artists and book lovers who were cut off from the world of publishing as big business.[39] Nevertheless, the term is somewhat misleading as the degree of 'privateness' of these presses varied. The earliest were certainly the pastimes of amateurs, such as the Daniel Press of Rev. Charles Daniel that from the late 1840s to the late 1910s produced but a few, though highly acclaimed titles; and even later, few would have been envisaged as commercially lucrative enterprises at the outset, although some did grow into modest businesses that came to be the main occupation of the people involved. It is therefore better to use the then current term 'small press' as a catch-all for all (relatively) small-scale ventures that designed their own books and did their own printing, although the latter sometimes using equipment owned by more commercial printing houses. What all Victorian small presses shared was a dedication to skilful printing by means of manual and therefore increasingly dated technology, whereby this restriction to old-fashioned methods, instead of being considered a setback, was approached as an opportunity for experimentation. The most celebrated small press of the nineteenth century was without a doubt the Kelmscott Press of William Morris, whose medievalist masterpieces also form the most enduringly famous work of the whole Revival. Morris worked with an old hand-press of the kind that was favoured by amateur printers, sought out delicate inks, and used especially manufactured hand-made paper. According to William Peterson, all these meticulous preparations were in aid of attempting to recreate the working conditions of early printers as much as possible: '[b]y selecting the Albion hand-press, Morris was able to turn to inks that were much thicker and slower-drying – and presumably closer in consistency and appearance to the inks employed by fifteenth-century printers'.[40]

Like Mackmurdo and Horne, Morris had worked in architecture after leaving university, but he soon turned to crafts on a smaller scale, such as furniture, decorated fabrics, wallpapers and eventually books, believing that here would be better prospects for some immediate improvement. As they believed so strongly in intrinsic analogies between the arts, downscaling from buildings to books did not seem a huge conceptual change to these artists. After all, the design and production of printed texts, just like that of buildings, had traditionally been a joint effort involving the labours of several workers, each providing different skills that needed to be harmonised in order to come up with an end product that would be regarded as a self-contained unit. The architectural metaphor, referring to a Total Art construct that is capable of harbouring several constituent art forms, returns time and again in applied art criticism of the period. The most famous artistic book of the nineteenth century, the 'Kelmscott *Chaucer*' (1896), was referred to by its illustrator Edward Burne-Jones as 'a pocket cathedral'.[41] In the *CGHH*, Horne too stated that 'a study of Architecture' alone can teach us 'the discipline of regarding the disposition of a work as a whole, and relating, both as regards form and mass, every one part to every other part, mindful always of fitness, harmony, proportion and symmetry'.[42] It is for this reason, as we shall see, that the last Aestheticist little magazine of the 1890s would be entitled the *Dome* (see Chapter 6).

Morris had learned the same lessons during his architectural training, and in applying these to texts he aimed for nothing less than the 'Ideal Book', explained thus in 1893:

> An illustrated book, where the illustrations are more than mere illustrations of the printed text, should be a harmonious work of art. The type, the spacing of the type, the position of the pages of print on the paper, should be considered from the artistic point of view. The illustrations should not have a mere accidental connection with the other ornaments and the type, but an essential and artistic connection. [. . .] This is the only possible way in which you can get beautiful books.[43]

Morris had been involved in the designing of his own literary publications before, in the emergent conviction of the necessity of 'reconciling type, border, initial and picture',[44] but his views on the matter were brought into focus in November 1888, when he attended a lecture by his Hammersmith neighbour and future associate Emery Walker on 'Letter-press printing and illustration' that for the influence it exerted on several audience members is often considered a breakthrough moment in the Revival of Fine Printing.[45] At that time, Walker was, amongst others, responsible for the printing of the illustrations in the *CGHH*, which was indeed the very topic of his lecture. Some years after the dissolution of the Century Guild and its magazine, Morris would also use a Greek font designed by erstwhile Guild member and *CGHH* regular Selwyn Image for Kelmscott books.

To late-Victorian readers who valued Fine Printing, the justly famous Kelmscott books, such as the edition of Ruskin's *The Nature of Gothic* (1892) quoted above that was tellingly one of their first publications (Figure 4), will instantly have recalled the *CGHH*. The magazine's front cover bore a woodcut by Selwyn Image, designed to confront the reader immediately with a visual summary of the interests and aims of the Guild (Figure 5). This well-known image of the knights whose lower extremities disappear into a caparisoned toy palfrey would dispel the popular misconception that there was no place for humour in Aestheticism. Perhaps next to the cause of civilising the Victorian middle classes, another hint that the magazine took from Arnold was its notable tension between 'high seriousness' and self-relativising irony, a mode that the urbane Image handled particularly well. This illustration is a visual pun on the magazine's name, referring to the so-called 'hobby-horses' used in folkloric Morris dancing (*pace* William), and a wink at how Victorian cultural nostalgia actually related to the medieval age that had furnished them with the example of the guilds.

Within, the magazine's letterpress, on hand-made paper and executed by the Chiswick Press that had also printed the *OCM*, has ample borders and only a single column of text in Caslon on every page (Figure 7). Mackmurdo, Horne and Image had a keen interest in typography and worked as book designers during their involvement with the magazine; from a comparison between any random page from the *CGHH* on the one hand, and *The Germ* (Figure 3) or the *OCM* (Figure 2) on the other, the advantages of little magazine editors participating in the material production of their publications will be plain. In the *CGHH*, woodcut decorated initials and other ornamental devices were especially designed instead of taken from the printer's stock as was standard practice, and the artists furnishing these devices were even credited in the magazine's table of contents. This was unheard of at the time, and brings these visual elements to the same level as that of the illustrations, which too are always credited among the other contents. 'Illustrations' might actually not be an adequate description of the pictorial art in the magazine, because these images usually are not representations of textual content. As noted in Chapter 1, there was among British artists working in print media a growing impatience with what Linda Dowling, following late-Victorian illustrator Joseph Pennell, calls the 'merely "explanatory" role' that was the norm up to this point.[46] As the etchings in *The Germ* were potentially autonomous but always still connected to textual items (see Chapter 1), the *CGHH* was arguably the first consistent attempt to address this discontent in a periodical. Whereas the original artistic and conceptual motivations of the Pre-Raphaelite illustrators are still relevant here, it additionally fits the political agenda of the Arts and Crafts Movement to question the dominant position of literature in periodicals, demanding that pictures in printed texts be considered as functionally illustrative but potentially autonomous works of art.

More importantly for a largely apolitical publication as the *CGHH*, however, such a levelling of content categories also enabled the Guild to further integrate verbal and pictorial art into the Total Art project that was their magazine. The art plates are sometimes referred to in the magazine as 'designs', which was no doubt not considered derogatory by the artists, as it adds another level to their contributions, functioning both on their own and as an integral component of the number of the magazine in which they appear. Following the example of the authors who were to consider illustrators as their equals, the pictorial artists too take a step down in the Victorian hierarchy of artistic media that assumed that certain skills are more valuable than others, and allow their status to be equalised with their colleagues working in book or periodical design, at the time generally considered a 'craft' instead of an 'art'. In the table of contents, the names of their designers as well as their engravers are listed, a clear statement that even the latter were valued as much as anyone else involved in the production of the magazine (Figure 8). With the *CGHH*, the Aestheticist little magazine becomes more than the literary organ of a particular group, or a mere repository for pictorial art. The paratextual aspects of the magazine come into focus and gain prominence in this 'Total' periodical, where artistic-literary content and paratextual presentation are conceptually integrated to achieve cohesion between the usually distinguished parts, as artistic crafts of equal value. In so doing, the *CGHH* tried to reform the allegedly insipid and unfair artistic practice of the age in the manner envisioned by Horne: 'not a merely negative protest, but a practical attempt to do otherwise'.[47]

Hobby Horse sans Century Guild: legitimising the trade

Even though they are usually treated as together constituting one single run, there are significant differences between the ***Century Guild Hobby Horse***, running from 1884 to 1892, and the 'New Series' published under the shorter name the *Hobby Horse* (1893–4). To distinguish more clearly between the two, we will henceforth keep on using *CGHH* for the magazine's 'Old Series', and use *Hobby Horse* for this 'New Series'. As we have seen, the *CGHH* presented itself as the official mouthpiece of the artistic craftsmen united in the Century Guild, a small but devoted organisation founded by architect and designer Arthur Mackmurdo in 1882. Although no specific date is on record for when the Guild was officially dissolved, its activities had largely petered out by the end of the 1880s. Other self-styled 'guilds' had recently formed that had a more centralised organisation than the Century Guild aspired to, and the latter had lost their role as a hub for artistic craftsmanship to publicity associations such as the Arts and Crafts Exhibition Society and pressure groups such as the National Association for the Advancement of Art and its Application to Industry (see Chapter 5). The Century Guild had played its part, and the final issue of the *CGHH* came out in October 1892. Horne, who had been editor from the second issue of the *CGHH* in 1886 until a quarrel with Mackmurdo got him dismissed at the end of 1891, continued for three more issues with a 'New Series' issued as the plain *Hobby Horse*.

The topics addressed in the magazine do not change significantly. In the letterpress, we still find original literary contributions as well as critical articles and more casual causeries on a variety of artistic topics. The fine and applied arts from book design to painting get as much attention as ever, and while Mackmurdo left, trusty Selwyn Image remained a regular contributor. At first glance, not much has changed in the presentation of the 'New Series', either. The magazine looks much like it did under its former title, and is surely still a prime example of Fine Printing. Instead of by the Chiswick Press it was now printed by the equally reputable firm of Folkard & Sons, which maintained its flawless setting and quality image reproduction. Although Mackmurdo did some acclaimed work in book design as well, it is likely that Horne had always been more involved in the typography of the *CGHH*, because he was the more active book artist. As he received fewer commissions for design in other media after the dissolution of the Century Guild, the book arts became his central occupation, and he was in demand with several central publishers of the 1890s. As a rare feat of integrated design, Horne had produced his sole collection of poetry *Diversi Colores* (1891), according to Jerome McGann a book so thoroughly designed by the poet/typographer as to facilitate a reading that perceives the visual presentation of the text itself as not only an enhancer but also a carrier of content, 'an aesthetic manifesto for an art of the "Total Book"'.[48] A magazine like the *Hobby Horse* is a different medium than the single-authored book because it as a rule yokes the expressive talents of several contributors, but here too Horne continued the experiments with integrated design that had begun in the *CGHH* during the 1880s. In this changed context, however, there were significant changes in how this bibliographic vision was being sold to the readership.

The relationship of the *CGHH* to George Allen and later Kegan Paul had always been kept intentionally vague so as not to cast doubt on the magazine's boasted independence, which it needed to cultivate to boost its avant-garde credibility. While the front matter of the *Hobby Horse* continues to assure us that the magazine is 'published for the proprietor', the 1893 prospectus for the 'New Series' tells a different story:

> Messrs. Elkin Mathews and John Lane beg to announce, that they have concluded arrangements with the proprietor of the 'Hobby Horse' by which they are now prepared to receive subscriptions for the issue of a New Series of that Magazine [. . .] formerly issued in a half-private manner.[49]

This makes it quite clear that the *Hobby Horse* was part of the publisher's list of Mathews and Lane, better known as the Bodley Head, arguably the most enterprising publishing house of the 1890s, which in the next few years would become publicly associated with well-known Fin-de-Siècle figures as Wilde and Aubrey Beardsley. By 1893, the firm was building a reputation for bringing controversial books with Revivalist design within the grasp of the common reader; harnessing a periodical that had done so much to establish the vogue for such books in the first place was an investment in their brand identity. The importance of the Bodley Head in promoting the 'affordably exquisite' Revivalist book and introducing the newest trends in 1890s literature to the uninitiated reader cannot be overstated.[50] Their reputation depended on the recognisable 'Bodley Head book', which

> came to possess a particular meaning and resonance for the public at large. A book issued by that press raised a quite specific set of expectations – expectations about contents and appearance – in a way that the products of no other firm did.[51]

Instead of slipping into an existing niche, the Bodley Head created a demand for a product that it was better placed to deliver than any other player in the market.

One of the first books that they published was a treatise *On the Making and Issuing of Books* (1891) by Charles Jacobi of the Chiswick Press, which had printed the *OCM* and the *CGHH* and was frequently used by the recently founded firm as well. Their association with this universally respected master printer was a declaration of their dedication to Fine Printing. However, the very first Bodley Head release *Volumes in Folio* (1889), by the firm's future publisher's reader and personal 'logroller' or purveyor of positive reviews Richard Le Gallienne (who in July 1892 – need it even be said? – contributed to the *CGHH*), was already a highly characteristic publication of their demonstrative bibliophilia.[52] This seemingly modest poetry collection announced several of its publisher's most recognisable characteristics. Content-wise it featured Aestheticist lyrics in the Swinburnian vein, transposing the Fleshly poet's signature erotic charge to Le Gallienne's own fetish for beautiful books. With 'its blue-gray "antique boards", its imitation vellum spine with raised bands, its Van Gelder handmade paper, and its tastefully designed title page lettered in red and black', and its setting in the Revivalists' favourite font Caslon, it was visually and materially made as seductive as possible too.[53] This collection may be situated within the then flourishing genre of 'book verse', to some extent a literary by-product of the Revival, of which enough appeared during the early 1890s for anthologies to be compiled. For instance, Joseph William Gleeson White, book designer and later editor of the art magazine the *Studio* and the annual *Pageant* (see Chapter 6), edited the anthology *Book-Song* (1893), published as part of publisher Elliot Stock's fittingly named 'Book-Lover's Library' series, which includes no fewer than six poets who had published with the Bodley Head, and is dedicated to that doyen of bookish singers, Le Gallienne. Gleeson White's dedication verses read 'I dedicate this sheaf of verse which then / You bade me gather', implying moreover that he even played some part in the anthology's inception.[54] The reviewer of *Book-Song* in the bibliographical periodical the *Library* (1888–) states facetiously that 'we are extremely pleased that there are so many minor poets [. . .] who are ready to profess their love for books in verses which are unimpeachable on any score, save that of dullness'.[55]

Of course, the *CGHH* had waxed lyrical about the material book as well, and for its associations with Fine Printing it was therefore a useful title for the Bodley Head to be associated with. In October 1889, for instance, Selwyn Image had contributed a characteristically sprightly essay on the joys of collecting books. He praised rare, centuries-old titles in terms similar to those that Revival of Fine Printing theorists were using to propagate their own canons of design that had been inspired by the revered early-modern 'Aldine, the Basle, or the Plantin Press [. . .]':

> How admirably disposed upon the ivory-coloured page lies, before our satisfied vision, the mass of choicely designed lettering! What a sense of proportion and propriety in the simple title-page; the headings with their ordered capitals; the initial letters and head-pieces [. . .]![56]

By telling his readers what to look out for in order to discern the distinct quality of old books, Image was by implication also praising the magazine in which his laudation appeared, and by extension the books designed by himself and his friends who also worked by the same principles. In this way, 'book verse' and prose appreciations like these were indirect advertisements that helped to establish the brand of the periodical or its publisher, and stimulated the development of new tastes in the public, as when Image states that '[a] mean, or vulgar, or unpleasing, presentation, therefore, of an author's spirit, causes in [him] a revolt, as at something puritanically unreasonable, and unmannerly'.[57] Subtly, the piece finishes with a contented sigh that although Image did not have the money for the truly great books, if he sought well enough, affordable gems could still be found. This is hardly subtle enough to qualify as subliminal advertising.

These must have been very welcome sentiments for a firm that wanted to cultivate in a wide audience a gusto for attractively designed books. The Bodley Head's literary marketeer Le Gallienne never pushed this agenda more blatantly than with the essay *Limited Editions, A Prose Fancy* (1893), later reprised as 'The Philosophy of "Limited Editions"' in *Prose Fancies* (1894), a collection of causeries on miscellaneous topics. Apart from a luxurious actually 'limited edition' of twenty-five vellum copies, the earlier version was ironically published in a regular edition of a thousand copies, which is several times that of the hitherto discussed little magazines, and more than most usual Bodley Head books.[58] It was preceded by the sonnet 'Confessio Amantis', which opens with a bathetic 'When do I love you most, sweet books of mine?', and then goes on to describe the booklover in his library:

> Ere lamplight dawneth, when low croons the fire
> To whispering twilight in my little room,
> And eyes read not, but sitting silently
> I feel your great hearts throbbing deep in quire,
> And hear you breathing round me in the gloom.[59]

Again, the purpose of the library is not (only) to store information: the speaker's 'eyes read not'. Books can also be nice to look at, and the pun on 'quire'/choir emphasises with a typical Aestheticist paradox that they can be artistically expressive even as non-communicating, material objects. Of course, what they express is the good taste of the collector. The speaker wants to bask in the exquisiteness of this collection, the sheer excitement of having acquired these beatified commodities. The fact that even the murmur of the fire is noticed implies that a contented contemplation of the library as a treasury of accumulated cultural capital is seen as its highest attainable bliss.

As Genette candidly remarks of book collecting, '[i]t is not enough to be happy; one must also be envied',[60] so an alternative answer to the blissful speaker's question as to when he loves his 'sweet books' the most would be: when the books are rare. In the following essay, Le Gallienne avers that

> [t]he ideal world would be that in which there should be at least one lover for each woman. In the higher life of books the ideal is similar. No book should be brought into the world which is not sure of love and lodging on some comfortable shelf.[61]

The Bodley Head promoted that sentiment by their standard policy of issuing a trade edition at 5 shillings, already attractive in comparison with books by other publishers sold at the same price, and besides this a more expensive limited edition. That would be printed on handmade Dutch Van Gelder paper, issued in a larger size and bound more luxuriously, and sold at twice to three times the regular price. Some had extra special editions that were printed on vellum, an expensive calfskin parchment, for an even more luxurious product. Le Gallienne, and several other authors publishing with the Bodley Head during its formative early years, offered the company an Aestheticist justification for such practices. Hereby not only content, form and production methods are being adapted to form a conceptual unity, even a less obvious feature such as the number of copies in an edition is conceptualised to fit in a Total Art project, although less to enhance the artistic value than to make the publisher more money.

Philip Cohen states that '[t]he heightened interest in collecting and rarity had engendered a healthy market for incidental bibliographical variants even of relatively common contemporary titles'.[62] Whereas for the Kelmscott Press the limited editions were primarily meant to be exceptional works of book art, surpassing even the regular editions, and were so limited because they were labour-intensive to produce and consequently too expensive to find many takers, for the Bodley Head speculation was undoubtedly the main objective. Artistic merit and financial profit are of course not necessarily mutually exclusive, but the deprecating tone in some assessments of the firm's publishing policy surely is not entirely unjustified. The assessment by Margaret Stetz that 'in a decade filled with social poseurs and literary masqueraders, the Bodley Head itself was a bit of a fraud' is representative.[63] While this is true, the problem with such a statement is that it presupposes that financially disinterested art is a possibility to begin with, and as such perpetuates the myths that makes it possible for hypocrites to flourish in the first place. The Bodley Head lucratively sought to 'manufacture[] in the buyer's mind the confusion of scarcity with quality',[64] but its cheaper editions were noteworthy productions as well, that were now disseminated to a wider audience that otherwise might have been stuck with shoddy work, and that ironically was not served by the socialists at the Kelmscott Press.

Because Mathews and Lane had the combined aesthetic taste and commercial genius to employ some of the best book artists of the age, and had their books printed by some of the most skilled printers and bound by the best binders, 'the Bodley Head was from the outset able to embody in its work the ideals and aims of the Revival of Fine Printing so often associated with the founding of Morris' Kelmscott Press'.[65] This even though the market positioning of the two firms was completely different, and Mathews and Lane lacked Morris's political motivations. Unlike the Hammersmith craftsman, they were nevertheless able to sell their splendid books at a small enough price to reach the lower middle classes. James Nelson elucidates their inventiveness in providing their books with an aura of 'daintiness', or implied refinement in the finished commodity:

> They did so by effective production practices which cut the cost to a minimum. For example, [they] employed larger-than-usual type sizes (above ten-point) and more leading than normal between lines. [. . .] This habitual use of relatively little text per book, of course, substantially reduced the cost of typesetting. Moreover, the partners printed their editions on remainders of fine paper which they bought at far below the normal price. In addition, they negotiated agreements which paid their [still upcoming] authors at best a modest royalty only after production costs had been paid.[66]

The dissolution of the Century Guild will inevitably have been a time of reflection and self-evaluation for the former Guild members, and

Horne's move to the roster of the Bodley Head, which was beginning to be known for such innovative marketing strategies, must have been a conscious repositioning within a changed market. For the Bodley Head, this was a good deal as well. Mathews and Lane had distributed periodicals before, which are rarely mentioned in critical studies. The Ruskin Reading Guild, which promoted the teachings of Ruskin after his death and were primarily active in Scotland, issued a London edition of their short-lived journals *Igdrasil* (1890–2) and *World Literature* (1892) with both George Allen and Elkin Mathews as partners, and the socialist Pioneer Club – not to be confused with Emily Massingberd's later feminist society of the same name – published their *Pioneer* (1887–91) with the Bodley Head; all three are rather newsletters for their respective societies than outwardly oriented propaganda organs, and were not much interested in new art and literature.[67] Even though the Bodley Head had also taken care of the distribution of Nos. 2 and 3 of the *Dial*, the *Hobby Horse* was the first magazine that the company effectively published, and this experience will have influenced their decision to take up the *Yellow Book* soon after in 1894 (see Chapter 4).

The *Hobby Horse* was only circulated by subscription, at the price of £1 per annum for four quarterly issues (though only three would actually appear). This breaks down to 5 shillings per number, twice as much as the *CGHH* had cost, and the price of a regular book or prestigious review periodical. With its forty pages of content per issue it does not deliver a lot of value for this amount of money, and this suggests that the Bodley Head meant it to be seen as another of its limited-edition publications. Its run of only three more issues may mean that it was not found expedient to keep the likely not cost-effective *Hobby Horse* alive for long after the foundation of the *Yellow Book* in 1894.

Like everything the Century Guild did, the *CGHH* had been barely solvent, which it hardly could have been because of its staunch refusal to include external advertisers. The *Hobby Horse* too only carries one advert in its three issues, and that is for the second issue of the *Dial* (in No. 1). This in many ways similar publication was distributed by the Bodley Head as well, and the cliques behind the two periodicals overlapped and were sympathetic to each other (see Chapter 3). The first issue of the *Dial* had been recommended to the readers of the *CGHH* with the message that 'without question, "The Dial" is a magazine to be bought',[68] and Horne contributed a poem to the second issue, now advertised in the *Hobby Horse*. This advertisement was probably not paid for, bearing in mind the constant financial troubles of the *Dial*'s editors Ricketts and Shannon, and their friendship with the *Hobby Horse* editor. Besides the *Dial* coterie themselves, the only party to benefit significantly from this advert would have been the clever *Hobby Horse* publishers and *Dial* distributors at the Bodley Head, who obviously had stakes in both periodicals.

When assessing the steep price of the *Hobby Horse*, however, the formal and material characteristics of the magazine have to be taken into account as well. The *CGHH*/*Hobby Horse* has not for nothing been declared 'perhaps the most complete example of an English "Total Art" periodical, with its hand-made paper, specially designed initials, borders and typography, and programmatic content'.[69] As the prospectus attests,

> the most scrupulous care will be expended upon the form and matter of the forthcoming series. A new title-page, and new ornaments, will be designed by the Editor; and all copper-plates and lithographs will be printed as India-proofs. The paper will be expressly hand-made for the Magazine, and will bear a special water-mark, and new type will be cast for the fresh series.[70]

The 'new title-page' in question is a stylish update by Horne of the earlier cover illustration by Image of the knights and their unlikely mounts (Figure 6). Whereas the first version, used throughout the run as the *CGHH*, incorporated thorny hedges, simultaneously symbolising organic development and the assertiveness of nature, this motif is now transferred to an ornamental frame. The thorns and their symbolism are thereby arguably contained, while the image of the hobby-horsed knight is allowed to step out of the frame and the self-conscious artificiality of the first version is yet increased. As Julie Codell has found, 'the *Hobby Horse* reflected a desire for poetic and mythic explanations with the realization that such explanations were no longer sustainable or appropriate'.[71] Of course, the old illustration was already partly humorous, but in this update for the Nineties, its 'Gothic' knightly valour is entirely gone. The steed has a jaunty cupid on its caparison, and what counts now is that 'Amor Omnia Vincit' or 'Love Conquers All', a final goodbye to the last residues of Arts and Crafts cultural nostalgia in the *CGHH*.

Horne also took other matters into his hands, as the 'new ornaments' mentioned above are, according to the table of contents of these three numbers, all 'from the designs of the Editor'. India proofs are normally trial prints on special paper that yield a finer registration of the image than would usually end up in a magazine, and that sometimes were sold in print shops. Concerning the choice of paper, a letter from Horne to Mathews reveals that he thinks '[w]e can have a special water mark, which will increase its value in the eyes of collectors', an idea that must have been music to the ears of his publisher.[72] Fletcher mentions that the sort of paper that they chose for the illustrations was Ingres paper, a high-quality but also conspicuously old-fashioned laid paper that was used by artists for prints, and would have been suitable for the India proofs.[73] Lay readers would not have known about this, but were informed by the prospectus that they should be duly impressed.

The *CGHH* was by and large a periodical by and for artistic craftsmen who expressed themselves clearly enough for lay readers to listen in (and maybe develop an interest), but now that the Century Guild was gone, the *Hobby Horse* appears to have shifted its attention somewhat to the uninitiated. For the second number, Image wrote three short causeries under the heading of 'A Ternary of Reflections', the middle one of which tells 'Of Certain Interleaved Volumes' that the author had recently obtained. The interleaving of books was a common practice well into the twentieth century, when these were often bought without (final) bindings, and the block of the book could still easily be tampered with. Study books in particular would receive such sheets of blank paper between the pages of text to serve for all kinds of annotations. Image reveals that such books are of interest to him for two distinct reasons. On the one hand, it is pleasant to ponder over the previous owners of the books, one of which in this case used to belong to Pitt the Younger, of whom many character traits might be derived from the preserved notes. On the other hand, the interleaves are usually not all scribbled over, becoming a source of high-quality 'Old Paper' that is much sought by '[t]hose of us, who are in the way of making pencil drawings, or printing etchings'.[74] The materiality of print publications is hereby emphasised by the author in the same way as it is in the prospectus for the *Hobby Horse*, teaching its readers once again to notice and appreciate such matters.

Though announced in the prospectus, no 'new font' would ultimately be cast for the 'New Series', as the *Hobby Horse* retains the reliable Caslon of the *CGHH*. Of course, the specific mention of there being a *new* font could have a special appeal to the readership of the *Hobby Horse* in the same way that they are told to be impressed by its paper. As with the emphasis on the design, on the care put into the printing of the illustrations and on the handmade paper, the fonts are hereby too related to the choiceness of the formal presentation of the magazine. There had been articles on typography in the *CGHH*, and Louis Dyer, a Classicist at Oxford, contributed to the third number of the *Hobby Horse* a review of 'A New Fount of Greek Types' designed by Image for the publisher Macmillan, likely the same Greek font that was used by the Kelmscott Press, as mentioned above.[75] The article highlights the scholarship that preceded the efforts of Image as type designer, who had been a prominent contributor to the *CGHH* since it started, and had been involved in its design.

The *CGHH* targeted connoisseurs, or at any rate readers who considered themselves as such, and reinforced the image of the Bodley Head as a haven for the more demanding reader like Le Gallienne's book verse had done before. As we have seen, this periodical wanted to educate its readership about art and show it the way towards the artistic craftsmanship of the Century Guild and its associates. In the *Hobby Horse*, the educational mission is subordinated to training its readership to be better consumers of Revivalist books. Not long after the third and final number of the *Hobby Horse* was released, a stormy break-up of the two partners in the Bodley Head firm followed that would end with Mathews leaving the business and setting up shop on his own. Although it would not be correct to discern a clear division between so-called 'decadents' and those more concerned with morality respectively assigned to Lane's and Mathews's now separate lists, Horne was certainly among those, like most members of the Rhymers' Club, who would side with Mathews because he was generally perceived as the more conscientious of the two. The *Hobby Horse* was among the items that Mathews eventually secured, while Lane landed lucrative projects like the *Yellow Book*. This led the poet Ernest Radford, an unwavering supporter of the Mathews faction, to reassure his publisher that '[t]he Hobby Horse is worth 1000 Yellow Books'.[76] Unfortunately, the *Hobby Horse* folded soon after, and the future was the *Yellow Book*'s. That future, as we will see in Chapter 4, would have its ups and downs as well.

Notes

1. Dowling, *Vulgarization of Art*, p. 25.
2. Mahoney, 'Work, Lack, and Longing', p. 224.
3. Hosmon, 'Oxford and Cambridge Magazine', p. 298.

4. 'The Century Guild of Artists'.
5. MCG [Mackmurdo], 'Guild's Flag Unfurling', p. 2.
6. Maidment, 'George Allen', p. 6.
7. Ibid., p. 8.
8. Howsam, *Kegan Paul*, p. 90.
9. Fletcher, *Rediscovering Herbert Horne*, p. 64.
10. Fletcher, 'Decadence and the Little Magazines', p. 183.
11. Grainger, 'Mackmurdo, Arthur Heygate', p. 763.
12. 'The Century Guild Work'.
13. Quoted in Mitchell, 'Century Guild Hobby Horse', p. 81.
14. Ibid., p. 81.
15. MCG [Mackmurdo], 'Guild's Flag Unfurling', p. 10.
16. Image, 'Lecture on Art', p. 47.
17. Mackmurdo, 'Forenoon Echoes of Love's Evensong', p. 71.
18. Rossetti, 'I. St. Luke the Painter', p. 160.
19. Mackmurdo, 'Century Guild Notes', p. 99.
20. Galton, 'Some Letters of Matthew Arnold', p. 47.
21. Image, 'Lecture on Art', p. 66.
22. Fletcher, 'Decadence and the Little Magazines', p. 179.
23. Horne, 'Century Guild', p. 298.
24. Morris, 'Influence of Building Materials upon Architecture'.
25. Horne, 'Some Considerations on the Nature of Fine Art', p. 85.
26. Hosmon, 'Hobby Horse', p. 165.
27. Morris, 'Preface', p. i.
28. Ruskin, *Nature of Gothic*, p. 15.
29. MCG [Mackmurdo], 'Guild's Flag Unfurling', p. 4.
30. Ibid., p. 11.
31. [Allen?], 'Century Guild Hobby Horse', p. 51.
32. MCG [Mackmurdo], 'Guild's Flag Unfurling', p. 2.
33. Brake, 'Pater, Symons and the Culture of the Fin de Siècle in Britain', p. 272.
34. Horne, 'Preface', p. 4.
35. Quoted from a mission statement printed on the verso of the front cover in several early numbers.
36. Image, 'Unity of Art', p. 4.
37. Ibid., p. 5.
38. Seiler, *Book Beautiful*, p. 17.
39. McLean, *Victorian Book Design and Colour Printing*, p. 164.
40. Peterson, *Kelmscott Press*, p. 111.
41. Quoted in ibid., p. 164.
42. Horne, 'Preface', p. 5.
43. Morris, 'Ideal Book', p. 67.
44. Peterson, *Kelmscott Press*, p. 164.
45. Ibid., p. 324.
46. Dowling, 'Letterpress and Picture', p. 118.

47. Horne, 'Century Guild', p. 298.
48. McGann, 'Herbert Horne's *Diversi Colores* (1891)', p. 161.
49. Quoted in Nelson, *Early Nineties*, p. 303.
50. Lambert, *Bodley Head*, p. 37.
51. Stetz, 'Sex, Lies, and Printed Cloth', p. 71.
52. Nelson, *Elkin Mathews*, p. 7.
53. Ibid., p. 9.
54. G. W. [Gleeson White], 'To Richard Le Gallienne', n.p.
55. 'Book-Song', p. 117.
56. Image, 'From a Secondhand Bookstall', p. 124.
57. Ibid., p. 124.
58. Stetz and Lasner, *England in the 1890s*, p. 5.
59. Le Gallienne, 'Confessio Amantis', n.p., ll. 9–14.
60. Genette, *Paratexts*, p. 36.
61. Quoted in Stetz, 'Sex, Lies, and Printed Cloth', p. 83.
62. Cohen, 'Richard Le Gallienne's *The Book-Bills of Narcissus*', p. 101.
63. Stetz, 'Sex, Lies, and Printed Cloth', p. 84.
64. Ibid., p. 74.
65. Nelson, *Early Nineties*, p. 37.
66. Nelson, *Elkin Mathews*, p. 9.
67. For more information on *Igdrasil* and *World Literature* specifically, see Maidment, 'Influence, Presence, Appropriation', pp. 73–8.
68. [Horne?], 'Contemporary Notes', p. 176.
69. Fletcher, *Rediscovering Herbert Horne*, p. 1.
70. Quoted in Nelson, *Early Nineties*, p. 303.
71. Codell, '*Century Guild Hobby Horse*', p. 46.
72. Ibid., p. 46.
73. Fletcher, *Rediscovering Herbert Horne*, p. 59.
74. Image, 'Ternary of Reflections', p. 43.
75. Dyer, 'New Fount of Greek Types', p. 84.
76. Quoted in Nelson, *Early Nineties*, p. 278.

Chapter 3

The Little Magazine as a Periodical Portfolio: the *Dial*, the *Pagan Review* and the *Page*

It should by now be clear that a notion of 'art' and 'commerce' as absolute opposites is untenable for little magazines, or for that matter for any kind of creative production that leaves the artist's studio or the author's desk to vie for attention with the output of others. As the previous two chapters have shown, little magazines were from the start in a peculiar predicament, poised against both the vulgarity of the mass-market magazine and the institutionalised authority of elitist publications. They posited themselves as an aesthetically and ideologically pure alternative to the outside world that they portrayed as artistically stale and corrupted by avarice, but at the same time they needed to engage with that world because they wanted to challenge its orthodoxy. For the circulation not to be limited to a few sympathetic readers personally known to the represented authors and artists, they sometimes had to play by the rules of the maligned mainstream. The concerns of the market seeped in through fissures in the magazines' integrated projects, which we have so far identified in advertisements for external supporters who had no direct connection to the magazine or its message, or through internal forms of publicity that are testimony to the simple need of its producers to make a living. In order to anticipate allegations that they were being contaminated or absorbed by the mainstream Culture Industry, two options were open to Aesthetic little magazines. They could attempt a strategy of aestheticisation to make the anomaly seem part of the artistic project, such as the 'medallions' offered for purchase in the *OCM* to decorate bound volumes of the periodical, or the notices of 'Century Guild Work' of the *CGHH*. If this was not possible, they could try to quarantine the threat, by zoning it off in a paratextual margin that arguably should not have been there in the first place but at least could be ignored, which is what *The Germ* did by banishing its one advertisement to the back of its wrappers. Either or both of these two practices can be found in every little magazine.

In fact, the disguised but inevitable commercial aspect of late-Victorian little magazines reaches deeper than this. It is an irony inherent to the genre that the little magazine, precisely because of its practice of publicly challenging orthodoxy, is in essence itself an advertisement for the people producing it, and by circulating their work the magazine generates immediate or future income. Each element of the magazine must be impeccable if it is to prove the full potential of the publication's principles. This not only serves the purpose of proselytising: it is intended to draw attention to the contributors, and hopefully also commissions. In the days of *The Germ*, the Pre-Raphaelite Brotherhood needed to sway the art market in their favour in order to sell pictures, and the Century Guild had to attract clients for its crafts. In the wake of the *CGHH* and its role within the Revival of Fine Printing, avant-garde journals began to showcase not only their contents, but also the skills involved in their design and material production, thereby soliciting work for their producers in the book arts. The use of the little magazine as such an easily circulated and affordable (collective) portfolio for its producers is a prominent characteristic of the genre in the late-Victorian period. In this chapter, we will see how three avant-garde publications of the 1890s, the first heyday of the little magazine, inventively exploited such opportunities for self-promotion.

The *Dial* as a coterie publication

Although the *CGHH* was instrumental in the development of the theory and practice of the applied arts in Britain, and especially furthered the cause of Fine Printing, for several years after its launch in 1884 no other little magazine was set up to follow in its footsteps. This changed in 1889 with the publication of the first number of the *Dial* (1889–97). Its editors Charles Ricketts and Charles Shannon claimed the now highly respected *Germ* as their precursor, which of course it was in the sense that the Pre-Raphaelite journal was the foundational text of the little magazine genre, but clearly the *Dial* borrowed more directly from the visual and material characteristics of the *CGHH*.

The *CGHH* did not often feature actual reviews, but as part of its mission to promote the work of likeminded artists and authors it did include 'Contemporary Notes' that recommended recent publications and other artistic initiatives endorsed by the Guild, and in October 1889 this section discussed a 'new periodical devoted to Art'. Herbert Horne, the likely author of this note, was a friend of the *Dial*'s well-connected editors, and appraised their magazine in a single, somewhat condescending paragraph:

> In recent years, no attempt of this kind has appeared in England, possessing so much interest and originality, or more full of promise of things to come. A modern magazine which does not descend to the abortive regions of magazine verse [. . .] is certainly to be welcomed. The literary portion of the periodical, however, is not technically satisfactory as prose, or equal in interest to the pictorial portion. The absence here of any severity of thought, without which prose cannot be said to exist, is felt, also, throughout the rest of the number. [. . .] But, without question, 'The Dial' is a magazine to be bought; and we sincerely hope it may have the success it deserves.[1]

This is as much as to say that there should be no mistake as to which of the two journals is superior. Of course, the general tone is favourable and will have been welcomed by the editors of the new periodical, and the *CGHH* would later go on to indirectly promote the magazine by using a lithograph by Shannon as a frontispiece in its April 1891 number. Horne also contributed an poem to the second number of the *Dial* in 1892, another sign that he supported the younger periodical. Nevertheless, the criticism in the above note does imply a misunderstanding of the real purposes of the *Dial*.

The undeniable similarities notwithstanding, there is one difference between the two publications which makes it necessary for them to be read differently. The *CGHH* was more explicitly programmatic because its editors wished it to be read as the official organ of the Century Guild, even if this organisation was made out to be a bigger affair than it in all likelihood ever was. It spoke on behalf of a larger network of contributors, established names as well as upcoming talent, whose contributions had to be contextualised through a (rudimentary) shared belief system that had to be rehearsed occasionally to remind the reader. The *Dial*, conversely, is a prime example of what is called a coterie publication. It should be considered a continuation in print of the meetings of a small group who had no interest in abandoning their individual trajectories by associating themselves formally with an organisation. Although they shared a frustration with the difficulties of gaining an audience for the type of work that they themselves valued the most, and appreciated each other's work, their involvement in this periodical was pragmatically motivated rather than driven by a shared manifesto.

The nucleus of the coterie behind the *Dial* was formed by the versatile artists Charles de Sousy Ricketts and Charles Haslewood

Shannon, who started the periodical at the beginning of their careers, when they had yet to firmly establish their reputations. Ricketts was mainly active as a book designer and illustrator before becoming a stage designer in the early twentieth century, and his work for several books by Oscar Wilde is still pointed out to graphic arts students today. In Shannon's career, painting and lithography predominated. Both, but especially Ricketts, did a considerable amount of illustration for mainstream periodicals as potboilers. That the two were a romantic item seems to have been suspected by everyone who knew them, and at the time they lived together in a house formerly occupied by James Whistler in an area of London known as the Vale, now indistinguishable from the rest of Chelsea, but then a glade in the urban jungle that was popular with artists. One of their regular visitors, the artist William Rothenstein, recalled that '[t]he Vale was then really a Vale, with wild gardens and houses hidden among trees'.[2] The house came to be known for its bohemian salon where one could meet countless authors and artists, such as Wilde or Yeats, but more often Katherine Bradley and Edith Cooper (publishing together as 'Michael Field' and known to friends as 'the Fields') and Lucien Pissarro, and the now lesser-known Thomas Sturge Moore, John Gray and Reginald Savage appear to have been there all the time. It was during the meetings of this 'tiny coterie', as Ricketts's biographer Paul Delaney calls it, and with the help of Savage and Gray in particular, that the *Dial* was planned and conceptualised.[3]

Each of the six core contributors of the magazine was in some way an outsider in the artistic and literary world of the late 1880s and early 1890s. Poets and playwrights Bradley and Cooper, like their hosts most probably a gay couple, are now among the most studied female authors of the British Fin de Siècle, but during their lifetimes they were notoriously elusive personalities. Fellow *Dial* contributor Thomas Sturge Moore, honouring his camaraderie with 'the Fields' that began at the Vale, edited a selection of their verse in 1923 and stated there that

> [t]hey had a wonderful reception in the eighties, announced by Browning and hailed as a major star; but their work, hurried by its welcome, disappointed this expectation, which was also dashed to discover that they were an aunt and niece and not some man unknown.[4]

As female poets, who additionally were in a suspiciously intimate relationship, they were according to Victorian mores doubly 'Odd Women', and their intense treatment of transcendent physical love made many readers uncomfortable. Bradley and Cooper contributed to the *Dial* from the second number, and Ricketts would later recall that the link between 'Michael Field' and himself was

> an occasional and very erratic magazine, *The Dial*, and it was through the numbers of this magazine, to which they later became contributors, that a chance meeting on a snowy winter day in Chelsea ultimately ripened into a friendship which lasted for over twenty years.[5]

The young poet Gray was at one point a protégé of Wilde's, but is notable in his own right for his efforts to introduce Britain to risqué Symbolist poets from Paris with whom he liaised on behalf of the London avant-garde. His *Silverpoints* (1893) is now considered as exemplary of Aesthetic poetry of the Decadent phase, as its immediately recognisable slender format with ornaments by Ricketts and Shannon is of the more experimental side of the Revival of Fine Printing, and was not coincidentally published at the Bodley Head. Gray struggled with his sexuality and was still plagued by doubts about his conversion to Roman Catholicism. In later years, looking back uneasily on his wild youth, the ordained canon remembered that his evenings at the Vale had been indispensable for his introduction to the literary circles of Paris and London.[6]

Sturge Moore may have been recognised as an illustrator, poet and playwright amongst his peers, but he never attained the wider recognition that friends like Yeats thought he deserved. In the late nineteenth century, he was trying to make a name for himself as an engraver, studying first with Shannon and then with Ricketts, who taught respectively at the Croydon and the Lambeth School of Art. At Lambeth he met fellow student Reginald Savage (1862–1932), now the most obscure member of the coterie despite his skilful illustration work during the 1890s and early twentieth century.[7] Savage is the least studied of the group because, according to the art critic Charles Holmes, he soon became frustrated by the impossibility of earning his livelihood with his mediaevalist woodcuts, and 'drifted off to make a living as an illustrator in a manner less exacting and much better paid'.[8] Finally, Lucien Pissarro, the son of French Impressionist Camille Pissarro who would years later himself be acclaimed for his work with the Camden Town Group, was then a wide-eyed expat in London, attempting as a painter to get out from under the shadow of his illustrious father. He developed a talent for book design under the supervision of Ricketts and would later participate in the Revival of Fine Printing through his own Eragny Press.[9]

Shannon and Ricketts were not only the most experienced artists, they also hosted the gatherings of this coterie and so slipped naturally into the editorship of the magazine that was their paper-and-ink continuation. Ricketts, Shannon, Gray and Savage filled the first issue, and from the second issue Sturge Moore and Pissarro joined in. The minor author and painter Walter Delaplaine Scull who published a few unnoticed literary works in the 1890s (No. 4), Herbert Horne (No. 2) and upcoming illustrator Laurence Housman (No. 5) each delivered one item, and the Fields have poetry and a prose vignette in Nos. 4 and 5. An untranslated French poem by Émile Verhaeren for No. 5, although in line with the regular focus of the periodical on French Symbolist poetry, is an unexpected twist. Ricketts uses the pseudonym 'Charles Sturt', with which he is credited for editorial work in some publications for the Vale Press (see below), for art criticism in Nos. 3 and 5, and he and Shannon sometimes have unsigned literary contributions in issues where they already have a signed essay, story or illustration.

Just like its precursor *The Germ*, the *Dial* features a small group of contributors who do not limit themselves to one medium. This multidisciplinarity is conspicuous, and intentionally so. Shannon and Ricketts often furnish illustrations, which like those in the *CGHH* are not always 'illustrative' in the sense that they do not refer to a text, but, as mentioned before, both also contributed essays and short fiction. Linked literary and pictorial items highlight a spirit of collaboration between the contributors, in the same way as in *The Germ*, but not with the same programmatic urgency of emphasising the cohesion of the producers. The frontispiece by Ricketts to the first number, with the rare luxury of being in colour, doubles as an illustration to the suggestive short story 'The Great Worm' by John Gray in the same number, daringly depicting a phallic monster leering at a nude maiden (Figure 9). In the last three issues, however, the frontispieces are no longer linked to a particular literary contribution. Sturge Moore has a poem in the second issue entitled 'On a Drawing by C. H. S.', which must refer to 'Charles Haslewood Shannon', but this does not seem to refer to a drawing of Shannon's in the *Dial*.

In the first issue there are also 'Notes', similar to those of the *CGHH*, being short mentions of topical events in the artistic scene, mostly provided by Savage. This may seem an odd feature in this ostensibly self-sufficient periodical, that otherwise took little notice of the outside world. The notes in question, however, concern events that were seen as congenial to the interests of the magazine, for example recent art exhibitions by Monet and the Brussels-based society 'Les XX', respectively in London and in Paris, that demonstrate that the *Dial* coterie felt it belonged to a wider, even transnational avant-garde. Longer articles address French inspirations in pictorial art such as Puvis de Chavannes (No. 1 – unsigned), Gustave Moureau (No. 3 – 'Sturt') and the Japanese painter and printmaker Utomaro (No. 5 – 'Sturt') whose influence can already be seen in the *japoniste* backdrop and erotica of the frontispiece illustration to the first number (Figure 9), and whose fame had reached Britain by way of French critic Edmond de Goncourt. There are laudatory essays on French authors, namely the Goncourt brothers (No. 1 – Gray) and Maurice de Guérin (No. 2 – unsigned), as well as a translation of a short story by the latter (No. 5 – Sturge Moore), and of poems by Ronsard (No. 3 – Sturge Moore) and Verlaine (No. 2 – Gray). Original poetry is dedicated to the recently deceased Rimbaud (Nos. 2 and 3 – Sturge Moore), and there is ekphrastic poetry on again Puvis (No. 2 – Sturge Moore). As we shall see, the *Dial* would pass on this French interest (which was already marginally present in recent numbers of the *CGHH*) to later publications such as the *Pageant* and the *Dome*. Next to French literature and art, particularly of the Symbolist school, the Pre-Raphaelites were a second important influence on the *Dial*. This home-grown inspiration is less obvious, but it for instance shows in the historical interest prevalent in some of the pictorial contributions, a 'taste for veiled allusions to the art and life of the past' Julie Codell believes the *Dial* to have inherited from the *CGHH*.[10] One clear instance of a revaluation of Renaissance art in the *Dial* is Savage's homage to the famous rhinoceros of Albrecht Dürer in No. 2 (Figure 10).

These two major inspirations are combined in an unsigned defence, unsigned but likely written by Ricketts on behalf of the group, against the ambiguous reception of the first issue, entitled 'The Unwritten Book' (No. 2). The reviews had mostly been guardedly positive, with critics seeing charm and originality in the magazine, but predicting a very limited audience and a short run for any publication of this kind. However, the *Magazine of Art* (1878–1904), one of the leading art publications at the time and although not hostile to avant-garde art per se intent on pleasing a wide readership, harshly dismissed the first *Dial* as incoherent in its contents, and full of 'hysterical and unhealthy [. . .] nudity and nonsense'.[11] Choosing not to reply to the allegation of immorality directly, the defence focuses on justifying the *Dial*'s editorial policy of an alleged 'reprehensible selectiveness'[12] by formulating a difficult but fascinating theory of art from which we can at once derive the aims of the magazine.

The title of the 'Unwritten Book' essay strongly recalls the French poet Mallarmé's unattained lifelong ambition of subsuming all of his diverse writings within the overarching project of *Le Livre* ('The Book'), already mentioned as one of the most committed Total Art projects of the nineteenth century in the Introduction to this book. Like other little magazines of the period, the *Dial* was faced with the problem of the characteristically open-ended format of the magazine, composed of the efforts of several contributors who all have their own interests, opinions and voices, which are collected in individual numbers that have to achieve some coherence on their own while still adding up with previous and future numbers to form one congruent series. If it was indeed too eclectic, as the *Magazine of Art* reviewer believed, then this would mean that it had come across as an inconsequential because fragmented text. The *Dial* tries to solve that by consistently referring to its numbers as 'Parts', implying that together these are segments of a greater whole beyond that of the individual number. Normally, the only closure that periodicals can achieve for themselves is that of each separate issue, or at best the annual volume, as the continuation of the series implies that each finished issue is not finished at all, but can be added to. Paradoxically, the *Dial*'s admission of incompleteness for each issue functions in the magazine's defence of its own eclecticism. By adopting the idea of the Mallarméan *Livre*, the *Dial* can defer the final coming together of the wide-ranging contents of its constituent 'Parts' to an unspecified moment in the future, when the self-sufficiency expected by its critics and demanded by the aesthetic of the Total Work of Art would finally be demonstrated.

Although he would only publish programmatic essays on the subject from the middle of the 1890s, Mallarmé had since the late 1860s declared that all his individual publications were to be considered mere 'feuillets' ('sheets'), or instalments towards his opus that would have no one prescribed meaning, but would be approachable from several angles dependent on the reader. This guarding of the text against the closure of a finished interpretation would detach it from its immediate moment of appearance and, according to Mallarmé himself in his essay *Quant au Livre* (1895), would permit the reader to bring to it, through the act of reading, the coherence of a 'a hymn, harmony and joy', expressing 'the links between everything'.[13] As a project of subjective meaning-making that involved not only the producers of the text but also the reader who brought in her/his personal history and inclinations, *Le Livre* was intended to add a dimension of audience participation to the Total Work of Art that is the text by elevating the reader from a passive spectator to an agent needed to activate the aesthetic potential of the literary text.[14] Mallarmé, arguably along with Verlaine, ruled the Parisian avant-garde, and these ideas would certainly be encountered by Ricketts and Shannon on their trips to Paris, where they met with leading Symbolist painters such as Puvis, or by Gray in his frequent correspondence with the critic Félix Fénéon, and through the latter with French Symbolist poets.

What the reader would have to pick up on immediately was the sole criterion for selection in the *Dial*: a symbolic representation of the interaction of man and the outside world. This symbolic representation, which the *Dial* group 'think common to all good art', is referred to as the 'Document': 'a [r]ecord of some remembered delight, record perhaps of a mere moment in a transfigured life' that the viewer of an artwork or the reader of a literary text can reactivate in their own mind. If the 'Unwritten Book' that is the Total project of the magazine breaks down into separate numbers or 'Parts', then each 'Part' would be a collection of such 'Documents':

> some exquisite detail in a masterpiece convincing to the spectator as a thing known, yet not of necessity the symbol of a borrowed story – possibly there, the mere symbol of time. [. . .] a thing, easily imagined away from a picture, but authoritative there, as gesture, or poetic recollection, the lattice-light cast upon the wall in Rossetti's *Proserpine*.[15]

David Corbett interprets the Document as an explanation for the *Dial*'s diverse contents because it would stand for 'an intense registration of experience that either is exotic or is allowed to be banal or abject in order to reveal or evoke unspecified meanings and emotions located beneath the surface of events'.[16] This would bring about a greater focus on the development of a personal style. The execution reveals the master, and not the represented topic, nor even the style the artist chooses to work in. This emphasis on the inherent qualities of the mode of representation makes it no longer possible for art to easily rely on institutionalised conventions for the sake of mere conventionalism, as was the rule in Academic painting and popular literature, and to reject given themes just because they have to date not found a place among the repertoire.

Corbett links this statement to the French Symbolist Manifesto, published in *Le Figaro* (1826–) by one of Mallarmé's disciples Jean

Moréas in September 1886.[17] There are certainly similarities: for one, an implicit rejection of the merits of literalist mimesis as favoured by the superseded avant-garde school of artistic and literary Naturalism, to which Moréas could 'in earnest only accord the value of a legitimate yet ill-advised protest'.[18] It was, however, not any less a part of the Pre-Raphaelite aesthetics of the *CGHH*, where in the very first issue (1884) Selwyn Image had attacked the same tendency in British illustration.[19] Realist art and literature, or its radical exponent Naturalism, is suspect for both currents because its main characteristic is the illusion of a direct representation of phenomena, which requires a false bracketing of the personal history and inclinations of the artist. Viewed from either a French Symbolist or a Pre-Raphaelite perspective, what comes to the forefront in the *Dial* is the idea that some aspects of art are more than simply mimetic of observed objects or intertextual references within cultural history, 'not of necessity the symbol of a borrowed story'. In her influential study of Fin-de-Siècle illustration, Lorraine Janzen Kooistra cites contemporaneous art critic Gleeson White's view in the *Pageant* (see Chapter 6) on the *Dial* as inspiring the 'unfettered illustrations' that can be found in many avant-garde books of the 1890s, which could accompany literary text or programmatic expositions, but would not assume subservience to these, and she sees the theory of the Document as a major development in this respect.[20] These artistic 'Documents' are self-referential, in the sense that they perform a necessary function in the context of the work; they can 'easily' be identified, or rather: 'imagined away'.

In this self-referentiality lies another link of the *Dial*'s Document to the Pre-Raphaelites. In the *Dial*'s defence, the 'Document' is referred to as 'a monument of moods', a hint at the opening lines of the introductory 'Sonnet on the Sonnet' in what since D. G. Rossetti's death in 1882 had become a core text of Aestheticism, *The House of Life*:

> A Sonnet is a moment's monument, –
> Memorial from the soul's eternity
> To one dead deathless hour. Look that it be,
> Whether for lustral rite or dire portent,
> Of its own intricate fullness reverent:
> Carve it in ivory or in ebony,
> As Day or Night prevail; and let Time see
> Its flowering crest impearled and orient.[21]

This sonnet, one of Rossetti's more straightforward statements of his opinions on poetry and pictorial art as well as the relationship between the two, is for several reasons an ideal inspiration for the editors of the

Dial. It claims an eternal validity for true art, even though all art originates in the artist's individual and transitory experience (ll. 2–3). It is important to note that this is a meta-sonnet, reflecting on the demands the conceit makes of the choice of style and even of the appropriate use of the chosen artistic medium (ll. 3–5). This means that the work of art is the stable representation of ideal content, and artists should be aware of what the medium brings to the work. To an even greater extent than in the *CGHH*, the quality of the materials used and the choice of techniques are central in the *Dial*. It is here that we must seek for the vaguely described 'gesture' that is mentioned in the magazine's defence, identifiable but not always intelligible, to be understood as the meaning contained in the material presentation.

The Pre-Raphaelites and the Artistic Craftsmen viewed the material aspects of the work of art as elements of central importance, because these created the medium through which any message could be transmitted. Even if they held that each issue of the *Dial* was but a 'Part' of a larger 'Unwritten Book' that would probably never be realised in the future, Ricketts and Shannon realised that this 'Part' too should be an artistic object. They followed the *CGHH* in elevating the production of their periodical, the work of art in question here, into an integral part of the creative process. Ricketts in particular was always very closely involved with the design and printing of the *Dial*. He initially wanted to secure a deal with George Allen, who had taken care of the 1884 issue of the *CGHH* and gathered further accolades since then, but failed to do so, and had to see the *Dial* through the press on his own.[22] The first issue was printed by Hazell, Watson and Viney (London), unfortunately not to the satisfaction of the editors. There were problems with the process blocks (a recent means of photographic reproduction of images), which explains why these only appear in this first number, and the lack of typographical distinction of the first number betrays Ricketts's lack of experience with page design.[23] For the following numbers the *Dial* moved to the acclaimed Ballantyne Press, a printing firm of high repute whom the demanding editors knew they could trust with their directions. Ricketts was advised to approach Ballantyne by the equally demanding James Whistler, who had printed his own meticulously designed book *The Gentle Art of Making Enemies* (1890) with them and, just like Ricketts would, had learned a great deal about the printer's craft from the association.[24] The first three numbers of the *Dial* were published privately, with distribution taken care of by the Bodley Head after 1892, and the last two numbers appear on the publisher's list of the newly founded Vale Press in 1896, which was owned by Ricketts and his patron, the barrister William Llewellyn Hacon, with the aforementioned Charles Holmes taking care the drudgery of daily management. It is telling that the Vale Press would later never keep actual presses of their own, but commission Ballantyne to print their books for them, of course under the close supervision of Ricketts himself. Ricketts stated that he could trust this firm to do as they were told, because the importance of 'the element of personal control which characterised the books of the revival' was respected at Ballantyne's much more than by other trade presses.[25] Tellingly, he even entrusted with them his pamphlet *A Defence of the Revival of Printing* (1899), which was actually a reply to critics of Vale Press books and therefore obviously had to be printed perfectly itself.

The *Dial* is not only typeset and printed with increasing confidence and success, but also stands out through its format. It is exceptionally large and unusual in size, from 12.2 by 9.4 inches (No. 1) to 14.2 by 11 inches (Nos. 2–5). In size at least, it is the largest little magazine of the period, closer to a folio than to the quarto or octavo sizes that were usually favoured. The fact that nevertheless none of the issues has more than thirty-six pages makes them very slender. From a designer's perspective, the size carries the advantages that the plates and ornaments can be bigger, and that there is more space for wide margins and letter spacing without ending up with unappealingly small blocks of text on the page. Not only are the pages oversized, the type is also noticeably large. According to Maureen Watry, 'the large point size was probably determined by economic considerations: lower composition costs for sizes above ten point with the added advantage that the rather scant text was stretched to a respectable length over a large format',[26] a trick, as discussed in Chapter 2, that was also used by inventive trade publishers like the Bodley Head who wanted to emulate Revivalist books. The used typeface is an old-style face similar to the Revival's pet font Caslon. When more intricate characters were wanted these were engraved, as is for instance the case with the text on the cover and title page (Figure 11); however, like the *CGHH* before it, the *Dial* is not cluttered with ornaments either. Occasionally, initials too were engraved for prose contributions; presumably the page layout for the consistently short poems was judged not to benefit from ornaments.

A notice in the prospectus for the second number drew attention to the fact that the included woodcuts and lithographs were directly printed from the wood or stone respectively, which is an important statement of the hands-on approach favoured by the Vale coterie. Shannon was an acclaimed painter, and the first number contains photogravures of two of his works, but after this none appear. Here the *Dial* is more radical than the *CGHH*, which featured both the old and newest methods of image reproduction, having photogravure reproductions of paintings in nearly every number, and even including some regular photographs in its 'Century Guild Work' section of objects designed by Guild members (see Chapter 2). From the second issue onwards, Ricketts and Shannon made a point of having woodcuts and engravings printed from the wood, as explained in a leaflet announcing No. 2, 'to ensure the greater sweetness in the printing',[27] but mainly to uphold the artistic craft they had both been trained in at the City and Guilds of London Art School under renowned master Charles Roberts. They responded to the recent obsolescence of their craft as a means of image reproduction precisely by no longer using engravings to *re*produce the pictorial work of painters and draughtsmen, but to produce original work straight away. Especially in the flagship second issue of the *Dial*, they are used as an expressive artistic medium in their own right, and are therefore no longer based on any other images, the artists working directly on the block. The 'craft' is in this manner placed on the same level as the 'art' to which it was formerly considered secondary, and the materials involved in the production of the magazine are aesthetically upgraded from humble means of image reproduction to the medium of original art.

Of course, in actual fact engraving was not so much upgraded as restored to this position of eminence. Ricketts advocated the need for a revival of engraving analogous to that of printing, which followed naturally from the ongoing Revival of Printing, in an article in the Aestheticist annual the *Pageant* (see Chapter 6). He states there that this artistic craft has been led astray since the Renaissance because it was no longer respected as an art in its own right, but forced to conform to unsuitable innovations in the other visual arts that it was now wont to reproduce:

> From the first, one of these evils was the detached draughtsman, from whom sprang an insistence upon the fashions in outline; the other element of failure at the root was the interpreter, with his callousness, his lack of responsibility, hence the great suggestive value of those few master-craftsmen who were designers and engravers at once.[28]

Savage's reference in his frontispiece to the second number of the *Dial* to Dürer (Figure 10), the most celebrated European engraver of all time, was a tribute to such 'master-craftsmen'. One of the tasks the artists at the Vale set themselves was to bring about the reconciliation of the creative and the technical aspects of engraving in one and the same artist, as historically had been the norm. Fellow *Dial* contributor Sturge Moore is praised in the *Pageant* article for his 'style of original wood engraving [that] is not here merely accidental, as of a trade engraver who is artist at his leisure, but in aim they show that directness of all work understood within the peculiar conditions of a medium'.[29] Ricketts hopes furthermore that such attempts at setting aright this deviation will be found 'in the pages of contemporary magazines',[30] no doubt meaning not least of which his own.

Other material aspects also receive due attention. Whereas the first issue of the *Dial* still has hazy lithographs and photographic reproductions, from the second issue onwards there is a marked improvement in the printing of the former, and as said the latter are entirely absent. It makes sense that a periodical which emphasised the importance of the 'Document', described as 'some exquisite detail', would take care to bring out its plates as clearly as possible. The introspection they had time for during the two-and-a-half-year intermission, aided by the technical know-how and experience of the Ballantyne Press, also resulted in a standardisation of the magazine's layout. From the second to the final issue, the same cover illustration is used with the slight difference that for Nos. 4 and 5 the logo of the newly founded Vale Press is substituted for the former mention 'Published by The Editors in the Vale, Chelsea' (Figure 11). From then on the issues at least looked the part of 'Parts' of a future greater whole, bringing a visual consistency that would possibly dispel misgivings about the magazine's internal eclecticism, just like the *CGHH* had done before. This image confirms this eclecticism by featuring references to the different arts: the melancholy female figure is standing behind a writing desk, below her there is a little sculpture, in the bottom left corner a violin represents music (although there is no music in the magazine, this might stand for poetry), and opposite is a painter's palette. However, all of these are subsumed within the one image, and therefore by implication integrated into the one Total Artwork for which this recurrent cover illustration stands. The female figure is sheltered by a rose bush, symbolising *sub rosa* intimacy with a chaste hint at secretive sexuality, and the Icarus figure of the painting resting on the easel by the palette is a common motif for a hubristic attempt at elevation beyond reasonable expectations, a fit emblem for the attractive hope-against-hope martyrdom of the avant-garde.

Also like the older magazine, the *Dial* had a strong interest in book design, and was produced by and for people who appreciated the recent Revival of Printing. Not only was Ricketts himself an acclaimed book designer, Sturge Moore and Pissarro were progressing in this applied art too. The *Dial* also played a role in the foundation of the aforementioned Vale Press. Several *Dial* contributors were at least marginally involved with this firm, albeit by having their work published as 'Michael Field' (who published most of their plays through this imprint), or by editorial work like Gray and Sturge Moore, the latter also furnishing illustrations. In the retrospective final publication of the Press in 1904, Ricketts recollects that his guiding principle was that 'a book is a living and corporate whole, the quality of beauty therein is all-pervading [. . .]. It is conceived harmoniously and made beautifully like any other genuine work of art. Unity, harmony, such are the essentials of fine book building.'[31] In other words, like others of his generation he considered books to require integrated or Total Art design. This conception of the book as a composite artwork is very important to Ricketts, as 'a work of art is a whole in which each portion is exquisite in itself yet co-ordinate'.[32] This 'whole' does not only refer to the material book considered as the sum of its paratextual elements, such as the bindings, choice of materials, decorations and illustrations, but also to the literary work that is printed, which should be the point of departure: 'fine literature, owing to its quality of permanence, suggests for that reason the desirability of a beautiful and permanent form for it'.[33]

Although the *Dial* never refers to the political aims of the Arts and Crafts Movement, which of course had been understated in its model the *CGHH* as well, Ricketts and his collaborators too prided themselves on their artistic craftsmanship by making sure that the readers of the *Dial* noticed the relevance of the applied arts that went into the production of the magazine and other publications on the Vale Press list. A clear example of this is the inclusion of a specimen of the 'Vale type' in No. 4 (1896), around the time of the establishment of the Press, that can be seen as the official launch of this font, Ricketts's first attempt at designing a typeface of his own. This item recalls the aestheticised advertising-by-demonstration strategy of the *CGHH* and the plain *Hobby Horse*, providing a supposedly disinterested sample of one's skill in order to solicit commissions. It is very similar in layout to the prospectus booklets that the Vale Press circulated around the publication of each new book, and – like the periodical in which it appears – it is therefore at the same time an advertisement for, and a conceptually justified demonstration of the design aesthetic that the Vale Press wished to be known for. The specimen is a four-page booklet in quality laid paper, smaller than the regular page size of the *Dial*, and is tipped in inside the periodical, halfway through an unrelated short story by Delaplaine Scull. It contains a page from the Vale Press edition of William Adlington's *The Excellent Narration of the Marriage of Cupide and Psyches* (1566/1897), a book that readers could of course buy if they were sufficiently impressed by this sample. This is a very liminal entry, and not only because it literally adheres so loosely to the material periodical. It is also at the same time a regular content item demonstrating an applied art, and a commercial publicity ploy. The third number of the *Dial* (1893) similarly features an illustration from the edition by Ricketts and Shannon of *Daphnis and Chloe* (also 1893). The excerpt printed here comes complete with the page number that the original image has in the book, which was the very first to appear with the Vale imprint, though it was distributed by the Bodley Head.[34]

After the Vale Press had been officially set up in business and the *Dial* from its fourth issue onwards became part of its list, it of course stands to reason that the only periodical that they would issue would be involved in the commercial strategy of the Press as a means of publicity. The shop sign at the offices of the Vale Press in Warwick Street read 'At the Sign of the Dial', suggesting that the *Dial* was deemed crucial to the reputation of Ricketts as a printing Revivalist. The fact that the eponymous periodical was already in its seventh year of existence by the time the Vale Press was founded implies that this image of 'the dial' was considered as a brand that stood for the entire firm, as it had done for the magazine. Linking this to the central idea behind the magazine as providing 'monuments of moods', the image of the dial could metaphorically refer to the text as a snapshot of the artistic world at the time of issue, a literal 'state of the art'. Fletcher additionally reads the magazine's title as 'a seeming promise of temporal determinism which the whimsical cycle of the periodical denies'.[35] The editors themselves adhered to the slightly underwhelming explanation that the title would reflect the magazine's appearance 'at such intervals as the sun of inspiration permits'.[36] From the second number onwards the added subtitle of the magazine became 'An occasional publication', which could not have been better chosen, as the five issues of the *Dial* appeared in a highly irregular frequency: No. 1 in 1889, No. 2 in 1892, No. 3 in 1893, No. 4 in 1896 and No. 5 in 1897. The fact that the first issue is simply subtitled 'The first number in the series', with no information about the projected pace of publication, suggests that the editors were not sure what frequency they could sustain for the periodical, and after the almost three years it had taken to bring out the second number, they wisely decided not to tie themselves down to deadlines.

The troublesome 'periodicity' of the periodical, which moved the *Dial* to refer to its issues as 'Parts', is also reflected by the characteristically whimsical comment that Wilde is reported to have made after seeing the first issue, that they should not 'bring out a second number, all perfect things should be unique'.[37] The Vale coterie's reasons for founding the *Dial* may have been pragmatic rather than programmatic, and they cleverly dodged allegations of a lack of focus by hinting at a Mallarméan project through which all of their interests would eventually come together, but the magazine's conceptual unity goes further than that. In the first issue, we find an anonymous editorial 'Apology', most probably written by Ricketts, which explains that

> [t]he sole aim of this magazine is to gain sympathy with its views. Intelligent ostracism meets one at every door for any view whatsoever, from choice of subject to choice of frame. If our entrance is *not* through an orthodox channel, it is not, therefore, entirely our fault; we are out of date in our belief that the artist's conscientiousness cannot be controlled by the paying public, and just as far as this notion is prevalent we shall be pardoned our seeming aggressiveness.[38]

We already know what the 'choice of subject' amounts to from our discussion of the contents, and the mention of the 'frame' confirms that the *Dial* was intended to provide an appropriate material medium for its contents. In its attitude of 'intelligent ostracism', the assertive avant-garde would aim solely 'to gain sympathy with its views', setting itself apart from an excluding and self-protective mainstream where lucre was the only accepted measure for artistic success. The 'seeming aggressiveness' of the little magazine is therefore always rather passive than directly assailant; the strategy of these avant-garde artists being to prove the feasibility of their own project through a stunning example of the new artistic practice. It is a defiant refusal to enter the logic of the market. The at times controversial content is presented by means of an intricately designed text that the editors hope to be bibliographically encoded with the artistic dignity of the coterie responsible for it. Despite the links to the Vale Press, the *Dial* is meant to present itself as an uncompromising alternative that explicitly rejects being part of any commercial strategy, positioning itself on the periphery of the periodical market.

Judging from the 'Apology', the editors seem to have had no false hopes about this. The ambitious design and production methods of the magazine, and the limited appeal to the market that was the result of an uncompromising editorial policy and its intimate circle of contributors, would have forced them to maintain a small circulation anyway. Nos. 1 and 2 both had a print run of 200 copies, 3 had 250, and 4 and 5 rose to a hardly impressive 270 (of which 250 were for sale). Small circulation of course implies higher production cost per copy. This could have been helped by including advertisements, but yet again as with the *CGHH*, the *Dial* lacks external advertisers and thereby forfeits another important source of income not declined by most 'regular' periodicals, or even little magazines. All this resulted in an exceptionally high price: the first number was priced at 7s. 6d, No. 2 at 10 shillings and the final three at 12s. 6d, making the *Dial* one of the most expensive periodicals of the 1890s. A leaflet held by the British Library announcing the publication of the second number announces that thirteen remaining copies of the first could be purchased in bound edition for the even higher price of 30 shillings, an interesting early instance of a periodical claiming a share in the upcoming vogue for rare and special editions instigated by the Bodley Head, by whom the *Dial* perhaps not coincidentally was from this second number distributed (see Chapter 2). This confirms that thanks to the work of the *Dial*, and the *CGHH* before it, beautifully designed periodicals were increasingly recognised as being of equal value to Revivalist books.

A prospectus for the fifth number of the *Dial* (1897), also in the British Library, announces in few words that this will be the final 'Part': '[t]he early parts were produced when it seemed impossible to launch original work in any other way. This is no longer the case, and the series ceases with the necessity for it.' Since then, the Vale Press had been established and brought in work for Ricketts and Shannon, who through the magazine, erratic though it was, had been allowed free rein and had reached with their own preferred work a wider audience than ever before. They now also regularly contributed to magazines, both avant-garde and mainstream, and took care of design and illustration for leading publishers of Revivalist books. Although they would never be as successful as their former teachers and hosts, Sturge Moore and Savage had received greater exposure as artists than they could have achieved on their own. For all four, the *Dial* had functioned as a circulating portfolio that had increasingly demonstrated their considerable talent. Gray lost interest in the avant-garde at the end of the 1890s, but had greatly benefited from the opportunity to aid the artistic causes that he felt most strongly about, and the Fields had been provided with a venue for the work that lay closest to their hearts.

The *Dial* was a marginal publication, but its place in the history of the little magazine genre should not be overlooked. It was the first periodical to appear in the heyday of British Aestheticism, the so-called 'Nineties'. Through its contents, it also did much to promote the French Symbolist inspirations so commonly associated with the Fin de Siècle, and the suspicion it was met with in some circles would become commonplace in the reception of Fin-de-Siècle little magazines, which soon were eyed suspiciously as likely purveyors of 'Decadence'. It seems significant for the rise in reputation of Ricketts and Shannon that the most damning review of the *Dial*'s first number appeared in the same periodical, the *Magazine of Art*, that published a highly positive account of its role in late-Victorian art and artistic printing close to the *Dial*'s folding in 1897. This article on Ricketts as a 'book-builder' was written by Gleeson White, whom we have had cause to mention as a critic and editor instrumental in the popularisation of the Revival before. It says nothing about the contents of the *Dial*, but reassesses the *Dial* as 'sumptuously-printed' for its 'invention in arranging ordinary types in well-balanced masses'.[39] We might say that the numbers are vital Documents in the history of British print design.

The many voices of the *Pagan Review*

With all of the little magazines that we have discussed up until now, we have seen that they were used as platforms for a given group, uniting to increase their impact on an often unwelcoming artistic orthodoxy. *The Germ* is thereby associated with the Pre-Raphaelite Brotherhood, the *OCM* with the Set, the *CGHH* with the Arts and Crafts organisation that it claimed to represent, and the *Dial* more opportunistically with the coterie that met at the Vale, albeit all four were sporadically joined by elect outsiders. We have furthermore discussed the different conceptual strategies available to these groups for presenting their periodical organs as collective efforts that would bear the stamp of their common vision and their internal collaboration, while still retaining some editorial focus and the high degree of conceptual unity that gradually came to be expected of Aestheticist journals. This could be a challenge, if only because of the characteristic instability of the magazine format. Margaret Beetham goes so far as to consider 'the variety and heterogeneity of their constituent genres and [. . .] diversity of voices' as the main characteristic of magazines.[40] This is true for the overwhelming majority of magazines, but to avant-garde artists and authors rules are made to be broken. Some individual little magazine producers, such as William Sharp of the *Pagan Review* (1892) and Edward Gordon Craig of the *Page* (1898–1901), felt the urge to assume control over their projects so strongly that they issued magazines which they not only edited and designed by themselves, but for which they alone supplied all, or nearly all, of the content.

Recalling our discussion of the history of the 'magazine' genre in Chapter 1, there described at its broadest, it might be a bit surprising to find that such a metaphorical storehouse of diverse information, from the beginning characterised by its heterogeneity, would only contain work by a single contributor, who is in charge of running and producing the periodical as well. Yet, there were precedents for such a counterintuitive choice. From the beginning of the eighteenth century roughly up until the 1750s, there were several so-called 'essay periodicals', the most famous of which included Joseph Addison and Richard Steele's *Spectator* (1711–12/15), Eliza Haywood's *Female Spectator* (1744–6) and Samuel Johnson's *Rambler* (1750–2), where each issue would be written by one author, and in the case of the latter two that one author wrote the entire series. The genre predates the magazines, however (as is so often the case) hazy the boundaries can be. Some of these publications already included a number of sometimes conflicting opinions debated in multiple 'voices'; the catch is that these were all provided by one author who assumed several personae. The short lifespan that essay periodicals tended to have was no doubt influenced by the demands they made on the solitary toilers behind them. They gradually were absorbed by the new periodical formats of the magazine in the second half of the eighteenth century, becoming the ancestors of the recurrent 'columns' in our magazines, newspapers and internet media of today.

There are not many well-known examples of magazines in the nineteenth century that were run on the same principle as the little magazines under scrutiny in this section, but one precursor likely known in the British avant-garde would be *La Dernière Mode* (1874). This was a French lady's fashion magazine edited and almost completely written by the ubiquitous Mallarmé. Although it is a strange exercise to consider a publication on such a topic a little magazine, de Gourmont, who as said coined the term 'petite revue', does include it among many indisputable cases in his little magazine bibliography as the 'rarest of journals'.[41] *La Dernière Mode* was certainly not intended to appeal to a minority audience and was not circulated in small editions, but it was indeed unlike any other women's magazine in the market at the time. Mallarmé wrote his articles under various pseudonyms, which corresponded to as many authorial personae, often female at that. He diversified his own writings, as it were, by implementing consistent voices for all of these masks, assigning specific specialist topics to each fictional contributor, which allowed him to present different aspects of his own views as well as to feature in the magazine contradictory opinions in ongoing public debates on fashion.[42] In an effort to help out his avant-garde friends, Mallarmé did allow in each of the eight biweekly issues a poem and a short story that were not written by himself, but by *Parnassiens* such as Coppée, Sully Prudhomme and Banville, and he included fashion plates and other illustrations that were commissioned from artists whom the inventive editor/author wished to support.

The bibliography of little magazines compiled by de Gourmont holds more surprises. The *Pagan Review*, entirely written in English and edited by the Scotsman William Sharp in a cottage in very English Sussex, finds a place in this overview of otherwise exclusively French-language magazines from France and Belgium. This periodical is described there as an 'imitation and parody of French Symbolist magazines',[43] a compliment that the bibliographer maybe wished to return by including the *Pagan Review* in the list. It was indeed one of the clearest examples of Gallic inspiration in the 1890s avant-garde, and Sharp had been an insider in Parisian literary circles since before the *Dial*'s Gray first crossed the Channel. Nevertheless, its appropriations from contemporaneous French journals are not simply derivative, and it would be wrong to view this magazine as a mere pastiche.

Sharp was born in 1855 into an upper-middle-class family in Paisley in Lowland Scotland. From an early age he was inspired by a spiritual devotion to the countryside around the family's Highland holiday home that would ultimately lead to his involvement in the Celtic Revival (see Chapter 5).[44] Arriving in London in the late 1870s, he soon had the considerable pleasure of becoming a protégé of Dante Gabriel Rossetti. Through Rossetti, Sharp became personally acquainted with most of the shaping forces of early Aestheticism, gaining a centrality in the literary salons of the period that is not reflected in the minor status he currently holds in literary history. He wrote prolifically in support of new fashions in art and literature, for instance as a critic for the Glasgow newspaper the *Herald* (1783–), and for the specialist *Art Journal* (1839–1912) that was often critical of the avant-garde. He also authored reverential biographies of his recently deceased mentor Rossetti (1882), Shelley (1887), Heine (1888) and Robert Browning (1889), in which the legacy of Romantic poetry is a recurrent interest. Furthermore, he contributed travel writing to popular publications such as *Good Words* (1860–1911) and even the highbrow but open-minded *Fortnightly Review* (1865–1954), insisting on the cultural determinism of natural environment and ethnicity; this interest would come to the forefront in his involvement with the later little magazine the *Evergreen* (see Chapter 5).

Although Sharp had published a novel and several collections of poetry, his breakthrough came with the emergence of his carefully guarded alter ego 'Fiona Macleod' in the early 1890s, which he only acknowledged on his deathbed in 1905. He had often been disappointed before by the reception of his literary work, which for its daring themes and experiments with form, both inspired by Continental literary Naturalism and Symbolism, generally was poorly received in the mainstream press. A rare counterpart to the countless Victorian women authors who wrote under male pseudonyms, the Macleod persona has been so central in assessments of Sharp's career that it has overshadowed the far larger amount of work he published under his own name. His two book-length biographies to date, an account by his first cousin and wife Elizabeth Sharp (1910) and a scholarly study by Flavia Alaya (1970), tellingly both mention the names Sharp and Macleod in the title. Sharp had a knack for this kind of masquerade, and the consensus is that this was at least in part a cunning strategy to dupe critics prejudiced against him. He invented several other personae, but none of these proved as productive as Fiona Macleod. The early 1890s form a particularly active period for this masked avenger, according to Alaya not by coincidence right after the publication of his book on Browning, in which he expresses admiration for the artful personae of the dramatic monologues. The artistic potential and challenge of writing (temporarily) under a fictitious guise must have been appealing, even more so as his own literary work had once again been misunderstood by critical opinion.

The question of how to reshape his career was a major consideration for Sharp in the early Nineties. His recent poetry collection *Sospiri di Roma* (1891) had been praised by important peers such as George Meredith, but its both poetic and sexual licence did not fare so well in the press. In this book, Sharp provided one of the earliest examples of free verse in Britain. Walt Whitman's *Leaves of Grass* (1855–92) and French pioneering texts such as Arthur Rimbaud's *Illuminations* (1886) were known, but mainly by the avant-garde, and although W. E. Henley's collection *In Hospital* (1888) had given the budding genre a respectable start in Britain, Sharp's unabashed celebration of sexuality and the obvious influence of more controversial poets like Whitman and

Baudelaire coloured the reception of his own collection. Alaya believes that '[t]he *Pagan Review* undoubtedly originated as a device for baiting the prudish critics who had responded so archly to his *Sospiri*'.[45] This is confirmed by a mention in a letter written to a friend on the reception of this collection, lamenting that

> [w]hether coming with praise or with blame and cast me to the perdition of the unrighteous, the critics all seem unable to take the true standpoint – namely, that of the poet. [. . .] It is no good to any one or to me to say that I am a Pagan – that I am 'an artist beyond doubt, but one without heed to the cravings of the human heart: a worshipper of the Beautiful, but without religion, without an ethical message, with nothing but a vain cry for the return, or it may be the advent, of an impossible ideal'.[46]

Sharp may have wanted to try how far he could push the envelope with this deliberately provocative magazine, which had but one number, published in September 1892. The magazine's motto was cleverly 'Sic transit gloria Grundi' ('thus passes the glory of [Mrs] Grundy', after the archetype of British prudishness); and the so-called 'paganism' of Sharp's editorial persona 'W. H. Brooks' (sometimes today still mistakenly assumed to have been a real person) propagates a hyperbolic version of the vitalism that Sharp had poetically explored before in the *Sospiri* poems. Elizabeth Sharp claims her husband wrote all contributions in a very short space of time in June 1892, and his diary indicates that he had finished most of them within a single week in 'a mental attitude [. . .] of sheer revelling in the beauty of objective life and nature'.[47] The tone of the 'Foreword' is confident or even defiant, not unlike the mission statement that we find in the *Dial*. The impossible task of converting the 'general public' to its pagan doctrine would never be the magazine's goal:

> Editorial prefaces to new magazines generally lay great stress on the effort of the directorate, and all concerned, to make the forthcoming periodical popular. We have no such expectation, not even, it may be added, any such intention. We aim at thorough-going unpopularity, and there is every reason to believe that, with the blessed who expect little, we shall not be disappointed.[48]

'Brooks'/Sharp goes on to state that his only hope is to reach 'the new generation', in whom 'the new paganism is a potent leaven'. This paganism is not set out in articles of faith, although we are assured that 'the Pagan Review conveys, or is meant to convey, a good deal by its title'.[49] The editor avers that 'this magazine is to be a purely literary, not a philosophical, partisan, or propagandist periodical', a side note that was perhaps deemed necessary because of the connotations of political partiality that the term 'review', as referring to a specific genre of periodical, still carried at the time. The fact that Sharp for a while considered reviving the periodical at a quarterly frequency[50] further confirms the suggestion that he wanted to hint (perhaps ironically) at the genre of the opinionated and learned quarterly reviews, as, for example, the *Yellow Book* would later do as well. Like earlier little magazines, the *Pagan Review* preferred to advocate its opinions by 'the transformation or reincarnation of them through indirect presentment', and would try to expound its points of view through 'artistic expression' rather than through 'such avocations as chronicling the ebb and flow of thought' in the everyday world.[51]

> It is *Life* that we preach, if perforce we must be taken as preachers at all, Life to the full, in all its manifestations, in its heights and depths, precious to the uttermost moment, not to be bartered even when maimed and weary.[52]

Denis Denisoff describes the notion of paganism in the late-Victorian avant-garde as ranging from the use of post-Romantic commonplaces of nature worship at its weakest, to at its strongest a fascination with the notion of a sophisticated non-dualist morality that would have been repressed after the spiritual conquest of Christianity, but notes that it often did not range beyond 'sensual nature worship'.[53] The 'Foreword' of the *Pagan Review* clearly exploits its pagan theme mainly for such provocation, but it does have some philosophical purchase. An interesting case for gender equality is made, on the principle that 'the supreme interest of Man is – Woman: and the most profound and fascinating problem to Woman is – Man'. Paganism would primarily be characterised by a frank attitude towards 'the myriad aspects of life', and, in a turn of phrase that indeed would have sent Mrs Grundy into a fit, 'it is natural that literature dominated by the various forces of the sexual emotion should prevail'.

Already in this first contribution, 'Brooks'/Sharp is speaking in the plural ('we'), intent on not being censored or otherwise checked in the hope of artistically representing all aspects of life. He declares his magazine representative of the 'new generation' for which he had high hopes. Similarly, the front matter on the back of the cover states that '[the *Pagan Review*] will publish nothing save by writers who theoretically and practically have identified, or are identifying themselves with "the younger men"', and though this implies that he has a more or less specific profile for his contributors in mind, it is never really clarified by which principles these 'younger men' would be characterised. Elizabeth Sharp does not supply a lot of information on this, merely stating that '[a]s he had no contributors, for he realised he would have to attract them, he himself wrote the whole of the Contents under various pseudonyms'.[54]

Attracting contributors was of course only made more troublesome by Sharp's pseudonymity in the magazine. It seems significant that he did reveal the truth to two American correspondents.[55] In a letter dated 13 August 1892 to the poet and critic Edmund Clarence Stedman, who was a major figure in transatlantic connections between Britain and the United States, Sharp hinted at a possible review in a future issue of work by Stedman and flatteringly confided in him about the worry of launching a new journal. Sharp had earlier sought the patronage of Stedman for publications in America, and in exchange had used his own interest in Britain in the latter's favour.[56] On the same day Sharp wrote to the Canadian-born Bliss Carman, who amongst many other periodicals wrote for the American counterparts to the British little magazines, inviting him to contribute, and asking him to mention the *Pagan Review* in the magazine *Current Literature* (1888–1925) with which Carman was then involved (neither would happen). The *Pagan Review* did invite submissions in the magazine itself, with the guidelines that '[n]o fiction can be considered, except short stories characterised by distinct actuality, whether "romantic" or "realistic"; and in no instance must these exceed 3000 words, while 2000, or even 1000 constitute a preferable length'.[57] For the projected following numbers, more was promised from the 'authors' already present in the first, and 'the collaboration of some of the most typical poets and romancists [sic] of the new movement in France and Belgium has been secured'.[58] One can only wonder if this was actually true, as no names for these 'typical' future contributors are given, and it would furthermore necessitate completely rethinking the concept of the magazine as set out in this first, and only, number. A letter dated 31 October 1892 does indicate that Sharp received at least one unsolicited manuscript, the only one confirmed by Mrs Sharp, from later *Yellow Book* contributor Robert Murray Gilchrist. Perhaps Gilchrist's early 'weird tales' would not have been out of place in the *Pagan Review*.

Rather than indolence in attracting other writers, Sharp's seclusion in his own magazine is once again a prime instance of the Aestheticist tendency to seize control of artistic projects to the largest extent possible. This allows the single person in charge to pursue her or his own vision less hindered by the need to make compromises. A conceptual unity of the Total Work of Art perhaps becomes more difficult to invoke as more people are involved, because it will always be an ideal construct stemming from the subjective judgement of a single mind, as it was with despotic personalities like Wagner, or at least of a close-knit group of collaborators who are willing to submit to the end result they collectively set out to achieve, as in the more formally and conceptually ambitious of our little magazines. When the diversity of personae in the *Pagan Review* is placed in the light of the editorial mission statement, announcing the treatment of all aspects of life while giving the author(s) freedom in their choice of literary style, it is clear that a form of equilibrium is needed to make sure that the included variety is conducive to this attempt at catching that pagan panoply of human existence. The art critic and poet John Addington Symonds, whose own pagan predilections were focused on the greater acceptance of same-sex relations in Ancient Greece, once praised Sharp in a letter as

> one of those who live (as Goethe has for ever put it), in 'the whole'. It is the great thing for modern criticism to get itself up out of holes and corners, mere personal proclivities and scholarly niceties, into the large air of nature and of man.[59]

The *Pagan Review* too hints at this experience of the Whole, and Sharp appears to have realised that, like every Total Work of Art, its conceptual cohesion would be marred by the never-closed and inherently miscellaneous genre of the magazine. Sharp wished to experiment with writing in different styles, and this had the additional advantage that he could make sure that each item was conducive to achieving a central message for the periodical, considered as a unified text.

The *Pagan Review* holds, apart from the opening 'Foreword' and a concluding 'Forecast', seven literary and two critical items. One of the latter, signed by 'S.' and therefore the one in which Sharp plays with his personae the least ingeniously, is a favourable review of the Franco-American poet Stuart Merrill's translations of French prose poetry *Pastels in Prose* (1890); the second is a gossip column entitled 'Contemporary Record' that under the epigraph 'Me judice' ('in my opinion') gathers a few bits of news from the literary world, for instance decrying recent work by Mrs Humphry Ward, Kipling and even Swinburne, seen as declining into respectable decrepitude. Meredith, whose *Modern Love* (1862) is also quoted extensively in the magazine's 'Foreword', Hardy, Whitman and Zola are commended for the inherent vitality of their writing.

The first literary contribution is called 'The Black Madonna', and signed 'W. S. Fanshawe'. It is a prose poem interlaced with short dramatic passages about the worship of a black statue of the Virgin Mary, here, however, blasphemously identified as a both beautiful and fearsome avatar of Astarte, a Middle Eastern deity of sexuality and war. This chthonic deity had before figured in D. G. Rossetti's double work *Astarte Syriaca* (1877) consisting of a painting and a poem, and more recently in the erotic verse collection *Astarte* (1891) by the French-speaking Flemish poet Pierre Louÿs, in both cases also personifying the unsettling power of sexuality. In the *Pagan Review*, the destructive might of sexual love is demonstrated when the statue comes to life after being worshipped by a votary, who seeks her out although he realises the tremendous danger this entails.

The contrasting lighter aspects of giving oneself over to infatuation are at the centre in the following item, a passionate love poem signed 'Geo. Gascoigne', that treats of analogies between love and nature. One of Sharp's poetry collections had been entitled *Romantic Ballads* (1888) in the conviction that a brief resurgence of Romantic poetry was inevitable in the near future, and the poetry in the *Pagan Review* too is full of post-Romantic tropes, as so much British poetry of the period was.[60] 'Poetry should be more vital than life itself',[61] as Sharp declared in the collection, and to this end the subject's moods are mirrored in descriptions of the elements in the *Pagan Review* as well. The titular 'Coming of Love' coincides with the budding of spring, and a lover addressed as 'flower of my heart' is told not to be in 'dread in thy heart of this divinest madness'.[62]

Then 'Willand Dreeme' (Middle Scots for 'dream willingly' or 'purposely') delivers a short story entitled 'The Pagans: A Memory', about how the acceptance of our natural desires can guide us in a contemporary world of respectable hypocrisy. The title of the story, and the placement of this item at the exact centre of the number, implies that the message we can deduct from it should be considered a programmatic statement for the magazine. The heterodiegetic narrator named 'Wilfrid Traquair' is a Scot leading a bohemian life in Paris, a mischievous autobiographical hint at the story's true author. Unlike the respective feverish Decadence and sublime Romanticism of the preceding items, this contribution stands out as a Realist treatment of the periodical's predominant theme. The *Pagan Review* is, as discussed above, not an openly political publication, but in the 'Foreword' the editor 'Brooks' had already declared the magazine's allegiance on the side of the rising female emancipation and what soon would come to be known as 'the New Women', and this story shares much with the fiction that was being published elsewhere in support of this movement. It even anticipates by some years Grant Allen's controversial novel on a similar subject, *The Woman Who Did* (1895). In the *Pagan Review* story, the narrator details his out-of-wedlock relationship with a fearless female artist who is eventually cut off because of this by her brother, described as a repressed pervert who takes out his frustration on the free, 'pagan' spirits, who seize this as an opportunity to live together unmarried. A second instalment is announced that would never appear, but some ominous foreshadowing implies that, like in Allen's novel, the matter will end in tears.

This is followed by two sonnets by 'Lionel Wingrave', together discussing 'An Untold Story' of heartbreak with – once again – metaphors drawn from nature. Here, the cycle of the planets beheld through the fog of the city is following a sublime cosmic order, while the spurned speaker is lamenting the coldness of his beloved who is unwilling to follow the course of nature by returning his affection.

The unsettling tale 'The Rape of the Sabines' about sexual violence in the Roman Campagna during the Wars of Independence follows, written under the guise of 'James Marazion'. Far from being a naïve commendation of free love, the *Pagan Review* interchanges such frank treatments of the risks of human nature with exemplary accounts of how our innate tendencies can be channelled towards a more positive liberation from the constraints of modern society, such as in the subsequent prose fragment 'The Oread' by 'Charles Verlayne', on a youth being seduced by the nymph of the title. Nature cast as a both beautiful but intimidating seductress is an important image recurring in several contributions, and is considered in the magazine through several different literary genres and a variety of settings and moods.

The final literary contribution is the dramatic fragment 'Dionysos in India', by 'Wm. Windover', a take on the Greek myth that Dionysos had been the first to conquer India, thought by the Ancients to be at the end of the world. This appears to be meant as an allegory for how our moral strength can be increased through overcoming social constraints and instead following the call of nature.

The concluding 'Forecast' claims that the *Pagan Review* will be 'above all else, national, and not a French bastard, or mixt-breed of any kind',[63] but the French references already spotted by de Gourmont are all too obvious. It is perhaps not irrelevant that the *Dial* too had downplayed the Continental influence despite abundant evidence to the contrary. Alaya states that '[Sharp] chose mostly French pseudonyms, [. . .] revealing his alignment with aesthetic movements on the continent'.[64] 'Mostly' is an exaggeration, as there are hints at British authors as well. Taking into consideration both the assumed names and the different styles associated with each persona, Swinburne, Lionel Johnson, Le Gallienne, and the eccentric poet and composer Theo Marzials are just some of the possibly referenced real authors in this at least partly satirical scheme. However, the *Pagan Review* lays its own similarities with French Symbolism on too thick for these to be disregarded altogether. Foreign readers were advised that the magazine was available in Paris through Léon Vanier, 'libraire-éditeur' on the Parisian left-bank Quartier Latin, who is significantly name-dropped in the *Pagan Review* story 'The Pagans' as 'that literary sponsor of so many of *les jeunes*'.[65] Vanier was an important player in the French literary field for having published Verlaine and younger Symbolist poets in the 1880s, including the earliest publications by Stuart Merrill, who gets reviewed in the magazine, and to those in the know the association will have boosted the credentials of the *Pagan Review* considerably. From two diary entries given by Mrs Sharp, we learn that Sharp at least for a while wanted to give the name *White Review* to his projected periodical, obviously thinking of the French *Revue Blanche* (1889–1903).[66] This magazine had published Verlaine (obviously echoed in 'Verlayne') and the early master of *vers libre* Gustave Kahn, an influence on Sharp's *Sospiri*.

When we take the modest design of the *Pagan Review* into account, the similarity to French Symbolist journals becomes more conspicuous. It is uncharacteristic of little magazines from Britain, as it is at first glance not very interesting from a designer's point of view, but it would not have stood out for this in France. French book design associated with Art Nouveau and other traditions was different in approach from the styles associated with the British Revival of Fine Printing, and even though people like Mallarmé were fervently experimenting with the way their works were being printed, this was usually limited to experiments with poetically functional typesetting rather than with other paratextual features such as ornaments or elaborate illustration. The *Pagan Review*, issued in what its own front matter refers to as a 'pamphlet form', with a small format, complete lack of illustration, unornamented paper covers, and standard typeface for its equally unremarkable typesetting, looks somewhat like the typically restrained French literary journals of the time, such as the then predominantly Symbolist *Mercure de France* (1890–).

However, although the *Pagan Review*'s sober wrappers (Figure 12) were less obviously designed, this does not mean that they were not meticulously planned. The most direct influence was no doubt once again Whistler, who as we have seen also loomed in the background with the completely different *Dial*. The *Pagan Review*'s design closely resembles the title page of the aforementioned *Gentle Art of Making Enemies* (Figure 13), conveniently delivering the kind of aesthetic distinction that could be managed in any print shop. In the representative example of Whistlerian typography, the asymmetrical letterpress is pushed into an upper corner, and except for a small woodcut depicting Whistler's iconic device of the butterfly, there is no illustration. With the *Pagan Review*, the text is arranged across the page instead of being conventionally centred, and in the lower left corner the magazine's playful motto is set in a fanciful pyramid of type, recalling a brand logo in the same way as Whistler's immediately recognisable butterfly. Just like Whistler's book, parts of which had also been published as pamphlets in the late 1880s, the *Pagan Review* was bound in plain brown paper wrappers. The typographical experiments of Whistler, who shortly after his death was characterised by Arts and Crafts artist and theorist Walter Crane as 'the complete antithesis of William Morris' in both artistic style and ideology, had constituted a toned-down alternative within the British Revival to the more obviously artistic style that Morris came to be associated with.[67] Some of Whistler's experiments were soon adopted by trade publishers such as his publisher Heinemann, who wished to provide visually distinctive books without spending much money on the often labour-intensive methods of the Arts and Crafts printers.[68] Whistler's book was a collection of his polemical writings inscribed to 'the rare few, who, early in life, have rid themselves of the friendship of the many', and cited (according to its subtitle) '*many instances, wherein the serious ones of this earth, carefully exasperated, have been prettily spurred on to unseemliness and indiscretion*'. As Nicholas Frankel has stated, its design 'represents graphically and dynamically [. . .] Whistler's assertion of the artist's prerogatives in the face of established critical authorities whose institutional weight had [. . .] gone largely unchallenged'.[69] In essence, it is an aesthetic of conspicuous frugality, wherein this creative resourcefulness signals a challenge to more prosperous opponents that is meant to emphasise the avant-garde position and courage of the author. By invoking the look of Whistler's print publications, Sharp could imply that he shared the rebelliousness of his famous model as well.

By adopting these economical design principles the production costs were kept down, and the *Pagan Review* could be sold cheaply at 1 shilling for a single issue; this is the same price as *The Germ*, but over forty years later. Readers were encouraged to subscribe for six monthly issues (6 shillings) or for the full year (12 shillings). This notice is accompanied by the amusingly prescient assurance that subscribers would be refunded in case of the periodical 'not living to its allotted term', Sharp having grasped that little magazines such as his usually do not have a long lifespan. Mrs Sharp tells us that

> the Review was well subscribed for, and many letters came to the Editor, and his secretary (myself) that were a source of interest and amusement [. . .] The Editor, however, swiftly realised that there could be no continuance of the Review. Not only could he not repeat such a tour de force, he realised that for several numbers he would have to provide the larger portion of the material – but the number had served his purpose.[70]

The primary 'purpose' of this little magazine appears to have been that of being a laboratory for new literary themes and styles. Sharp felt that the experience had purged him of his artistic inhibitions after the bad reception of his earlier publications under his own name, and that the use of the masks in the *Pagan Review* had 'exhausted a transition phase that had passed to give way to the expression of his more permanent self'.[71] At the back of the issue, advertisements were included for upcoming books 'to be issued privately' by the fictional 'Fanshawe' (to be named *Vistas*), 'Gascoigne' ('a drama in prose' called *The Tower of Silence*), 'Verlayne' (the 'barbaric studies' *La Mort s'Amuse*), the 'romance' *The Hazard of Love* by 'Marazion' and the full version of *Dionysos in India* by 'Windover'. Now the additional purpose of the *Pagan Review* as an authorial portfolio becomes clear. The first two listed titles get elaborate adverts to address 'readers of the *Pagan Review* who may care to have their names put on record in advance as subscribers on publication. Only a few copies will be disposable in any case.' This is a clever trick, almost working like a popularity survey: Sharp could hereby determine which of his personae was most in demand and thereby most likely to result in a critically acclaimed and commercially viable publication. Thereby, Sharp would in fact be writing on commission from his public. The titles that do not get actual advertisements may never have been intended to be written in the first place, and the fact that the 'Gascoigne' book never materialised likely indicates that it did not generate sufficient response.

The advertised *Vistas* would actually appear, two years later in 1894, but under Sharp's real name. It contains causeries and prose poems, including 'The Black Madonna'. In his letter on the *Pagan Review* to

Bliss Carman, Sharp already indicates that 'at present' (i.e. August 1892) he did 'not wish "William Sharp" to be read into "W. S. Fanshawe"', which suggests that he had been considering publicly owning up to the authorship at a later stage.[72] 'Dionysos in India', still only 'a fragment', and the *Pagan Review* poems 'Gascoigne' and 'Wingrave' were included in Sharp's posthumously collected *Songs and Poems, Old and New* (1909).[73] It is unclear whether the mention of these titles in the *Pagan Review* was a mere effort of Sharp's to boost speculation about his fictitious coterie, or whether he at that point genuinely intended to keep in use all or at least some of his authorial personae. Two books not directly linked to the magazine are also recommended to the reader's attention. One was the recently published *English Poems* (1892) by his friend Le Gallienne, and the other *Living Scottish Poets* edited by the poet and later *Evergreen* contributor George Douglas, which presumably was a working title for the anthology *Contemporary Scottish Verse* (1893) that would appear in the publisher Walter Scott's 'Canterbury Poets' series, of which Sharp was the general editor. The opportunity to promote Scottish literature must have been too tempting for the cultural nationalist Sharp to pass up for a small risk of being identified, and the advert even mentions him as one of the contributing poets.

A month after the publication of this first and only number, the subscribers of the *Pagan Review* received a card, dated 15 September 1892, stating that,

> [r]egretted by none, save the affectionate parents and a few forlorn friends, The Pagan Review has returned to the void whence it came. The progenitors, more hopeful than reasonable, look for an unglorious but robust resurrection at some more fortunate date. 'For of such is the Kingdom of Paganism'.

The very prompt demise of the *Pagan Review* suggests that the magazine had always been intended to be a one-off publication, and, as argued, primarily an experiment in artistic expression and literary marketing for its editor and author. It is difficult to assess the role of the *Pagan Review* in Sharp's career. The 1890s were a decade of unprecedented activity for him, and we will, as announced earlier, come across him again in the discussion of the later journal the *Evergreen*. That publication, though vastly different in design and content, may be argued to be such a hoped-for 'resurrection', but before that other little magazines would appear that put the principles of the *Pagan Review* into practice in a less eccentric manner. The *Pagan Review* will always deserve attention as one of the most unusual publications of the British Fin de Siècle.

A book of samples: the *Page*

The *Pagan Review* was not the only little magazine in the 1890s to be largely the result of the labours of one mind and two hands. Edward Gordon Craig's *Page* is another example, and an interesting counterpoint to Sharp's journal. Whereas the *Pagan Review* was purely literary in interest, in the *Page* the emphasis lies on visual art and material craftsmanship, and of a highly idiosyncratic sort. Born out of wedlock to the legendary actress Ellen Terry and architect and interior designer Edward Godwin, an important figure in early Aestheticism, Craig was introduced into artistic circles at an early age, and as a child had shared the stage with such immortal thespians as his godfather Henry Irving. In the early twentieth century, he was to become one of the most important designers, directors and theorists of modernist theatre, and drama historians mention him in the same breath as his contemporary Adolphe Appiah, with whom he shared the conviction that drama should provide an integrated experience of text, acting and scenery in which each aspect would be finely tuned to suit the other; often to the point that their ideas were thought implausible and discarded. According to Christopher Innes, Craig believed that

> [t]he theatre is a branch of art both equivalent to, and as unique in expression as poetry, music, and architecture. As such, it should have the same standards of aesthetic unity as the other arts. This could be achieved only if it were the work of one man.[74]

Like other adherents of Total Art in stage design, Craig was a nightmare for directors to work with, because he 'insisted on total control over any production he was involved in, and his refusal to compromise meant, in fact, withdrawing from the theatre'.[75] Not surprisingly, this happened a few times over the course of his career.

After giving up professional acting in his early twenties, Craig pursued an interest in woodcuts that started off as a modest pastime, but soon became more serious. He had been introduced to the art by his friends the poster artists James Pryde and William Nicholson, who would became his occasional collaborators. Pryde and Nicholson designed posters and other forms of advertisements on commission under the name of the 'Beggarstaff Brothers', and Craig was sometimes invited to assist. Of an enthusiastic disposition, the otherwise unemployed Craig soon put this new-found skill to use in providing him with some needed extra income. In 1897, only four years after finishing his first woodcut, Craig started a small business as publisher of items of 'artistic printing', but what mainly kept him busy at the time was his little magazine the *Page*, for which he was the publisher, editor, designer and main contributor. He had sat idle for months after quitting the busy world of the London stage, and as he had a tendency towards nervousness that occasionally turned into fits of mental illness, his then wife May approvingly 'saw the *Page* as an occupation that might keep Ted [Craig's nickname] out of trouble'.[76]

The *Page* was one of the most unconventional titles in a genre priding itself on its unconventional attitudes. Its frequency, for one, was irregular even by the standards of little magazines. The *Page* started out as a monthly publication during its first year (1898), then became quarterly for 1899 and 1900, and finally in 1901 only two half-yearly numbers were issued. The price at least remained stable at 1s. 2d per number, or 10 shillings for a yearly subscription. It does not have page numbers, and Craig's son and biographer Edward describes it as 'a magazine that existed of eighty-five percent decorative illustrations and fifteen percent irrelevant reading matter', which is not widely off the mark.[77] Most of the content consists of woodcuts done by Craig, and the included textual items are on such randomly disconnected topics that it does seem as if the actual choice of texts was considered of almost no consequence, and the opportunity for formal presentation of the letterpress was of more importance to the editor/entrepreneur. As we will see, the *Page* functions on three levels: it is a means of circulating Craig's woodcuts, it is a testing ground for him to experiment with typography for later use in his books, and, not unimportantly, it is in a way also a sly brochure for his publishing business.

There are in the *Page* occasional references to services provided 'at the Sign of the Rose', his ever small publishing venture. Like with Ricketts's Vale Press founded a few years earlier, it is a matter of debate to what extent the Rose could consider itself an autonomous printing venture. Although Craig designed all his books himself, he would always release them through an external publisher, and as he kept no presses himself he was not their printer either. There were even no fixed premises for the Rose, which welcomed correspondence wherever Craig happened to be staying at the time – often at the homes of friends, in Croydon and rural Surrey. Already in the front matter to the first issue of the *Page*, a notice clarifies the focus at the Rose: 'Each month we shall publish two bookplates, one already in use and one looking for a master. Occasionally we shall print an example of a menu (a woodcut). The menu would be glad of a master or mistress.' Regularly throughout the run of the *Page*, Craig offers his services in such 'Artistic Printing', inviting commissions. Although Craig's output has nothing in common stylistically with the Arts and Crafts Movement, his periodical fulfils for him a similar use as the *CGHH* did for the Century Guild and, although Craig claims no Pre-Raphaelite or Symbolist inspirations, as the *Dial* did for the book artists of the Vale coterie. The *Page* is thereby a palpable demonstration of its designer's skill. The Vale Press also offered similar services to the Rose's, albeit of a less domestic nature. Ricketts issued through his Press catalogues of art exhibitions by supported artists, and Vale Press prospectuses offered to publish 'small editions for Societies or Private Persons', and the design of personalised book bindings and bookplates. Craig's menus are maybe more surprising than these items that all pertain to book arts, but surely by the standards of the *CGHH* these too were forms of applied art.

Designing bookplates was common for artists in the 1890s, as is attested by the fact that the more high-minded Ricketts offered them too. There was a market for artistic bookplates during the Victorian era that came out of the bibliophile craze of the Fin de Siècle. Historical or original examples of the art can be found in other little magazines that will soon be more familiar to us, such as the *Yellow Book*, *Savoy* (both Chapter 4) and *Dome* (Chapter 6). The so-called 'ex libris' was at the time considered a noble applied art that allowed owners to show off their librarian sophistication, and can therefore be seen as a by-product of the Revival of Fine Printing. For artists it was a nice opportunity to work in a very particular medium, to make some money, and humour possible patrons. The bookplates printed in the *Page* included some that were inscribed, or 'already in use' (Figure 14). These included, for instance, several made for Craig's doting mother Ellen Terry, who was one of the most famous actresses of the Victorian age. To bookplate collectors, a bookplate inscribed to a celebrity was of additional interest because they admired it not only for the skill of the artist, but also for the information on the tastes and inclinations of its owner this commissioned piece conveyed. While arguably one the more humble forms of print design, bookplates were important enough to Craig for him to republish his work in that medium (including some that had appeared in the *Page*) in the tellingly named collection *Nothing or the Bookplate* (1925). He explains there that during his few years away from the theatre, '[w]ood-engraving and drawing for journals helped me too, but bookplates were the main source of income for me. So I always remember this, and always feel grateful toward the whole world of bookplates and bookplate collectors, users, and makers.'[78]

These collectors were a target audience of the *Page*, which like some other little magazines of the 1890s occasionally included supplementary gifts.[79] Artistic magazines like the *Magazine of Art* habitually contained loose or easily detachable plates reproducing artworks discussed within the magazine that could be hung on the wall as a cheap source of artistic prints or collected in commonplace books by readers. The *CGHH* too already had these during the 1880s, when it would, for instance, loosely insert its frontispieces that were grayscale photographic reproductions (in the jargon called 'halftones') of paintings. Those of the *Page* usually took the form of a loosely tipped-in print on higher-quality paper, and were often hand-coloured. The above-mentioned first woodcut Craig ever successfully finished a few years before setting up the *Page*, a portrait of Walt Whitman, was issued as a gift supplement with the second number of February 1898 (Figure 15).

Craig Jr referred to the texts printed in the *Page* as 'irrelevant reading matter', which is an understandable description as these seem randomly chosen and inconsequential, but they make a lot more sense when they are considered as not primarily meant for reading. These texts mostly consist of short extracts and some short poems and literary prose vignettes, forming together a whimsical miscellany that, if it adds up to any message at all, is that of a nonchalant relativism that the reader just needs to go along with. Sometimes the only text on a page is a single inspiring quote, from such diverse sages as Marcus Aurelius, Thomas Carlyle or R. L. Stevenson. That the choice of textual content was not completely random is demonstrated by the fact that Craig chooses to do a few quite long-running series, sometimes lasting a year or more. For instance, there is the interesting 'School scenes from Naya Polyana', being anecdotes by Tolstoy of his experiences with alternative education systems. This source could have been favoured because the editor identified with Tolstoy's mild anarchism that consisted of a denial to accept the pointless exigencies of nineteenth-century society. However, it is hard to come up with a rationale for another series, entitled 'Concerning confectionary', consisting of recipes for pastry, marmalades and sweets by Guglielmo Jarrin, 'Ornamental Confectioner in the Reign of King George the Fourth'. Neither was original, the Tolstoy series being a translation of extracts from the (in turn) French translation *L'École de Yasnaia Poliana* (1888), and the Jarrin bits taken from that author's *The Italian Confectioner* (1820).

Both examples, however, lent themselves perfectly to the primary purpose of the magazine, because they could be cut up into short snippets of text that could function for Craig as a test case for page design (Figure 16). They are then a more captivating variant of the 'Lorem ipsum' section from Cicero that twentieth-century graphic artists would use to demonstrate their page designs and the different possibilities of new fonts. This would also explain the difference in genres represented in the magazine because this would allow Craig to experiment with the demands and opportunities of particular categories of letterpress; poems and recipes are not usually set in the same composition patterns. None of the letterpress contributions are more than a few pages long, and even then there is usually very little print on every page, especially in the first two years. Holbrook Jackson, early connoisseur of the 1890s and its contributions to the Revival of Fine Printing in particular, was generally complementary about Craig's later forays into book design, but called the *Page* 'crude and naïvely pretentious because it aims at distinction with uncertain taste and insufficient experience of book designing at a time when typographical influences were not always reliable guides'.[80] In contrast to the orderly set and sober typography that we find in the other little magazines of the Nineties, the *Page* has more of a collage of various kinds of illustrations and snippets of text. It shows the deliberate jumble of typefaces that the Revivalists had tried to move away from, and these can change several times over the course of only a few pages. In the *Page*, playbill faces are typically interchanged with the regular old-style types, in what seems to be little more than a deliberate statement of typographical anarchy, or perhaps, as Colin Franklin has argued, an ironic imitation of the worst of Victorian printing.[81] The *Page*'s design aesthetic was born out of necessity and then dignified by means of a self-satirising bohemianism; but it can also be seen as defying the medieval and early-modern style in the Revival of Fine Printing that was past its peak after Morris died in 1896 but still informed the design of Ricketts and the designers working in the Arts and Crafts tradition.[82] Nothing about the *Page* is even remotely Pre-Raphaelite.

These visual and material aspects of print and plates are certainly the most striking features of the *Page*. Its name already attests the self-conscious materiality that is characteristic of the ambitiously conceptualised books and periodicals in the Nineties. A recurrent motto in the periodical is a quote from Byron's *Don Juan*, 'History with all her vast volumes, hath but one Page' (Canto 4, stanza CVIII), which first appears as one of many quotes hovering through the magazine as the only isolated scrap of text on the pages where they occur. In *Don*

Juan, this metaphor refers to the repetitive patterns of all-too-human behaviour that keep reappearing throughout history, and, on a deeper level, to themes and tropes that recur in the writing of histories both real and fictional. Placed in the particular context of the *Page*, there are additional materialist implications. Most of its numbers close with a one-page advert section that only contains notices for publications by Craig himself. The *Page* is also publicised here of course, with, as is customary, a list of excerpts from reviews in a wide array of periodicals. Ever the jester, Craig here amusingly placed among these press opinions the Byron quote discussed above, as if it were a review. What is more important, is that in the description of the magazine in these adverts, the *Page* is not referred to as 'a magazine', but as 'a volume of pages'. Strikingly, the publication is hereby described as a combination of standalone and self-referentially material objects, viewed in abstraction from one another. This is emphasised by the fact that it is not paginated, not even for the letterpress. Apart from making the task of the periodicals scholar more troublesome, this choice also demonstrates how to Craig the *Page* was more than anything else a collection of samples, examples of what he was capable of in the creation of an artistic publication; it is both an aesthetic experiment, and a sample catalogue for his print design business. Every copy is also hand-numbered, of course, to give them added value for the book/periodical collector, but conceptually this also makes each copy a unique work of art.

As if all this disregard for convention were not enough, there is an additional peculiarity in Craig's fanciful use of pseudonyms that can contend with that of Sharp in the *Pagan Review*. His son tells us that, already before the start of the magazine,

> Jimmy [James Pryde] suggested that [Craig] could sign some of his work by other names and so invent new 'blokes' like the Beggarstaff. [. . .] They tried to think of other names. Ted's favourite 'Bath Oliver' biscuits were lying on the table – 'There you are', said Jimmy, 'Oliver Bath', and this became the first of the many pseudonyms that were to follow.[83]

Funnily enough, Craig took the conceit so far as to design a bookplate for this 'Oliver Bath', and printed it in the *Page* (No. 2.2 of 1899) (Figure 14). For some reason the plate depicts a thistle. Perhaps it was part of the mythology behind this crispy character that he was to be imagined a Scotsman. Be that as it may; this was to be one of the most productive pseudonyms found in the *Page*, and certainly the most developed. In Nos. 1 and 2 of 1901, he is credited as 'The Late Oliver Bath', and the latter even carries an obituary for this fictional artist, written by the also make-believe 'Drayton', who is said to have prepared a novel, *The Book of Penny Dreadful Joys*, that would have been illustrated by the lamented young artist. This title is an obvious wink at Craig's own woodcut collection *The Book of Penny Toys* (1899), which is advertised in the magazine, and of which some examples are used as illustrations in the *Page* to what appear to be children's poems. Bath, allegedly son of 'Lady Georgiana Bath', is said by Drayton to have belonged to the 'Beardsley-Hardy School of Art' (see Chapter 4). This at first consideration quite nonsensical categorisation could be a jest at the outrage that only a few years before had surrounded the work of Beardsley, arguably the greatest black-and-white artist of the Fin de Siècle, and the similar controversy around Hardy's Naturalistic novels such as *Tess* (1891) and *Jude the Obscure* (1895). It might also have been a way to jocularly place the *Page* in the tradition of controversial magazines like the *Yellow Book* and the *Savoy*. Both were commonly associated with Beardsley, and the latter had carried in its sixth number a defence of the critically maligned *Jude* by Havelock Ellis. All of this is of course intentionally silly, as the woodcuts supplied by 'Oliver Bath' are in no way more provocative than the other ones in the *Page*, and as a matter of fact none of the illustrations seem meant to shock the readers anyway – at least, not morally.

The critical reception of the magazine was markedly positive, the overall tone amusingly being that the playfulness of the periodical was so obvious that few reviewers wanted to be a spoilsport. Of course, it was not explicitly belligerent against any perceived enemy, or serious enough to be a competitor to any other journal either. For instance, in the *Dome*, Charles Holme assures that us the *Page* is 'an imitation of nothing else on heaven or earth', and like us noticed that

> [i]t was made up of a very few leaves printed on one side only, so that each rivulet of type not only meandered through the familiar meadow of margin, but also drained a far-spreading western hinterland formed by the blank back of the page but one before. To look at all the cuts and read all the letterpress took so much less than ten minutes.[84]

The magazine is recognised as an 'experiment', and Craig's originality is praised, even though Holme has some reservations about the crudeness of some of the illustrations. The *Dome* editors must have liked it well enough, as shortly before a promotional poster for the *Dome* had been designed by Craig, which was reprinted in the same issue as the review appeared in. This reduced plate was also inserted as a supplement in the *Dome*, and in its December 1899 issue the *Dome* featured two contributions by Craig, one of which was the Whitman portrait (Figure 15) that had been issued before with the *Page*. This exchange of content between one periodical and another was common in the Victorian age, but in little magazines, where originality of content was a major concern, it only happened in instances of explicit homage. Once again, this stresses the provisional nature of the *Page*, and it proves that the magazine was correctly interpreted at the time to be above all a means for Craig to make his art known to the public. 'He felt he must keep the *Page* going at all costs, since it was his only contact with the public, however small: he knew that if he did not keep before the public, he would perish.'[85] The *Page* was so peculiar that it could of course never draw very large audiences, but Craig did make an effort to increase its circulation. In the issue for May 1899, he announces 'a competition', the rules of which would be that whoever brought in the most subscribers would be awarded a guinea. Maybe the small print, indicating that there was a minimum of fifteen signatures to be collected, discouraged potential participants; two numbers later we get the disappointing news that the prize has not been earned. The *Page* nevertheless helped Craig to get his illustrations into the *Dome*, and soon after into the popular weeklies the *Sphere* (1900–64) and the *Lady's Pictorial* (1880–1921).

After the first two years, the *Page*, though still an unusual publication, seems to be managed by slightly less erratic principles. The margins of the letterpress shrink to more usual sizes allowing for more text on the page and longer literary items, and the magazine plays host more frequently to guest contributors. The range of artists who contribute is as surprising as the items they deliver, which are mostly not the kind of work commonly associated with them. Burne-Jones, for instance, contributes a sketch for theatrical costume, and the famed actor Henry Irving delivers a very competent drawing. It is probable that Craig's mother, who before becoming romantically involved with Godwin had been Mrs G. F. Watts and therefore knew many artists, and who not long after Craig was born became both professionally and romantically linked to Irving, was useful in furnishing such connections for the young editor.[86] Other occasional contributors include his collaborators Pryde and Nicholson, and more famous artist friends William Rothenstein, Max Beerbohm and Laurence Housman.

The unreliability of the *Page*'s publication frequency makes it an oddly reliable guide to how much work Craig had on besides the magazine, for instance in stage design, which was soon to become his main vocation. Craig ended the *Page* after the fourth year because of his new responsibilities and because he no longer had any leisure (or perhaps need) for his periodical adventure.[87] He would return to periodical editing for another little magazine, the *Mask* (1908–29), in which he once again made inventive use of personae, and more restrained though still experimental typography. This later periodical gets more attention in design histories, arguably because at this point Craig had become an established figure in modernist theatre. For those of us who like to go back to the source, and for lovers of artistic oddities and literary curiosities, Craig's earlier exploits in the *Page* will retain their peculiar fascination.

Notes

1. [Horne?], 'Contemporary Notes', p. 176.
2. Rothenstein, *Men and Memories*, p. 166.
3. Delaney, *Charles Ricketts*, p. 43.
4. Sturge Moore, 'Preface', p. 11.
5. Ricketts, *Michael Field*, p. 1.
6. McCormack, *John Gray*, p. 32.
7. Gwynn, *Sturge Moore and the Life of Art*, pp. 14–28.
8. Holmes, *Self & Partners*, p. 165.
9. Whitely, *Lucien Pissarro in England*, p. 15.
10. Codell, 'Century Guild Hobby Horse', p. 46.
11. 'The Chronicle of Art: December 1889', p. xi.
12. [Ricketts?], 'Unwritten Book', p. 25.
13. 'l'hymne, harmonie et joie [. . .] des relations entre tout' (Mallarmé, 'Quant au Livre', p. 378).
14. Arnar, *Book as Instrument*, p. 49.
15. Ibid., p. 26.
16. Corbett, 'Symbolism in British "Little Magazines"', p. 105.
17. Ibid., p. 104.
18. 'auquel on ne peut accorder sérieusement qu'une valeur de protestation, légitime mais mal avisée' (Moréas, 'Le Symbolisme', p. 1).
19. Image, 'Three Notes on Art: II', *passim*.
20. Kooistra, *Artist as Critic*, pp. 33, 100.
21. Rossetti, 'Sonnet on the Sonnet', p. 127.
22. Watry, *Vale Press*, p. 6.
23. Ibid., p. 5.

24. Ibid., p. 19.
25. Ricketts, *Bibliography*, p. ix.
26. Watry, *Vale Press*, p. 6, n. 17.
27. 'Advertisement', leaflet announcing *Dial* 2 (1892).
28. Ricketts, 'Note on Original Wood Engraving', p. 253.
29. Ibid., pp. 265–6.
30. Ibid., p. 266.
31. Ricketts, *Bibliography*, p. vi.
32. Ibid., p. vii.
33. Ibid., p. v.
34. Nelson, *Early Nineties*, p. 44.
35. Fletcher, 'Decadence and the Little Magazines', p. 192.
36. Quoted in Watry, *Vale Press*, p. 97.
37. Quoted in Nelson, *Early Nineties*, p. 304.
38. [Ricketts?], 'Apology', p. 36. Emphasis original.
39. Gleeson White, 'At the Sign of the Dial', p. 305.
40. Beetham, 'Magazines', p. 391.
41. 'journal rarissime' (de Gourmont, *Petites Revues*, p. 11).
42. Furbank, *Mallarmé on Fashion*, p. 4.
43. 'Imitation et parodie des revues symbolistes françaises' (de Gourmont, *Petites Revues*, p. 18).
44. Alaya, *William Sharp – 'Fiona Macleod'*, p. 19.
45. Ibid., p. 103.
46. Quoted in ibid., p. 185.
47. Sharp, *William Sharp (Fiona Macleod)*, p. 201.
48. Brooks [Sharp], 'Foreword', p. 1.
49. Ibid., p. 2.
50. Sharp, *William Sharp (Fiona Macleod)*, pp. 205–6.
51. Brooks [Sharp], 'Foreword', p. 3.
52. Ibid., p. 2.
53. Denisoff, 'Dissipating Nature of Decadent Paganism', p. 442.
54. Sharp, *William Sharp (Fiona Macleod)*, p. 200.
55. Sharp, 'Section IX'.
56. Scholnick, *Edmund Clarence Stedman*, p. 154.
57. [Sharp], 'Forecast', p. 64.
58. Ibid., p. 64.
59. Quoted in Sharp, *William Sharp (Fiona Macleod)*, p. 112.
60. Boyiopoulos and Sandy, 'Introduction', *passim*.
61. Sharp, 'Dedicatory Note', p. viii.
62. Gascoigne [Sharp], 'Coming of Love', p. 19.
63. Brooks [Sharp], 'Forecast', p. 64.
64. Alaya, *William Sharp – 'Fiona Macleod'*, p. 103.
65. Dreeme [Sharp], 'Pagans', p. 25.
66. Sharp, *William Sharp (Fiona Macleod)*, pp. 203, 207.
67. Crane, *Decorative Illustration of Books Old and New*, p. 271.

68. Berman, 'Whistler and the Printed Page', p. 67.
69. Frankel, 'James McNeill Whistler and the Politics of the Page', pp. 242–3.
70. Sharp, *William Sharp (Fiona Macleod)*, p. 204.
71. Ibid., p. 204.
72. Sharp, 'Section IX'.
73. Sharp, *William Sharp (Fiona Macleod)*, p. 201.
74. Innes, *Edward Gordon Craig*, p. 112.
75. Ibid., p. 111.
76. Craig, *Gordon Craig*, p. 106.
77. Ibid., p. 241.
78. Craig, 'Foreword', n.p.
79. Claes, 'Supplements and Paratext', p. 206.
80. Jackson, *Printing of Books*, pp. 132–3.
81. Franklin, *Fond of Printing*, p. 34.
82. Ibid., p. 39.
83. Craig, *Gordon Craig*, p. 102.
84. Holme, 'Reviews and Notices: The *Page*', p. 168.
85. Craig, *Gordon Craig*, p. 113.
86. Booth, 'Terry, Ellen'.
87. Craig, *Gordon Craig*, p. 137.

Chapter 4

Selling the Yellow Nineties: the *Yellow Book* and the *Savoy*

Colour-coding the Fin de Siècle: the *Yellow Book*

It may be different in palaeontology or geology, but in the Humanities periodisation is far from an exact science. When asked to do the impossible, and pinpoint the exact moment when a cultural-historical era ends and another begins, literature scholars often resort to quoting Virginia Woolf. In her essay *Mr. Bennett and Mrs. Brown* (1924), Woolf ironically remarked that 'in or about December, 1910, human character changed', separating the new Georgians from the old Edwardians.[1] She was being that specific because she wanted to draw attention to what she called the inevitably 'arbitrary' character of historical periodisation: distinguishing distinct eras relies on decisions that can always be called into question, but we cannot do without some compartmentalisation of successive realities if we want to make sense of the unwieldy mass of time that is human history. Even mere decades have gathered associations that have become so fixed to them as to become proverbial, such as 'the Sixties' or 'the Noughties', although contradictory connotations inevitably operate side by side.

It seems no coincidence that from around the time when Woolf said that 'human nature changed', so around 1910, the decade between December 1889 and January 1900 began to be treated as a distinct cultural epoch, known as 'the Nineties' for short. A forward-looking Georgian generation was gaining confidence to disown the legacy of the Victorian age and become fully-fledged modernists, but realised that too many literary, artistic and philosophical phenomena in the final years of the nineteenth century did not fit their clichéd view of the Victorian age, by then increasingly dismissed as having mainly produced literature and art that reflected its sexual repression and social conformism. Holbrook Jackson delivered an enduringly relevant study of the period with his *The Eighteen Nineties* (1911), and defends there his choice to discuss this discrete period by stating that it had 'already become a distinctive epoch in the minds of those who concern themselves with art and literature'.[2] The popular image of the Nineties dates back to the last few years before the First World War.

Normally such distinctions go out of fashion as the distinguished decades fade from living memory, but this term is still in use today. It is sometimes qualified as 'the Yellow Nineties' when critics wish to make clear that they are specifically referring to that portion of the decade's literary and artistic output that is seen as challenging orthodoxy, assumed to have been exceptionally large in this period. This yellow colour coding can be traced back to an association with a publication that Jackson refers to on the first page of his opening chapter, and that another early study of the 1890s refers to as 'a momentous event in the history of aesthetics generally': the (in) famous *Yellow Book*.[3] Up until today, this magazine remains the most studied periodical of the Nineties, and it is routinely discussed in university courses on the Fin de Siècle. The *Yellow Book* is often made out to be the quintessential avant-garde publication of the period, but as this chapter will show, that is not quite true. What it was instead, was a singularly successful attempt to gain entrance for the avant-garde into the living rooms of a broad readership that liked the idea of owning beautiful books, but that was ultimately more interested in scandal and sensation than in new literature and art.

As we shall see, the *Yellow Book* has several important claims to our attention. It sold better than any more typical little magazine while still presenting itself as part of that category, through cultivating for itself the image of an uncompromising avant-garde periodical that was going to beat the mainstream at its own game. At least initially, it accepted work by the most uncompromising avant-garde figures of the period. For the largely hostile press coverage that it attracted and its mention during Oscar Wilde's trial for gross indecency (legalese for all male homosexual intercourse short of penetration), it is often seen as the most controversial periodical of its time. Since then, it has been permanently associated with Aubrey Beardsley's depictions of debauchery that can be found in any book on the period (including this one), already during his short lifetime making him the most recognised artist of British 'Decadence' (Figure 17). Yet, like the usually more chaste *CGHH* in the 1880s, it also obtained contributions from authors and artists who could be discussed in polite society, such as Henry James (on no fewer than four counts) and Royal Academy president Frederic Leighton, who between its covers featured side by side with provocative young upstarts with surprisingly few explicit clashes in style or message. This coexistence of commercial success and notoriety was not a fluke, but the result of careful marketing on the part of editor Henry Harland, and above all the publisher John Lane at the Bodley Head, whom we have discussed before as the most resourceful entrepreneur of British Aestheticism (see Chapter 2). It is oddly fitting that the opening item of the first issue was James's short story 'The Death of the Lion', which features the adventures of a young journalist who sums up the business of the late-Victorian British press as 'just to create the demand we required'.[4] The *Yellow Book* was so successful because of its twin strengths of creating a recognisable visual-material format for itself, and managing to fascinate its sensationalist readership with controversial content.

As we have seen, Lane and his initial partner Elkin Mathews had garnered some experience with publishing and selling little magazines by taking on the dissemination of the *Dial*, and becoming co-proprietors for the temporarily revived *Hobby Horse* (see Chapters 2 and 3). The *Yellow Book*, however, operated on an entirely different level as compared with these earlier magazines that mainly circulated within the avant-garde itself. Whereas the previously discussed journals only managed a run of a few hundred copies at best, the *Yellow Book* released 7,000 copies of its first number and 5,000 of the second.[5] These did not have to be ordered from a *primus inter pares* contributor acting as the magazine's proprietor either, but were available from all major booksellers, not least of which the newsagent chain W. H. Smith that was present in all major railway stations to catch the many potential readers who now commuted or otherwise travelled by train. From the first issue, a parallel edition was issued in the United States, by the firm Copeland and Day of Boston, which also sold well. The association with these earlier, more typical little magazines had reinforced the Bodley Head's credentials as publishers, and it suited their enterprise to take away those innovations of the Revival of Fine Printing that were compatible with commercially viable methods of book production, aimed at an audience who did not have much money to spend or time to invest but might still like to buy into the idea of Aestheticism.

The prospectus for the first number of the *Yellow Book* stresses the merits of its material presentation, which would make the magazine stand out amongst its competitors:

> In point of mechanical excellence the Yellow Book will be as nearly perfect as can be made. The present announcement shows the size and shape of the paper (now being especially woven) on which it will be printed, as well as the type that will be used, and the proportion of text and margin.[6]

This is as patient an explanation of Fine Printing principles as you will find, recalling the prospectus they issued for the also outreaching *Hobby Horse* (see Chapter 2), showing once again that the editors and publishers were not aiming for a small readership of initiates. The *Dial* and the *Hobby Horse* had been exclusive prestige ventures for the Bodley Head, furnishing the firm with credentials, and that reputation could now be put to use to help sell the easily obtained *Yellow Book*. The purpose of this prospectus, like with many other Bodley Head publications, is clear: to 'create the demand [they] required' for affordable, beautiful books among layman readers who would not have realised the value of Fine Printing themselves, or as the prospectus puts it, 'a book that will make book-lovers of many who are now indifferent to books'.[7] This is exactly what the firm had already been doing, with some success, by means of its earlier publications of gushing bibliophilic essays and fetishistic 'book verse' by the likes of Richard Le Gallienne (see Chapter 2), but now if anything was doing more effectively, as each number of the new magazine would outsell several times any other book or periodical on Lane's list.

As Margaret Stetz has pointed out, there is a cultivation of class aspirations in many advertisements of Bodley Head publications.[8] The *Yellow Book* prospectus too makes liberal use of vacuous descriptors like 'charming' and 'distinguished' that appeal to the middle-class sentiment that although one may not have the funds required to purchase the high end of book art, or the leisure and know-how to track down the next new thing, that does not mean that there are no alternatives by which to demonstrate that one has as discerning tastes as affluent collectors or scholarly connoisseurs. The boarded, cloth-covered binding of its octavo 'Volumes' (as it meaningfully styles its individual numbers) is of a quality rarely seen in periodical publications. Beerbohm later stressed the importance of the binding, 'not a paper thing, a board thing, a book', because the magazine should last longer than a mere 'quarter of a year', that is, until the next issue came out, and that 'we contributors in those days always spoke of the Yellow **Book**'.[9] It was meant to be considered a genuine 'book', to be displayed alongside other genuine books like novels, poetry collections and art histories in one's private library. The magazine had new cover designs every number that are instantly recognisable, especially in the early numbers designed by Aubrey Beardsley. A periodical does not become nearly synonymous with the decade in which it is published without developing a strong brand.

Several contributors would later state in their memoirs that they had been aware at the time that they were part of a commercial enterprise. Two juvenilia by the poet, novelist and playwright Maurice Baring appeared in the *Yellow Book*, and the magazine figures – by intention peripherally – in his reminiscing essay on 'The Nineties' (1931). After going through a list of cultural phenomena that shaped his personal experience of this decade, most of which do not correspond with the popular image of artistic, political or sexual non-conformism, he suddenly starts:

> I have forgotten to mention the Yellow Book. That I should have forgotten it shows the part it really played in the epoch: a quite insignificant part, although later historians and students of the period have taken it as a symbol representing the whole epoch. Apart from Aubrey Beardsley's drawings which came out in the earlier numbers, it was exactly like any literary review which has appeared in England before or since.[10]

Baring alludes here ironically to a second reason, besides the striking visual and material branding, why the magazine managed to leave such a mark on cultural history. Le Gallienne, a more regular contributor than Baring and a front-line observer, mused in his memoirs that 'it is hard to realise why [the *Yellow Book*] should have seemed so shocking', and said of its success in the marketplace that '[t]his was shrewd Lane's doing'.[11] Both commentators found that the main novelty of the magazine was that it was intentionally marketed as controversial by its publisher John Lane; not to scare away the philistines as was ostensibly the case in some of the earlier little magazines such as the *Dial* or the *Pagan Review*, but rather to entice them in.

As we have seen in the critical response to the *Dial* (see Chapter 2), Aesthetes and Francophile bohemians had obviously been frowned upon before. By the early Nineties, the media had lit upon a new cliché that would become a focal point for media sensationalism: the bugbear of 'Decadence'. The term had originated in Continental cultural-pessimist milieus, where it denoted a morbid tendency to escape through self-destructive practices from the rules that kept society in check, a dangerous monomania read into a range of culturally heterodox discourses by those who identified with the orthodoxy of established social, political and aesthetic norms. The term was never widely appropriated by the artists and authors to whom it was applied, and an appreciation of 'The Decadent Movement in Literature' published by Arthur Symons in *Harper's New Monthly Magazine* (1850–) in 1893, which links the literature of the Fin de Siècle with 'the Greek, the Latin, decadence: an intense self-consciousness, a restless curiosity in research, an over-subtilising refinement upon refinement, a spiritual and moral perversity', is one of a very few cases in which it is given serious scrutiny by an avant-garde insider.[12] 'Decadent' literally means 'falling-off' or 'degenerate', and cultural critiques from the 1880s onwards often discussed the targeted phenomena as the result of over-sophistication. In one of the most internationally influential texts of this tendency, the Austrian journalist Max Nordau's *Entartung* (1892) that had an audience in Britain before its English translation *Degeneration* (1895), there are chapters devoted to diverse, supposedly unwholesome, pan-European phenomena such as the Pre-Raphaelites, Symbolism, the 'Richard Wagner Cult', 'Parnassians and Diabolists', 'Decadents and Aesthetes', Ibsenists and 'Zola and his School'; in short, just about all of the major inspirations to the authors and artists of the British avant-garde in the 1890s.

In 1890s Britain, the various creeds grouped together under the heading of Aestheticism were obvious targets, as their resistance to utilitarianism and (to various extents) questioning of moral values clashed with the drive towards self-improvement and the institutionalised morality that were characteristic of the Victorian age. During the 1880s, popular media such as the satirical weekly *Punch* (1841–2002) depicted Aesthetes as affected and effete dandies and sickly-looking women who were obsessed with the Pre-Raphaelites and *objets d'art*. As Kirsten MacLeod has shown in her splendid study on the subject, the backlash shifted from mockery to outrage when this ridiculed but mostly harmless escapism was combined in literature with the rising influence of French Naturalism, importing from there an unprecedentedly frank depiction of unmentionable social ills such as substance abuse and sexual violence. This was most notably the case with the publication of *The Picture of Dorian Gray* (1890), arguably the moment that the term 'decadent' became current in the critical jargon of British periodical criticism.[13] This was perceived as a threat to public morality, because the rising literacy and changing economics of publishing put such literature within reach of a wider audience than ever before, potentially influencing the ever distrusted 'masses'. In the years leading up to the launch of the *Yellow Book*, one event with huge consequences for the perception of the latest trends in literature was the 1888 trial of the publisher Henry Vizetelly, who went to prison for obscene libel when he refused to cease publication of a translation of the French Naturalist Émile Zola's novel *La Terre* (1887). A young generation of British authors such as Symons, Lionel Johnson and Ernest Dowson were piqued by the possibility for self-assertion offered by this frank new style, and in their work increasingly dwelled on intoxication and the urban decay depicted by the French Naturalist novelists and Symbolist *poètes maudits*, and the *Yellow Book* would be a greedy taker of this sort of provocative material.

This seemed to confirm the threat that had been the motivation for Nordau to write his polemical study, that this multifaceted Fin-de-Siècle degeneracy could spread out from the perverted avant-garde to the vulnerable man in the street. Although at first only a minority are drawn to 'the new tendencies',

> this minority has the gift of covering the whole visible surface of society, as a little oil extends over a large area of the surface of the sea. It consists chiefly of rich educated people, or of fanatics. The former give the *ton* [trend-setting example] to all the snobs, the fools, and the blockheads; the latter make an impression upon the weak and dependent, and intimidate the nervous.[14]

Later *Savoy* contributor Edgar Jepson would remark that 'they sent poor Mr. Vizetelly to prison for charging only six shillings each for his translations of the novels of Zola'; that is, for making them available to the general public.[15] Such fears help explain why the success of the *Yellow Book* made some critics nervous from the very start. Here was a periodical that unlike the little magazines of the past could be picked up by unwitting travellers, drawn in by its alluring design, and corrupt them in the space of a railway journey.

In the many reviews that appeared of its inaugural issue, three items were discussed with particular horror: Beardsley's cover designs and plates with their depiction of grotesque *demimondaines* who leered at the reader from the very cover; Max Beerbohm's essay 'A Defence of Cosmetics' that appraised artificial over natural beauty; and the poem 'Stella Maris' by Arthur Symons that blasphemously transferred the titular epithet from the Virgin Mary to a prostitute. Whereas Beerbohm's essay seemed to programmatically argue the principles of Decadence with dangerously charming wit, the bordering art of Beardsley and the poem of Symons seemed to glorify the nefarious consequences of Beerbohm's principles when put into practice.[16] Speaking of Beardsley's art that was all over the magazine, John Alfred Spender, a zealous hunter of Decadents since the days of *Dorian*, prodded the *Westminster Gazette*'s readership among Liberal Party parliamentarians for 'a short Act of Parliament to make this kind of thing illegal'.[17] Beerbohm claimed in the second number to have been shocked at the reaction his piece had elicited, especially when one reviewer called it 'the rankest and most nauseous thing in all literature'.[18]

That is certainly a harsh verdict. Strangely, however, no scholar has yet been able to trace it to a published review, and it is more than plausible that this is not a quote at all, but a little exercise in poetic licence on the part of our eloquent author, inserted with the agreement of his editor and publisher. It was not unknown for the *Yellow Book*, and its spin-off the *Savoy*, to explicitly cite negative reviews in its adverts, when said reviews came from publications that they wanted to antagonise or from which they wanted to emphasise their differences. Laurel Brake has argued that the *Yellow Book* made good use of the contemporaneous rise of 'New Journalism' (not to be confused with the 1960s phenomenon of the same name) and its investment in celebrity culture and sensationalism.[19] This was one of the major innovations in the history of journalism, which can be said to constitute the watershed between nineteenth-century and twentieth-century reporting, popularising such later staples of the periodical press as the interview. This is in fact one of the major themes of Henry James's aforementioned 'Death of the Lion', that opens Vol. 1 of the *Yellow Book*. Formerly, the press had only been genuinely interested in the personality of the highest ranking public figures, but the focus of New Journalistic periodicals such as the *Pall Mall Gazette* (1865–1923) under William Thomas Stead on personal character made it possible to market literary authors and artists as personalities, now in every sense 'characters' in the true or romanticised stories of their lives. In contrast to the partisan aggression of the press before this point, New Journalism made possible the generally applied ad hominem style of the later tabloid papers, and quickly found that nothing sold better than a scandal. With clever manipulation, authors who did not mind what exactly was being said about them could remain in the public eye. Wilde, for example, understood and exploited it well until this strategy backfired, and made his immoral Lord Henry famously quip that 'there is only one thing in the world worse than being talked about, and that is not being talked about'.[20]

Instead of hushing up the most damning critiques, the *Yellow Book* basked in their outrage and was eager to draw attention to them. It consistently resisted the tendency of little magazines to establish collective positions from whence to engage with the outside world, and is itself a zone for debate on its contents. Beerbohm responded to his critics with a 'Letter to the Editor' in which he explained that he had not been completely serious; the *National Observer* (1888–97), a newspaper led by W. E. Henley that welcomed new art and literature but was always cautious of public morality, would afterwards admit that it had been taken in, but stubbornly insisted that this misunderstanding 'only shows that nobody has any idea where these decadents will stop'.[21] Vol. 2 also has a review of the first issue by the respected art critic Philip Gilbert Hamerton, which is balanced in its judgements and not at all a standard puff piece. Hamerton was a generally respected authority who had written for leading art journals since the 1860s, and although never controversial, he had a reputation for open-mindedness. A qualified admirer of Ruskin and the Pre-Raphaelites in his youth, he never politicised artistic production to the extent the Arts and Crafts Movement would, and allowed for artists to work within the economic constraints of the age. In his much-read essay collection *Thoughts About Art* (1862/1871), Hamerton pays a lot of attention to the role of the artist in society, and, arguing that 'the position of talent in the world would be sounder if its real relation to capital were thoroughly understood', he does not call on artists to rise against the forces of the market.[22] He might thereby be relied upon to understand the marketing policies of the *Yellow Book*. In his review, Hamerton does defend the magazine against its less understanding critics, but even he states frankly of Symons's 'Stella Maris' that

> the choice of the title is in itself offensive. It is taken from one of the most beautiful hymns to the Holy Virgin (Ave, maris Stella!), and applied to a London street-walker, as a star in the dark sea of urban life. We know that the younger poets make art independent of morals, and certainly the two have no necessary connection; but why should poetic art be employed to celebrate common fornication?[23]

However gently phrased, this is a severe criticism, and the fact that a magazine would print such an interpretation of its own contents proves that it intentionally sought moral controversy. As a rare instance of moral concern, the first volume had already featured an essay by Arthur Waugh on 'Reticence in Literature', a guarded apology for literary Realism that condemns the excesses of Naturalism: '[m]idway between liberty and license, in literature as in morals, stands the pivot of good taste, the centre-point of art'.[24] This prompted a response under the same title in Vol. 2 by the young British exponent of Naturalist fiction Hubert Crackanthorpe, expressing annoyance at Waugh's presumptuousness in recommending self-censorship, and retorting that 'the essential is contained in the frank, fearless acceptance by every man of his entire artistic temperament, with its qualities and its flaws'.[25] This attitude, he expected, would triumph over the reactionary critics in the future, who inanely yell 'decadence, decadence: you are all decadent nowadays'.[26] Through initiatives like the *Yellow Book*, '[a] new public has been created – appreciative, eager and determined'.[27]

Beardsley, who had arguably caused the most outrage of all, is just as conspicuously present in the second issue as in the first, and instead of attempting to lessen the association of the magazine with this artist, he was honoured by the inclusion of a portrait by Walter Sickert to turn notoriety into celebrity. While in earlier little magazines this would have been an innocuous gesture of camaraderie within the avant-garde akin to collaboration between artists, or a declaration that the magazine would stand by its attacked designer and art editor, in the sensational *Yellow Book* this at least additionally has a more commercial purpose. In later issues, other contributors are cleverly promoted by means of a series of six 'Bodley Heads', which are portraits of Le Gallienne and John Davidson (Vol. 4), 'George Egerton' (Vol. 5), Kenneth Grahame (Vol. 8), George Slythe Street (Vol. 11) and Evelyn Sharp (Vol. 12). Other authors to be portrayed, contributing to the *Yellow Book* though not publishing with the Bodley Head, are for instance Henry James (Vol. 2), George Moore (Vol. 4) and Ada Leverson (Vol. 5). These do not necessarily occur in numbers which have a contribution by the pictured authors, so they were simply calculated to play on an implied celebrity status, counting on the fact that readers would know who these people were. Yeats, who contributed to the magazine too, remembered that he and Symons were occasionally recognised in the street at the time of the Wilde trial, so it appears that even minor poets could become (minor) celebrities in those troubled days.[28]

Its sensationalism is not the *Yellow Book*'s only appropriation of features that were associated with the popular press. Some of its formal characteristics can be interpreted in this light as well. The magazine excelled in the genre of the short story, usually of a suitable length to be read in one sitting, for instance ideal as railway reading. Though it is true that the long interval between the magazine's quarterly issues would not have encouraged the serialisation of longer texts anyway, the prospectus for the first number announced that '[the *Yellow Book*] will publish no serials; but its complete stories will sometimes run into considerable length in themselves. Thus the tiresome "choppy" effect of so many magazines will be avoided.'[29] The older little magazines in our corpus had all featured short fiction, and as Winnie Chan discusses at length in her monograph on the market position of the short story during the 1890s, the *Yellow Book* was obviously not the first periodical to present itself explicitly as a venue for this literary genre, but the way it did this was significant. An important earlier example is the *Strand* (1891–1951), which was one of the first magazines to specialise in short stories, for instance publishing Conan Doyle's immensely popular 'Sherlock Holmes' series. While the Holmes stories are narratologically more complex than many early readers probably realised, much short fiction in magazines of the early 1890s 'pleased popular tastes by affirming objectivity and confidence in the narrator as a social authority'.[30] Noting the commercial appeal of this format, the *Yellow Book* seized upon it, and adapted it to the experimental styles for which it wanted to be known, specialising in 'thematically emphasised controversial subjects and formally emphasised heightened subjectivity'.[31] Its securing of the highbrow author Henry James for the first number was a masterstroke, as this Historian of Fine Consciences was one of the instigators of 'heightened subjectivity' in nineteenth-century fiction, and the controversial note was gladly furnished by younger short story writers such as the Naturalist Crackanthorpe, and New Women such as Ella D'Arcy and George Egerton. The genre continued to be one of the strengths of the magazine throughout its run.[32]

There was of course a tradition of critical condescension towards periodical publication engrained in high culture, a position of prestige that little magazines could not reach because they could not court the necessary institutional backing without losing their avant-garde status, but which they nevertheless had to engage with and possibly surpass for their challenge to established mores and taste to succeed. A year before the launch of the *Yellow Book*, the *Hobby Horse* had dismissed the nosiness of contemporary journalism for the debilitating effect it might have on the general public as part of a laudation for the great opponent of New Journalism Matthew Arnold, in an issue already published by the Bodley Head.[33] Now, the publishers sought the attention the popular press to sell one of their newest publications. Arnold had attacked the excesses of sensational journalism, associating periodical literature altogether with 'extensive' quick consumption – which the short fiction in the *Yellow Book* facilitated – and the cultivation of a short attention span that would soon spoil its readers and make it impossible for them to deal with literary texts that sustained or even demanded more 'intensive' reading.[34] The design concept of the *Yellow Book* was to suggest visually and materially that it constituted an asset of permanent value, and that this particular periodical would not be summarily discarded after quick consumption, unlike the widespread hack writing that is slighted in Bodley Head publications like John Davidson's *Fleet Street Eclogues* (1893), excerpted in Vol. 5 of the *Yellow Book*. A further justification for the magazine's preference for short stories over serialised fiction in instalments was therefore that each number could thereby be implied to conceptually form an autonomous publication, a self-contained '*[b]ook*'. The policy to have a different cover design for each issue, and different title pages in most, may have been inspired by the *Dial*, but it certainly accommodates the conceptual uniqueness of every single issue. The magazine's most conspicuous paratextual features serve to keep at bay all possible associations with disposable literary production. At 5 shillings the magazine was within reach of a wide audience but certainly more expensive than it had to be in order to make a profit. Its price was no doubt intentionally kept close to that of the trade editions of Bodley Head books that were usually priced at 6 shillings, or of review periodicals that went for the same price. The magazine met its new middle-class readership halfway by providing content that they might be taught to relate to, but this financial investment was an important component of its commodified Aestheticism, as the reader was paying for the privilege of feeling part of an elite community.

Like the little magazines before it, the *Yellow Book* places itself at least partly in the tradition of the Total Work of Art. The conceptual integration of form and matter implied in Beardsley's view that it was to be 'a complete book'[35] was, however, again as much a marketing ploy as an aesthetic consideration. Several of its material features refer to redundant practices that are functionally and aesthetically useless, and were clearly meant to evoke a sense of false daintiness in the novice bibliophiles among its readership. The first mannerism that they will have noticed is that the *Yellow Book* was sold 'unopened', meaning that the sheets out of which the pages were made had not been cut, and readers needed a penknife before they could start reading. While this was a normal feature until the end of the nineteenth century, by then most books and periodicals would come with machine-cut pages, so this is a deliberate anachronism meant to set the magazine apart from its competitors and force readers to engage with the material volume. Also, in the early issues illustrations are covered by a functionless, tipped-in piece of tissue guard paper. The fact that the publishers eventually dropped these is sufficient proof that they realised full well that they were unnecessary, as there should be no problem with ink offset with process blocks, the photographic printing procedure that was the default method for image reproduction in the magazine. Other little magazines of the period do not have them, or only for frontispieces, and are none the worse for it, and it is significant that Beardsley would never bother with them in the *Savoy*, where like in the early *Yellow Book* he was art editor. It is quite likely that they just had these to suggest preciousness. Even today tissue papers, which are not popular in bibliographical circles because they usually serve no purpose, are still occasionally used for purposes of ostentation.[36] As a third and final example, again in its early numbers, the *Yellow Book* featured so-called 'catch-words', a quaint affectation possibly copied from the third issue of the *Dial*. Hereby the first word of the following page is printed in the tail margin of each page, originally meant to facilitate easy collation of the pages in the right order in old manuscripts and in printed publications before the industrialisation of printing in the early nineteenth century. As already remarked by Hamerton in his review of the first issue laconically included in Vol. 2, catch-words are simply pointless in a publication like the *Yellow Book*.[37] As Linda Dowling states, this too was a 'deliberate anachronism' to draw attention to the presentation of the text in its handsome Caslon font, surrounded by copious margins.[38]

Several commentators have commented on the *Yellow Book*'s consistent separate listing of its literary and pictorial contributions in the table of contents, distinguished in Vol. 1 by means of the literal terms 'Letterpress' and 'Pictures'. It is perhaps significant that this already changed to the more conventional 'Literature' and 'Art' in the second number, after Hamerton had remarked in his review that this 'seems unfortunate, because "letterpress" is usually understood to mean an inferior kind of writing, which is merely an accompaniment to something else, such as engravings, or even maps'.[39] While this is true, using these terms does fit with the publisher's early campaign of presenting itself as the leading purveyor of Fine Printing, as 'letterpress' is the technical term for 'printed matter from type as distinct from lithographic or plate printing',[40] in the words of the Chiswick Press's Charles Jacobi in his aforementioned printing and design manual issued with the Bodley Head. This would draw attention to the craftsmanship behind the meticulously designed and printed page. Reading the *Yellow Book* in the way we are urged to by the editors, is not to immediately read past the material text, but also to appreciate the presentation of this content at the same time.

The separate listing of 'literature' and 'art' is itself an important factor for the relationship between both content categories within the magazine. This suggests a different approach to the Total Periodical than that of *The Germ* and the *Dial* which highlighted cross-medial collaborations in art and literature, or the horizontal collaboration of the arts in the Arts and Crafts journal the *CGHH*. As we have seen, both were motivated by a resistance to the conventional hierarchy of art forms, and specifically the subordination of the illustration to the illustrated text. Both the verbal and the visual elements of this partnership needed to at least potentially function as autonomous works of art, while commenting on each other with equal authority. In the *Yellow Book*, this defence of the dignity of pictorial art is as pronounced, but in most cases the function of the picture as commentary on the text has been discarded altogether. This was the plan from the beginning, as it was announced that '[t]he pictures will in no case serve as illustrations to the letterpress, but each will stand by itself as an independent contribution'.[41] The separate listing of the Art made it possible for illustrators to evade their conventional obligations to Literature. Despite this strong denunciation of cross-medial links in the prospectus, there are some cases where texts and images are placed in close proximity and cannot but influence the way each is interpreted when approached in this bibliographical context. We most notably have to exclude from the *Yellow Book*'s general principle the juxtaposition in Vol. 1 of 'Stella Maris' by Symons, a poem about a prostitute, and the immediately preceding picture 'Night Piece' by Beardsley (Figure 18), that seems to portray the 'Juliet of a night' whom the poem addresses. Considered separately, either contributor might convince some naïve doubters that the controversy existed only in the mind of the reader or eye of the beholder, but the editorial decision to place them next to each other makes that particularly hard to believe.

Though such thematic unity between pictures and text in individual contributions is rare, all are tied together through the previously discussed conceptualisation of each Volume as a self-sufficient or 'complete book'. The design of the *Yellow Book* was not meant to represent the cohesion of a set of contributors, or a given ideological position or aesthetic principle that needed to be reinforced through a harmonious interplay between contributions. Rather, it draws attention to the beautiful and precious object as which the magazine was marketed. Laurel Brake has gone so far as to compare it to 'a coffee-table book', a kind of fashionable commodity to have lying around to casually show off one's taste.[42] True to the social aspirations of the middle-class readers whom it enticed, 'Books Beautiful' like the *Yellow Book* may suggest cultural capital when flaunted by their owners, along with an attractive disdain for conformity.

The *Yellow Book* provided more such opportunities to make it part of one's lifestyle. At the back of Vol. 4 (January 1895) a 'Double-page Supplement: Frontispiece for Juvenal' was inserted (Figure 19). This drawing by Beardsley was actually never used for publication in a book, though Beardsley made several particularly bawdy (unpublished) drawings inspired by Juvenal during the 1890s. It shows two monkeys in oriental livery carrying a sedan chair with an androgynous dignitary inside, a familiar image because it was parodied by Edward Linley Sambourne in *Punch*, with a transvestite Beardsley instead of the simian carriers, and several typical Beardsleyan characters for passengers in a dustman's cart (Figure 20). This supplement is tipped in, like similar items in the *CGHH* and the *Page*, and can be taken out without causing damage to the book block. It is also, like other visual art contributions to the magazine, preceded by an all but blank page bearing its title and the name of the artist, so that it seamlessly forms part of the mother periodical when left in. What is peculiar about the parody in *Punch* is that it targets the whole Bodley (or rather 'Bogey') Head enterprise, while on earlier occasions that Beardsley's contributions to the *Yellow Book* were parodied in *Punch*, the magazine itself had been specifically targeted. The caption 'Rubbish may be shot here', a notice commonly found at garbage disposal sites, next to a dustbin full of drawings and texts, applies to the publisher, and the caricaturist is implying that Beardsley's artwork can stand in for the entire list of the publisher, by depicting him as literally pulling the firm. Additionally, the parody means that the supplement is in fact a success, because *Punch* is treating it (though ironically) as a representative advertisement for both the magazine and the publishing firm for which it is a flagship. Lane brilliantly also sold from his offices *Yellow Book* ephemera such as prospectuses and posters for a small fee or even gave them away free of charge, effectively using them as merchandising.[43] These posters, especially the sensational early ones by Beardsley such as his sickly woman reader browsing for disposable literature at a railway bookshop that is also on the cover of the prospectus, are still on sale today as prime examples of Fin-de-Siècle poster art (Figure 21). That some of these posters too were parodied by *Punch*, in the same way as the gift supplement and regular illustrations in the magazine, is testimony to their wide circulation.

A final significant discrepancy between the commercial ambitions of the *Yellow Book* and its little magazine background is the large advertisement sections that it carried. The magazine divided its adverts over three separate sections that could easily be removed, being inserted prospectuses, external advertising sections, and Lane's own publisher's lists. It is difficult to ascertain whether these items were issued consistently, because readers and librarians did expurgate them from their copies, and there may not be a single publicly accessible holding of the *Yellow Book* which contains them all. As is often the case, such ephemera will lightly be discarded, and even in detailed studies of this periodical, any mention of them is rare.

The prospectuses, bearing the cover illustration to the present issue and giving the contents for the present and past issues of the *Yellow Book*, are when present usually found tipped in, pasted to the endpapers at the front of the periodical. These were adhered very loosely and could therefore, like the supplement, be removed without damaging the Volume. Readers could purge their *Yellow Book*s of such mundane necessities, which are never referenced in the periodical itself, no doubt so as not to infringe on the magazine's principle that each Volume was complete in itself. The actual advertisement sections, on the other hand, were bound in with the periodical, but in a separate section at the back that with some care can also be removed without resorting to more drastic measures like rebinding. These are divided into two parts: 'The Yellow Book advertisements' and 'List of Books in Belles Lettres'. The first part features external advertisers, and is sometimes preceded by a small contents page entitled 'Publisher's Announcements'. The second is actually the list of the Bodley Head, which was also often included in the regular books published by the firm. For books that have already been published reviews are excerpted, and details for price, format and publishers of licensed American editions are supplied throughout.

The advertisement sections have a different pagination from the main text, and their two parts are also paginated separately from each other. The number of pages of these sections differs for each issue, as does their relative size. We can discern a gradual evolution towards a smaller 'Yellow Book advertisements' section in favour of the 'List of Books in Belles Lettres', until the former finally disappears after October 1895 (Vol. 7), returning once more in a very slim version in Vol. 9 (April 1896), but disappearing altogether for the final four numbers. In most issues, the 'Advertisements' are preceded by the above-mentioned title page, which usually lists the advertisers. The 'Belles Lettres' are always accompanied by a title page bearing the publisher's device, which from Vol. 7 (October 1895) onwards is replaced by an elegant drawing of the façade of the Bodley Head office with the new title 'Catalogue of Publications in Belles Lettres'.

The advertised books span all genres that would then have been seen as 'belles lettres'; there is fiction, poetry, history, criticism and philosophy. J. M. Dent advertise their *Morte d'Arthur* (1893) here, which is not surprising as it had been illustrated by Beardsley; and as Laurence Housman was a contributor too, Swan Sonnenschein could be expected to advertise Housman's collaboration with George Meredith, *Jump to Glory Jane* (1892). Heinemann understandably lists titles by Turgenev, Björnson, Ibsen and Villiers de l'Isle-Adam, all popular references among the contributors to the *Yellow Book*. Kegan Paul, Trench, Trübner & Co. could also count on finding takers for their titles on bibliography and printing history, written by experts with Revival credentials such as Herbert Horne.

True to John Lane's image of resourceful businessman, he also managed to attract less obvious adverts. The fact that the advertisement section could be removed does of course enable the magazine to distance itself from these in the most literal sense of the word, another compromise between aesthetic purism and commercial cunning. Books alluding to respectable domesticity are rare, though Vol. 3 (October 1894) holds Dean & Son's list, advertising the *Baby's Souvenir*, a scrapbook meant to record important moments in the life of infants. This publisher also pushes the no doubt charming but hardly artistic *Our Friend the Dog*, '[a] complete practical guide to all that is known about every breed of dog in the world'.

More to the purpose, however, is that Vol. 4 (January 1895) advertises, as part of a Chatto & Windus advert, Robert Buchanan's anti-Decadent play *The Charlatan* (1894). Although Buchanan had publicly apologised for his harsh opposition to 'The Fleshly School of Poetry' after the death of Rossetti, he was still no friend to the Fin-de-Siècle avant-garde, and this play was meant as another timely warning against their influence. Buchanan was in this period tangled up in a polemic with Le Gallienne on the role of Christianity in literature and society at large, that had started when the latter had ridiculed his poem *The Wandering Jew: A Christmas Carol* (1893) in a review. Lane had insisted that Le Gallienne publish his essay *Religion of a Literary Man* (1893) as soon as possible to take advantage of the ongoing public attention.[44] By having his work advertised within the periodical home of Le Gallienne, Buchanan's publisher in turn could profit from their association, making them unlikely bedfellows in the publicity scheme of the *Yellow Book*. Similarly, Bentley & Son see no harm in promoting the work of the anti-Decadent novelist Marie Corelli in the first issue (April 1894), who, in her bestseller *Wormwood* (1890) on the physical disintegration of a young Frenchman addicted to absinthe, had explicitly warned her British readers not to fall under the spell of Decadence.[45] She was hereby promoted in the commercially most successful publicity organ that the British counterparts to the maligned French avant-garde ever had. Because moralist and amoral authors wrote about the same themes and emulated each other's style, they appealed to the exact same audiences, and the magazine would have been purchased by readers who might not care whether the sensationalist depictions of immorality were intended as romanticised celebrations or as foreboding auguries. This is yet another instance of how supposedly Decadent and self-declared anti-Decadent authors in this period took advantage of the opposite side's fame or infamy.

Some other periodicals advertised here as well, such as the artistic periodicals the *Art Journal* (1839–1912) and the *Studio* (1893–1964), which while avoiding controversy were at least sympathetic to the newest currents in fine and applied art; *Chapman's Magazine of Fiction* (1895–8), which must have anticipated overlaps in their readership because of the *Yellow Book*'s short stories; and *Scribner's Magazine* (1887–1939), of New York, which was likely drawn by the *Yellow Book*'s transatlantic audience through its American edition. With these overlaps in mind, Baring's remark about the *Yellow Book* being 'exactly like any literary review' becomes a lot clearer. Except for the *Dome* (see Chapter 6), the *Yellow Book* included a wider array of advertisers than any other little magazine, which as a rule kept to advertisers from the coterie of the editors, or who would otherwise have a demonstrable link to their production. The critical outrage after the first issue does not yet seem to have affected its popularity with the advertisers in Vol. 2, as it still has more or less the same firms as the previous one. By the third Volume, the reputation of the new periodical was arguably well established, and we see this reflected in an even larger advert supplement for Vol. 4 in which more major publishers are listed, with for instance Chatto & Windus joining in for the first time.

In early April 1895, Wilde was arrested, and the magazine's piquant notoriety quickly turned into danger of ostracism. Although there is a risk of overstating the contrast, Linda Hughes has helpfully suggested a division of the run of the *Yellow Book* into two phases: 'BT' or 'before the trial', and 'AT' for 'after the trial'.[46] The fifth issue of April 1895 was due to be ready by the fifteenth, but the fact that it only appeared on the thirtieth is a clear sign that there was much confused mending to be done, as for instance all of Beardsley's contributions were rejected.[47] As is common knowledge, at the time of his arrest Wilde had been spotted with a French *livre jaune*, a cheap type of novel that was probably an ironic inspiration for the *Yellow Book*'s title, and that was mistaken in excited press reports for the magazine itself. Despite the risks that the magazine had been taking, Harland and Beardsley had in fact agreed upon founding the magazine that Wilde would never contribute, out of a sense that his contributions would monopolise the whole enterprise, one of the few times when the editors prevailed upon Lane not to enforce upon them a Bodley Head author.[48]After this misunderstanding had spread, the for once innocent magazine was severely implicated in the affair, to the point that its publisher's offices were vandalised by an angry mob.[49]

What followed was a major clash between what we might call the moralist and the amoralist factions of the firm's authors, and also within the magazine the heterogeneity of the contributor stall now became a problem for the first time. From the first issue, established authors who had not come close to endorsing moral corruption themselves had been under some suspicion of lending their support to Decadence, such as happened to Henry James who found that especially the American press openly worried for his spiritual well-being because of the company he seemed to keep in decrepit old London.[50] Closer to home, a review of the first number in *The Times* (1788–) had stated that '[o]n the whole the New Art and the New Literature appear to us to compare in this singular volume far from favourably with the old, and we doubt if the representatives of the latter will much relish the companionship [. . .] in which they find themselves', in particular the president of the Royal Academy 'Sir Frederic Leighton [. . .] who finds himself cheek by jowl with such advanced and riotous representatives of the New Art as Mr. Aubrey Beardsley and Mr. Walter Sickert'. The reviewer also tried to bully the allegedly 'tamer' authors 'Mr. Henry James, Mr. Edmund Gosse, Mr. George Saintsbury, and Dr. Richard Garnett' into dissociating themselves from the more objectionable contributors.[51] The Wilde affair was more a catalyst for such resentment than the event of a whole new crisis. Successful Bodley Head authors like William Watson and Alice Meynell, who had friends among the Aesthetes but were averse to all moral controversy, and ostentatiously proper outsiders such as the novelist Mrs Humphry Ward (lampooned for her respectability in the *Pagan Review*), now demanded the ousting from the publisher's list not only of Wilde himself, but also of

Beardsley and Arthur Symons. Besides having supplied the most consistently provocative material to the magazine, Beardsley was associated in the popular press with Wilde because of his illustrations for *Salomé* (1894), and Symons likely had made the mistake of associating himself too openly with Decadence through his aforementioned article in *Harper's*. Lane gave in, barring both from contributing to the *Yellow Book*, and firing Beardsley from his position as its art editor. The magazine in the 'after-trial' phase was to avoid overly daring content and, more importantly, after the loss of Beardsley it never looked the same again.

We do not yet see a sharp decrease in the number of advertisers in Vol. 5 (April 1895) that came out in the month of the trial, but the difference with the following issue is dramatic. There is not a single external advert left in Vol. 6 (July 1895), as all the space is taken up by Lane's own publications. By Vol. 7 (October 1895) there are a few once again, though suspiciously, Lane put some of his own adverts in with the external ones, while retaining the normal separate section for his own books besides. This had only occurred once before, in Vol. 4 (January 1895), with an advert for the high-profile 'Keynotes Series', a successful series of low-priced novels that was started to further capitalise on the success of the short story collection *Keynotes* (1893) by George Egerton. It mostly consisted of shorter work on then popular Naturalist, Aesthetic-Decadent or New Woman themes, and later opened up to other styles and genres. All were designed by Beardsley until he was dropped by the firm, and together with the *Yellow Book*, which initially had a similar marketing strategy to it, it was the most successful publishing scheme at the Bodley Head.

In the seventh number among the cosmetically enlarged advertisement section, four fairly innocuous books (Kenneth Grahame's children's story collection *The Golden Age*, Frank Swettenham's travelogues *Malay Sketches*, and the short story collections *Monochromes* by Ella D'Arcy and *Grey Roses* by Harland) were advertised separately with large single adverts, and with an unusually high number of favourable press notices from the most diverse newspapers and periodicals. This may have been a ploy to inflate the 'Yellow Book advertisements' section, to make it seem as if the magazine was unaffected and the Bodley Head had been incorrectly assumed to be the official house publisher of the maligned Decadents. Here we also note the absence of an introductory sheet which would normally list the (now absent) external advertisers, which might have been an attempt to cover up this stratagem. As said above, after this act of desperation the external adverts were dropped altogether, and more of Lane's list was included instead.

Nevertheless, the Wilde affair was not the end for the magazine, which would after all be around for another two years or eight numbers after his arrest. With Beardsley out of the picture, a host of visual artists could move in who formerly had been backbenchers or not present at all. The illustrator Patten Wilson temporarily took the helm, probably as much due to his talent as to his stylistic remoteness from Beardsley. In contrast to the instantly recognisable originality of his predecessor, Wilson's covers were compositions of references to all that was fashionable in book art from Continental Art Nouveau line patterns over Whistlerian peacocks to *japonisme*, and, importantly, he steers clear of any lubricity. Wilson furnished all cover designs for the following two numbers (Vol. 5 of April and Vol. 6 of July 1895), although Vol. 5 retains the former Beardsley design for the back. For the following numbers a recurrent back cover design by Wilson is used, making him after all an underestimatedly central figure in the after-trial magazine. Another way in which Patten Wilson was rewarded for the dexterity with which he was able to supply material at the eleventh hour during the time of need, was that he took over from Beardsley the job of designing the 'Keynotes Series' as well.

As the ousted Beardsley had been in charge of the visual branding of the magazine, his sudden absence forced the magazine to partially reinvent itself. His successors in its cover design, such as Patten Wilson or Nellie Syrett, delivered fine work, but few critics would say that they equalled his vision. According to Katherine Mix, Beardsley's editorial judgement was also missed by Harland and Lane, who were now faced with the responsibility for the visual art as well as for the letterpress:

> In three numbers Harland shifted the responsibility to other shoulders, presenting in Volume VII only work from the Newlyn School in Cornwall, an offshoot of the New English Art Club, in Volume VIII twenty-five pictures and one photograph of a piece of sculpture from the Glasgow School, [. . .] and in Volume IX decorative designs from the Birmingham School.[52]

Outsourcing the pictorial art was a clever solution, as it made the job of the remaining editor easier, while adding an interest to the magazine for readers who wished to keep up with new developments in British art. However, accommodating these stylistically divergent groups of course did not help the magazine to maintain a uniform appearance or – for the *Yellow Book* practically the same thing – brand identity, which is one of the reasons why the after-trial *Yellow Book* coheres even less than the 'before-trial'. It is telling, however, that artists such as Arthur Gaskin and Ernest Treglown of the Birmingham School, regulars in the Aestheticist but soundly anti-Decadent *Quest* (see Chapter 5), could be induced to work for a purified *Yellow Book*. Stetz and Lasner argue that this new-found attention to artistic centres outside London was a conscious choice to continue offering captivating pictorial content after Beardsley's dismissal.[53] Some unity in design was preserved within each number, as the artist delivering the cover illustration would also furnish a design for the title page of the respective number. From Vol. 6 onwards, the same back cover design by Patten Wilson is used, featuring an image of a ship with a sculpture of a (British?) bulldog on its bow, with the sailors attempting to set sail with the anchor still lowered (Figure 22). This may have been a visual metaphor for the stick-in-the-mud attitude of the British establishment that had caused so much trouble for the magazine and its contributors during and after the Wilde trial.

The same Vol. 6 contains a reproduction of Gertrude Demain Hammond's painting *The Yellow Book* (Figure 23), the original of which was in Lane's office.[54] This is a strangely self-referential image of a man showing a bashful young woman an opened *Yellow Book*, which can significantly be identified as Vol. 2, itself the most self-referential in the series for its review of the preceding first number by Hamerton and the justifications by Beerbohm and Crackanthorpe. Little is known about the genesis of the painting, but the artist may have started on it during the moralistic backlash against the first numbers. Two readings of this image are possible. Stetz and Lasner interpret it as part of a campaign by the *Yellow Book* to gain the trust of its readership after the recent crisis, especially that of the female readers who might be most concerned about its respectability. By depicting a conversation about the magazine between a woman and a man set in a living room, the painting would suggest that it was a proper topic of domestic conversation. Stetz and Lasner suggest that 'the painting hinted, moreover that the *Yellow Book* could forward the intimacy between (innocent) women and (experienced) men in the courtship process and, therefore, provide a sort of public service by smoothing the workings of bourgeois life'.[55] While it is perfectly plausible that this is how the image was received, it does seem a safe reading, and an alternative, more radical interpretation might be suggested. The artist was an outspoken advocate of equal opportunity for male and female artists, and she had been interviewed on the subject in the New Woman weekly the *Woman's Herald* (1891–3) in one of its first issues. Asked the tendentiously phrased question 'whether anyone can draw properly the human form divine unless they have studied from the nude', considered indispensable for the training of male artists but usually withheld from women as a skill unnecessary for the types of work that they were supposed to produce, she replies: 'Most decidedly no. It is an impossibility', and that she 'would have fared very badly' if she had not been given that opportunity during her training at the Lambeth School of Art (where Ricketts also taught). To the interviewer's question whether she has exhibited with the Society of Lady Artists that was founded in 1855 for the promotion of female painters, she states that she has not, because she prefers to place her work 'in juxtaposition with that of male artists, that I may be fairly judged and criticised'.[56] Given these opinions, it seems odd that Hammond would have wanted to depict such a condescending scene as this, or that it would be encouraged by the same firm that two years before had published George Egerton's aforementioned *Keynotes* with its stories about sexually active, independent women. Readers interested in such literature, amply provided by the *Yellow Book*, might not appreciate such a lesson either. An alternative interpretation could be that the depicted woman is being lectured by a male authority figure on her unrespectable reading. This would fit in the defence of the magazine as well because it connects moral censorship in the late-Victorian era with patriarchy holding back female emancipation as well as the development of art and literature.

From the beginning, the magazine had published New Woman fiction by authors such as George Egerton, Ada Leverson and Evelyn Sharp (no relation), in which gender norms were questioned and the institutionalised sexism of romantic and social life was exposed, and the New Woman author Ella D'Arcy acted as an editorial assistant to Henry Harland. Significantly, Hammond's painting is placed between a short story by Egerton and a poem by the socialist and feminist Dollie Radford. In this 'Song', the lyrical subject – suggestively of undisclosed gender – describes itself as surrounded by a 'hedge of roses / Which walls my garden round' (ll. 1–2). Outside of this beautified fence '[l]ies fresh unfurrowed ground' (l. 4). Now that 'labours all have ended / Within my fragrant wall', the speaker sees the addressee and proceeds to 'break my barrier through / And leave all it encloses, / Dear one, to follow you'.[57] Although the *Yellow Book*, as said, resists interpretation of pictorial matter in the light of surrounding literary copy, readers could be forgiven for reinterpreting the preceding image when they next come across the active agency of this lyrical subject, who appears to be a woman breaking out of the rose-hedged prettified framework provided for her by society. Read as an allegory for female authorship or artistry, both become a plea for allowing women access to the same material, and the same themes, as the privileged males who should be their peers.

As the *Yellow Book* had previously always marketed itself as a publication defying public opinion, and had recently capitulated to pressure to dissociate itself from its most two defiant contributors, it had to find new ways to exercise its rebellious spirit. New Woman authors like Egerton and Radford, though marginally implicated in the Decadence scare too as they published through the same publishers and journals, and had the same visual iconography in their book art (provided initially for Egerton by Beardsley, and by Beardsley's successor Wilson for Radford), were a safer option. This corroborates the argument of Linda Hughes that in the after-trial phase, the homosocial discourse of the first issues that either has no interest in women or tends to objectify them, is pushed to the background to the advantage of female poets, like Radford, often implicitly supporting New Woman tenets.[58] These new opportunities for female authors constitute the main value of the later *Yellow Book* to readers interested in avant-garde literature.

A second attempt: the *Savoy*

Even though the *Yellow Book* is from a purist's point of view not the most inspiring avant-garde journal of the 1890s, its (initial) commercial success certainly influenced other publications that wanted to move beyond the 'littleness' of the little magazine and address a larger audience than had been deemed possible, or desirable, before it had set the precedent. In Chapter 6, for instance, we will meet the *Pageant*, published during the final two years of the *Yellow Book*, and the *Dome*, which started around the time when it went defunct, but neither of these shows such a clear, nor such a troublesome relationship to the trendsetter as the *Savoy* (1896).

There are several contradictory anecdotes about how the *Savoy* came into the world, a common problem when researching this period, because many central figures as well as bystanders tried to overstate their importance during the early-twentieth-century boom in mythologising memoirs of the Nineties, mentioned at the beginning of this chapter. The bare facts of the matter appear to be that after having been turned out by the *Yellow Book* and its publisher the Bodley Head, Beardsley and Symons were looking for a new outlet for their creativity and, of course, a new source of income. Beardsley's drawings had often been parodied and plainly castigated for their immorality, as was the poetry of Symons for its Decadent lassitude or the blasphemy of 'Stella Maris', and during that calamitous spring of 1895 both were continuously disappointed by publishers who had felt no misgivings about their work before. For example, David Nutt, nervous about having published Wilde's *The Happy Prince and Other Tales* (1888), declined Beardsley's nude depiction of the god Amor as a frontispiece for a collection by the homosexual poet André Raffalovich, although he had commissioned several illustrations by Beardsley before. Similarly, Lane reneged on his earlier agreement with Symons to publish his poetry collection *London Nights* (1896), which contained two poems included in the *Yellow Book* – the above-mentioned 'Stella Maris' (Vol. 1) and the lesser-known 'Credo' (Vol. 3) justifying 'the joy of sin' (l. 12) – and which was later rejected by Heinemann as well.[59]

Luckily for both, a new and fearless publishing firm had just started up business. Leonard Smithers, who up until then had made a living selling rare antiquities and under-the-counter erotica from his London bookshop, was willing to take them in. He had been publishing dangerous materials since the late 1880s as an associate of the illustrious pornographer Harry Nichols, among others helping the famous Sir Richard Burton with pursuits even more exotic than that author's translation of the *Arabian Nights* (1885). Ignoring the above-mentioned Vizetelly trial which before the Wilde affair was the major instance of public outrage against immoral literature of the entire Victorian era, the intrepid Smithers had published new translations in 1894 of no fewer than six Zola novels, among them the infamous *The Earth*, by daring young men like Symons, Ernest Dowson and the essayist and sexologist Havelock Ellis, though with the wise precaution of selling this novel expensively at 2 guineas (£2 2s.) so that he could not be accused of corrupting the common man.[60] By now taking up the newest batch of tarred authors, Smithers had in effect ignored the two biggest scandals of the literary late nineteenth century. He provided Beardsley with several commissions, and published not only Symons's *London Nights*, but also work by other authors, like Dowson, who had not been targeted as badly but out of sympathy had abandoned Lane of their own accord. Smithers fits the period perfectly as an upcoming publisher investing in the newest literary trends and in Print-Revivalist production principles, but who had the business sense to make these pay their way. He thereby moved into the niche carved out by the Bodley Head, and made no attempt to hide the rivalry between this firm and his own.

When he met with a vengeful cabal consisting among others of former *Yellow Book* contributors Symons, Beardsley, Dowson and the artist Charles Conder, who wanted a chance to spite their former periodical outlet, Smithers instantly recognised the potential in this situation. He had all but usurped what was left of the market for 'Decadent' books in the wake of the Wilde trial, and felt he could do the same for periodical literature by launching a journal edited by Beardsley and Symons. The eighth Volume of the *Yellow Book* (January 1896), which was in direct competition with the first number of the *Savoy* (planned for December 1895 but coming out a month late), was not coincidentally the bulkiest issue in that magazine's history, over 400 pages thick and, besides featuring the well-known George Gissing also containing the first contributions by several upcoming authors. These included two authors that are now rarely associated with the magazine: John Buchan and H. G. Wells. These were not strangers, as Buchan at the time worked as reader for the Bodley Head and was to publish with them his short story collection *Scholar Gypsies* (1896), while Lane had recently published Wells's essays *Select Conversations with an Uncle* (1895).[61] Their work in other periodicals had been favourably received, and, above all, both wrote accessible work that was not controversial. Kate Macdonald argues that the inclusion of an author like Buchan would have been a statement that the *Yellow Book* wanted to diversify the increasingly formulaic content of the magazine, which according to reviewers was becoming predictable.[62] Wells too may have been able to help portray the *Yellow Book* as a versatile periodical attracting contributors of varied profiles, that, although it would remain the best place to find the newest in art and literature, would not limit itself to the proceedings of any avant-garde sect.

This was wise, because the new *Savoy* was vying for a similar market position. In the 'Editorial Note' for the first issue, Symons and Beardsley declared:

> All we ask from our contributors is good work, and good work is all we offer our readers. [. . .] We have no formulas [. . .] We have not invented a new point of view. We are not Realists, Romanticists, or Decadents. For us, all art is good, which is good art.[63]

This echoes the promise in the prospectus for the first *Yellow Book* that '[i]n many ways its contributors will employ a freer hand than what the limitations of the old-fashioned periodicals can permit'.[64] The reason for this stipulation in the *Savoy* was probably twofold. First, of course, they had learned from the press reaction to the *Yellow Book* that they would inevitably be pigeonholed as 'Decadent' and wanted to contain the damage; but they also wanted to set themselves apart from more strict little magazines that were perceived as linked to a single coterie or association.[65]

There are more similarities between the two magazines. The first issue of the *Yellow Book* had 'A Defence of Cosmetics' that made Max Beerbohm a target for negative reviews because of its (actually parodic) Baudelairean/Huysmansian celebration of artifice, and its pastiche of the maxims of Wilde. The first issue of the *Savoy* featured George Bernard Shaw's more clearly parodic 'On Going to Church', a prescription for how to enhance the experience of everyday life through more innocent stimuli, 'in a world which, unable to live by bread alone, lives spiritually on alcohol and morphia'.[66] Some of the names from the early issues of the *Yellow Book* return as well, most prominently of course Beardsley and Symons, and although the *Savoy* does not boast big names like Henry James or George Saintsbury, with Shaw and Joseph Conrad (No. 6) it can at least match the rising stars championed by Harland and Lane. Notably, a significant number of the most important avant-garde poets of the Nineties – united in the so-called Rhymers' Club that featured amongst others Symons, Le Gallienne, Herbert Horne, Lionel Johnson, Ernest Dowson, John Davidson and most famously Yeats – shifted from the *Yellow Book* to the *Savoy* and, despite the fact that the Bodley Head had published the two *Books* (1892 and 1894) of this informal society, now published either with Smithers or with Lane's former partner Elkin Mathews. Apart from the obviously central position of Symons, Yeats contributed several times to the new magazine while he had appeared only once in the *Yellow Book*; there is also more by Dowson and Lionel Johnson; and a short story by Ernest Rhys, the Welsh poet and future founding editor of the 'Everyman' series for J. M. Dent. Even though both magazines were interested in French literature, and sometimes even included French verse, the *Savoy* benefited from the closer contacts Symons had in Paris to excel here too. A review of the first issue of the *Savoy* by the French poet and critic Gabriel de Lautrec spoke of 'Mr Arthur Symons, of whom the name is, together with the previously mentioned [Dowson], one of the most cherished in Paris among those of the young men of letters who are in favour in

London.'[67] Both magazines also recruited often from their respective publisher's list, with Smithers proving himself as good at product placement as Lane, several *Savoy* items being extracts from soon to be released books.

All of this does not mean that the two magazines were interchangeable. The full extent of the differences between them can only be gauged when the paratextual level is taken into the equation. Whereas the *Yellow Book* is, obviously, yellow, the *Savoy* is pink, but the most prominent visual characteristic of the *Yellow Book* had (also obviously) been the fact that it was designed to be a 'book'. The *Savoy* does not have the sturdy cloth-covered boards of its predecessor, only sporting paper wrappers. It had two good reasons for not copying this ambitious look. Anticipating that comparisons between the two magazines would be inevitable, the founders realised that in the foreseeable future any periodical that looked like the *Yellow Book* would be automatically treated as derivative, but Beardsley especially realised that the chances of a fair reception would be compromised if the public recognised in the *Savoy* the tainted format of the publication that they were convinced Wilde had been carrying around at the time of his arrest.[68]

The second reason was production costs, Smithers not having much capital to invest into the venture and being eager to keep the price down. Understanding that the bibliophile interest of the *Yellow Book* certainly was a force to be reckoned with, they nevertheless accommodated readers who wished to add value to their copies themselves by means of a unique supplement. The concluding 'Publisher's Note' to the second number states that

> for the convenience of such subscribers as desire to bind up 'The Savoy' into volumes, is appended a print of the covers of No. 1 and 2, pulled on white paper, which may be bound in, in substitution for the pink cardboard covers.

These supplemental prints continued throughout the run of the magazine, and do not occur in any of the other little magazines of the period. Whereas the *Yellow Book* has its book format to suggest for itself a longevity beyond the ephemeral character of other periodicals, the *Savoy* hereby cleverly suggests to readers the possibility of binding their own copies, and gives them an opportunity to customise their bound volumes.

This fundamental difference between the two contenders was obviously noticed. The gossip column of the satirical weekly the

Pick-Me-Up, after stating of the first issue of the *Savoy* that it was 'preternaturally dull' in comparison with the *Yellow Book*, coldly added that '[t]he cover is tinted a delicate shade of pink. Presumably the new quarterly is blushing for its sorry appearance.'[69] However, such measures of economy allowed the *Savoy* to price itself at 2s. 6d, only half as expensive as its primary competitor, even though we have to take into account that the *Yellow Book* was usually almost twice as bulky. This discrepancy in size is solved after the first three, also quarterly, issues of the *Savoy*, when it becomes a monthly, only slightly slimmer with an average length of about ninety pages, and a price drop to 2 shillings. As Brake has noted, the quarterly frequency had been intentionally opted for by the *Yellow Book* because quarterlies are associated with different implied readers than monthlies. Quarterlies, however, also require a particular marketing strategy that ties the readers to their periodical of choice, making them consistently identify themselves with the implied readership, as was the case in the traditionally quarterly reviews that explicitly advocated certain ideological or artistic points of view. Monthly magazines, conversely, have a potentially broader audience that can be attracted on an issue-by-issue basis, because attention for the periodical may be renewed every month. Smithers probably hoped that by trying to 'enter a potential mass market of monthly magazine readers [. . .] the high production costs of a high-quality, illustrated magazine would be offset by numerous sales'.[70]

In the 'Editorial Note' to the *Savoy*'s third issue announcing that henceforth the magazine will be issued monthly, we also learn that 'the opportunities of monthly publication will permit of the issue of a serial, and arrangements are being made with Mr. George Moore for the serial publication of his new novel, "Evelyn Innes"'. This serialisation of what was to become one of Moore's most successful novels never came to pass, unfortunately; however, at that time the *Savoy* actually included two series already, which are certainly worthy of note. Havelock Ellis, who delivers several daring defences of contentious literature like the novels of Zola (No. 1) and Thomas Hardy's *Jude the Obscure* (No. 6), also contributes three lengthy introductory articles on Friedrich Nietzsche, giving context and informative summaries of all his major works in layman's terms, to the second, third and fourth number. These were instrumental in the propagation of Nietzsche's thought in Britain, where the 'Philosopher with the Hammer' had not received much attention up till then. Already in the first and second numbers, we find one of the *Savoy*'s better-known serials, being the first few chapters of Beardsley's unfinished novella *Under the Hill*, based on the Tannhäuser legend that had earlier been adapted by Wagner and Swinburne. Two versions of this work would later be published. The one most often reprinted and anthologised is the uncensored version later published by Smithers under the name *The Story of Venus and Tannhäuser* (1907). This later version is an erotic fever dream, but the text that was published in the *Savoy* is less explicit, though still not remotely prudish. This series makes it to only two instalments, before being suspended due to the illness of the author and illustrator that would lead to his untimely death in 1898. After that, there was a series of three articles on 'William Blake and His Illustrations to the Divine Comedy' by Yeats (Nos. 3–5), and the two-part novella 'Beauty's Hour' by Olivia Shakespear (Nos. 4 and 5). The *Yellow Book*, as said, never featured serials; not just because this would be impractical due to its quarterly frequency, but also so as not to impinge on its central concept that each number could function as an autonomous rounded-off 'volume'. Such concerns did not apply to the *Savoy*.

Like the *Yellow Book*, the *Savoy* divides its content into 'Literature' and 'Art', but these categories are less isolated from each other in the *Savoy* than they were in the *Yellow Book*. As we have seen, there the pictorial art was intentionally curated as if the magazine were an art exhibition, each exhibition piece warded off from surrounding literary contributions by means of an introductory page announcing the title of the piece and the name of the artist, and in the earliest issues a redundant tissue guard, and we are told repeatedly that the plates 'in no case serve as illustration to the letterpress'.[71] In the *Savoy*, not only are such material markers of distance entirely absent, there is also more often a direct relationship between bordering literary and pictorial contributions. *Under the Hill* is a case in point, as the major charm of the piece is that it is illustrated so generously by Beardsley in his trademark style. Another clear example is a translation of Villon's famous 'Epitaph in Form of a Ballad' by Theodore Wratislaw in No. 6 (October 1895), on the opposite page to which in the same opening is an austere illustration by William Horton of four hanged corpses entitled with the poem's common French designation, 'Ballade des Pendus' (Figure 24). Or, in the correct Aestheticist attitude to illustration, we could of course also reverse the precedence between the two items, and say that the poem is printed opposite the plate. However one looks at it, there are plenty of completely autonomous pictures and literary contributions as well. The choice whether to cooperate cross-medially with other contributors was left to the authors and artists themselves in accordance with the professed freedom of artistic expression in the magazine, which was only limited, as our old acquaintance Selwyn

Image adds in the first number, 'with that one proviso of blanching the libel-court'.[72]

Despite these later successful instances of artistic synergy, there is a striking mention in the first 'Editorial Note' that the editors 'desire no false unity of form and matter'. This seemingly offhand remark is a sneer at the *Yellow Book*, but it has far-reaching programmatic repercussions. Even though the *Savoy*, with its Beardsley covers, impeccable page layout and choice content, is no mean achievement in form as well as in content, it appears, as stated above, to consciously reject the Total Work of Art aesthetic. Image, who fulfils a role similar to Hamerton's in the *Yellow Book* of an established authority bestowing his blessing on the younger generation, applauds that

> [t]he writers shall have no further care than to say precisely what each of them thinks and feels on the matter in hand, unhampered by the least concern of supporting any tradition, or by a dread of contradicting, even flatly, what someone else, or their own selves, may have written in the same paper.[73]

This may seem to be a strange statement for someone who had been so involved in such a thoroughly conceptualised magazine as the *CGHH*, but it may be explained by the fact that the *Savoy* was simply understood to have different aims. It comes closer to the miscellaneous character of monthly literary magazines than earlier little magazines, and does not share the *Yellow Book*'s inclination to hide this concession to the mainstream through distracting formal characteristics.

This is borne out by the relative carelessness with which the *Savoy* handles its advertisements. Whereas the *Yellow Book* had still taken trouble to present its adverts in a loose supplement that could be cut out if desired, the *Savoy* seems to have had no qualms about its advertisement sections. 'The Savoy – advertisements', as they are referred to in the header on each page, are always placed at the back of the periodical, in the first issue paginated separately but for the following ones simply paginated continuously from the body text of the magazine. Yet, it is confusing that an 'Editorial Note' to No. 7 claimed that the *Savoy* was 'without advertisements',[74] which could only be true if the editors thought of the advertisement sections as supplemental and therefore not strictly belonging to the magazine proper, unlike those of many magazines that had adverts scattered throughout. The *Savoy*'s adverts are also never listed in the table of contents. By these means, a minimal distance is still implied between magazine and the worldly necessities in addendum.

The larger part of the *Savoy*'s adverts are for Smithers's publisher's list, only four external advertisers being found in its pages during the short lifespan of this magazine. Like the Bodley Head with the *Yellow Book*, Smithers saw the *Savoy* as a perfect way to ensure his catalogues had a larger audience than he could otherwise hope to reach. It is undoubtedly no coincidence that the last issue of the *Savoy*, No. 8 of December 1896, has the largest Smithers list of all, running up to eight pages, whereas the average number for the rest of the run is about four. Like Lane before him, Smithers provides excerpts from reviews for all advertised books, of course taken out of context and therefore often quoted to advantage. Books that needed to be marketed as edgy, like poetry collections by Symons and Theodore Wratislaw, would sometimes teasingly be accompanied by quotes that warned about their candour and voluptuousness, although all too harsh dismissals were always avoided. Smithers, despite his embonpoint silhouette that is repeatedly parodied by Beardsley in the magazine (Figure 25), was surprisingly good at walking the tightrope.

The external advert that recurs most often is an ornamented full-page one for 'Designer, Engraver on Wood and Photozincographer' Paul Naumann, who is credited on the 'Art Contents' pages as responsible for the image reproductions in the magazine. As such he is closely linked to the production of the periodical, in the same way as his competitor Carl Hentschel was affiliated with the *Yellow Book*. An ornate advert for bookbinder Cedric Chivers appears in Nos. 4 and 5, and there is a far soberer one for publishers H. Henry & Co. (see Chapter 6) in No. 4. The latter's adverts for the Nietzsche editions seem linked with the essays on the German philosopher by Havelock Ellis that were appearing in the *Savoy* at the time. Ellis, one of the most versatile thinkers of the late-Victorian period and a regular contributor to the magazine, wrote his much-praised introductions to Nietzsche's ideas in order to advance these in the English-speaking world, so this was an opportunity not to be missed by the first English publisher of his translated collected works, who would later that year also launch the Aestheticist annual the *Pageant* (see Chapter 6). In the first issue, an almost hidden notice for the Stickphast company also appears – 'paste stick' manufacturers whom we will also encounter in the little magazine the *Quest* (see Chapter 5) – enclosed by adverts for Smithers.

It is difficult to ascertain whether the *Savoy* was issued with any other supplemental items besides these advertisements and the above-mentioned white paper covers. The first issue was launched with a tipped-in Christmas card by Beardsley (Figure 26), which would have been more timely if the magazine had reached its earlier December deadline, but of course it would keep for at least a year. Its inclusion among the 'Art Contents' could have prevented sale of the periodical without this gift supplement, making sure readers were not cheated and could appreciate the value they were getting for their money from a simple glance at the contents list. A Christmas card may seem to be a very un-Aesthetic and mundane object, but it is in fact an excellent example of an everyday object that could be easily claimed as a locus for applied art in this period dedicated to intensifying our experience of the everyday. In the Victorian period, Christmas cards were often preserved in albums instead of binned after the holidays as is usually the custom today, and the permanence thereby accorded to the card makes it a seasonal gift to be cherished like any other. This card was an isolated promotion scheme for the launch of the periodical that unfortunately (and ominously) came too late to fulfil its function. The delay had been caused because of Beardsley's characteristic mischief, and, yet again, his feud with the *Yellow Book*. The first version of the cover featured a naked putto urinating over what was clearly a copy of the hated rival publication. Luckily, the last-minute interference of other contributors kept the magazine, in Selwyn Image's phrase, from 'blanching the libel court'.[75]

Generally speaking, this avoidance of too dangerous controversy worked out quite well, perhaps even a bit too well. Reviewers would of course compare the *Savoy* with the *Yellow Book*, and the challenger usually did not come out victorious. The 'dullness' that *Pick-Me-Up* complained of is, surprisingly, not a rare verdict, and the *Savoy* was repeatedly rejected as an unnecessary spin-off. *The Times*, which had fulminated against the *Yellow Book*, wrote of the first number that it would

> be something of a disappointment to those who expected to find this offshoot of 'The Yellow Book' more antinomian than its respectable parent. To us it seems to be very much like what we have seen elsewhere, except that there is a little more of Mr. Aubrey Beardsley in it.[76]

Despite the cautiously positive though underwhelmed evaluation of the *Savoy*'s contents, one big logistical problem did arise that was directly caused by the public image of the magazine. A reproduction of Blake's nude Antaeus in No. 3, though not it any way smutty by itself, had frightened the Head of Purchases at W. H. Smith, and subsequently the chain refused to stack the *Savoy* in their numerous shops. Yeats recalled that

> when Symons pointed out that Blake was considered 'a very spiritual artist', [the bookseller's manager] replied, 'O, Mr Symons, you must remember that we have an audience of young ladies as well as an audience of agnostics.' However, he called Arthur Symons back from the door to say, 'If contrary to our expectations the Savoy should have a large sale, we should be very glad to see you again.'[77]

In a letter to Richard Garnett, Symons would later confide that they 'could not get [the *Savoy*] to pay its way; for as you know, the price was reduced to meet the requirements of Smith's bookstalls'.[78]

In the short 'Causerie: By Way of Epilogue' that concludes the last number, Symons lists this as one of the three reasons why the magazine failed. As W. H. Smith was then, as now, the biggest proprietor of railway booksellers in Britain, being barred from its stalls must have been a blow to the sales of any periodical that aimed at the monthly magazine market. Another reason given by Symons was 'giving so much for so little money',[79] a publication as cheap as the *Savoy* needing to sell many copies before achieving its break-even, which it never did. 'And then, worst of all, we assumed that there were very many people in the world who really cared for art, and really for art's sake.'[80] Then follows a bitter denial of the viability of avant-garde little magazines entering the mainstream periodical market, a mistake they would never make again. There seem to have been quite specific plans for how the magazine could possibly make its return:

> [I]n our next venture we are going to make no attempt to be popular. We shall make our appearance twice only in the year; our volumes will be larger in size, better produced, and they will cost more. In this way we shall be able to appeal to that limited public which cares for the things we care for.[81]

Significantly, what this would have amounted to would likely have been a return to what little magazines did before the *Yellow Book* set out to fight the mainstream with its own weapons.

Of course, other reasons for the failure could be suggested than those Symons admits himself. The *Savoy* had been stuck in an undesirable position, as due to the uncompromising reputation of the editors they were deemed untouchable by most advertisers and distrusted by the major distributors of periodical publications such as W. H. Smith, but the critics and the readers whom they were hoping to tantalise through edgy content apparently felt that they had seen it all before, and were not impressed by a cleaner version of the before-trial *Yellow Book*. Shortly after hearing of the impending demise of the *Savoy*, Hubert Crackanthorpe contacted publisher Grant Richards, who was then just starting out, to invite him to take over the magazine together. Crackanthorpe, whose mother was the well-connected journalist Blanche Crackanthorpe and who had himself briefly edited a magazine focusing on short fiction called the *Albemarle* (1892), believed his to be a 'more valuable' name than that of Symons, and Richards's name an improvement on that of Smithers. He wanted to break away from what he calls 'the Beardsley tradition', blaming the lack of success on the enduring association of the magazine with the two contested figures of Symons and Beardsley.[82] Nothing would come of this palace coup, and Crackanthorpe shortly after committed suicide at the age of twenty-six, true to the type of what Yeats called the 'Tragic Generation'.

Smithers, true to his character, found a way to profit from the end of the magazine, even during and shortly after it was being closed down. The eighth number was entirely composed of contributions by the two editors Symons and Beardsley, which suggests that it was only released to stretch the run of the magazine to an entire year. This was also needed for the magazine to be reprinted and re-released in the set of three complete volumes, bound in blue cloth, that are already announced in the 'Editorial Note' of No. 7 as having 'a cover of Mr. Beardsley's designing'. The *Savoy* merchandising does not stop there. For readers who already had the separate original numbers and did not wish to purchase the bibliophile bound volumes, they offered in the advertisements to No. 8 'artistic blue cloth cases with elaborate cover design in gold by Aubrey Beardsley'. It is not rare for little magazines to be reissued in different formats at a given stage, but this kind of option is quite rare. Next to the supplemental covers that were included with the magazine's numbers, this was another opportunity for loyal readers to customise their own *Savoys*. This way the magazine could appeal to collectors as well as to the average reader. The advertisement section in the last number is not only the biggest of all, it is also the only one out of eight that carries illustrations, being cover illustrations from the advertised books. One of these, for Beardsley's upcoming *Book of Fifty Drawings* (1897), is listed among the regular 'Art Contents' in the table of contents, the only time ever that the advertisement section is referenced there.

As if 'the Yellow Nineties' were not quite compact enough, Max Beerbohm, in an essay published in the month that the *Savoy* folded, honoured his friend by stating that everything changed for the avant-garde after 'the Beardsley period', now decidedly over after this second disappointment.[83] The ever ailing Beardsley would outlive his 'Period' only for a short while, as he died of tuberculosis in March 1898, at twenty-five years old. Ironically, 'The Beardsley Period' would also be the title of an essay on the Nineties authored by Osbert Burdett in 1928, and published by Beardsley's old adversary Lane. The cautious publisher had in fact soon after Beardsley's death deemed it opportune to recall his former friendship with the artist whom he had once so abruptly disowned, and published several studies of his work that avoid discussing their relationship during the mid-Nineties. He himself wrote a pamphlet on *Aubrey Beardsley and the Yellow Book* (1903), which is hardly more than a catalogue of recent Bodley Head publications cashing in on the artist's legacy, including a reprint of the three volumes of the *Savoy*, the rights for which were likely acquired soon after Smithers went bankrupt in 1900. Beardsley's dismissal from the *Yellow Book* and the 'Keynotes Series' is deftly glossed over:

> as an editor and a draughtsman [Beardsley] was always a practical joker, for one had, so to speak, to place his drawings under a microscope, and look at them upside down. This tendency, on the eve of the production of Volume V., [. . .] rendered it necessary to omit his work from that volume.[84]

Professional publishers, like the common reader complained of by Symons, tend to not really care 'for art, and really for art's sake'. Perhaps they cannot afford to.

Notes

1. Woolf, *Mr. Bennett and Mrs. Brown*, p. 2.
2. Jackson, *Eighteen Nineties*, p. 14.
3. Ibid., p. 17; Blaikie-Murdoch, *Renaissance of the Nineties*, p. 18.
4. James, 'Death of the Lion', p. 8.
5. Nelson, *Early Nineties*, p. 288.
6. 'Prospectus', n.p.
7. Ibid.
8. Stetz, 'Sex, Lies, and Printed Cloth', p. 76.

9. Quoted in Mix, *Study in Yellow*, p. 3. Emphasis original.
10. Baring, 'Nineties', p. 103.
11. Le Gallienne, *Romantic '90s*, pp. 227–8.
12. Symons, 'Decadent Movement in Literature', pp. 858–9.
13. MacLeod, *Fictions of British Decadence*, pp. 2–7.
14. Nordau, *Degeneration*, p. 7.
15. Jepson, *Memoirs of a Victorian*, p. 244.
16. Felstiner, *Lies of Art*, pp. 6–7.
17. 'Yellow Book', p. 3.
18. Beerbohm, 'Letter to the Editor', p. 283.
19. Brake, 'Endgames', pp. 59–60.
20. Wilde, *Picture of Dorian Gray*, p. 6.
21. 'Dullness in Yellow', p. 359.
22. Hamerton, 'Picture Buying', p. 125.
23. Hamerton, 'Yellow Book', p. 181.
24. Waugh, 'Reticence in Literature', p. 204.
25. Crackanthorpe, 'Reticence in Literature', p. 269.
26. Ibid., p. 266.
27. Ibid., p. 268.
28. Yeats, 'Trembling of the Veil', p. 324.
29. 'Prospectus', n.p.
30. Chan, *Economy of the Short Story*, p. 51.
31. Ibid., p. 51.
32. The *Yellow Book* is discussed with a representative selection from the contributions by less famous and avant-garde authors in Boyiopoulos et al., *Decadent Short Story*.
33. Image, 'Ternary of Reflections', p. 44.
34. Wald, 'Periodicals and Periodicity', p. 423.
35. Interview with the *Critic* (5 May 1894, p. 301), quoted in Kooistra, 'Modern Illustrated Magazine', p. 134.
36. Carter and Barker, *ABC for Book Collectors*, p. 217.
37. Hamerton, 'Yellow Book', p. 182.
38. Dowling, 'Letterpress and Picture', p. 125.
39. Hamerton, 'Yellow Book', p. 179.
40. Jacobi, *Making and Issuing of Books*, p. 61.
41. 'Prospectus', n.p.
42. Brake, 'Endgames', p. 51.
43. Stetz, 'Sex, Lies, and Printed Cloth', p. 75.
44. Nelson, *Early Nineties*, p. 258.
45. MacLeod, *Fictions of British Decadence*, p. 84.
46. Hughes, 'Women Poets and Contested Spaces', p. 850.
47. Mix, *Study in Yellow*, p. 147.
48. Stetz and Lasner, *Yellow Book*, p. 20.
49. Lambert, *Bodley Head*, p. 107.
50. Mendelsohn, *Henry James, Oscar Wilde*, pp. 203–4.

51. 'The Yellow Book, An Illustrated Quarterly', p. 3.
52. Mix, *Study in Yellow*, p. 191.
53. Stetz and Lasner, *Yellow Book*, p. 34.
54. Ibid., p. 29.
55. Ibid., p. 29.
56. 'Interview: Gertrude Hammond', pp. 177–8.
57. Radford [Maitland], 'Song', pp. 121–2.
58. Hughes, 'Women Poets and Contested Spaces', *passim*.
59. Nelson, *Publisher to the Decadents*, p. 58.
60. Jepson, *Memoirs of a Victorian*, p. 244.
61. Lambert, *Bodley Head*, p. 59.
62. Macdonald, 'Buchan and the *Yellow Book*', p. 49.
63. 'Editorial Note', n.p.
64. 'Prospectus', n.p.
65. Beckson, *Arthur Symons*, p. 127.
66. Shaw, 'On Going to Church', p. 13.
67. 'M. Arthur Symons dont le nom est, avec celui du précédent [Dowson], un des plus sympathiques à Paris parmi ceux des jeunes littérateurs en faveur à Londres' (quoted from *Courrier Français* (2 February 1896), in Garbáty, 'French Coterie of the *Savoy* 1896', p. 612).
68. Nelson, *Publisher to the Decadents*, p. 67.
69. 'Notions', p. 13.
70. Brake, 'Marketing Notoriety', p. 174.
71. See 'Prospectus', n.p.
72. Image, 'Criticism and the Critic', pp. 143–4.
73. Ibid., pp. 143–4.
74. [Symons], 'Editorial Note', n.p.
75. Nelson, *Publisher to the Decadents*, p. 70.
76. 'Books of the Week', p. 8.
77. Yeats, 'Trembling of the Veil', p. 324.
78. Quoted in Bishop, 'Re:Covering Modernism', p. 296.
79. Symons, 'Causerie', p. 92.
80. Ibid., p. 92.
81. Ibid., p. 92.
82. Quoted in Crackanthorpe, *Hubert Crackanthorpe*, p. 131.
83. Beerbohm, 'Be It Cosiness', p. 235.
84. [Lane], *Aubrey Beardsley and the Yellow Book*, p. 6.

Chapter 5

Politicised Aestheticism outside London: the *Quest* and the *Evergreen*

As we have noted in the previous chapter, until the *Yellow Book* after the redundancy of Beardsley started inviting artistic groups specifically from outside London to furnish its designs and illustrations, lay readers might have been excused for thinking avant-garde art and literature was the monopoly of the British capital. All the little magazines that we have so far discussed, including even the *OCM*, were published in London. This is in keeping with the standard view of the British avant-garde during the 1890s, which has been studied mainly as a metropolitan phenomenon. Most of the pioneering authors whom the poets and artists in the 1890s little magazines looked to as examples had also been based in the metropolitan centres of their day, where Baudelaire's Parisian flâneur took 'a bath in the multitudes' or D. G. Rossetti has his lyrical subject meet the prostitute 'Jenny' one Saturday night at the London Haymarket. When they wrote about contemporaneous settings, the earliest British Aestheticist poets and artists often sought out controversial social issues that 'our learned London children know' (in Rossetti's cynical phrase from the same poem) and that Victorian orthodoxy would only permit to be referenced with explicit disapproval. Among the allegedly *décadentes* French inspirations of the 1890s, Naturalist novelists, while specialising in filth and depravity, usually focused on smaller towns or rural settings, and because of the focus on the abject nature of these scenes there is no element of justification, nor an implied incentive to emulate the debased characters. Somehow, the urban setting of much Parnassian and Symbolist literature facilitated a coexistence of antinomian morals and attractive bohemian urbanity. The same applies to associated styles in painting and illustration of this period.

In the 1890s several of the British artists and authors pigeonholed as Decadent copied from these their frank depictions of urban squalor that could be read as glorifying immorality, an interpretation encouraged by alleged Decadents themselves. When Beardsley or Walter Sickert depicted scenes of libertinism and intemperance in the *Yellow Book* and the *Savoy*, they played to a middle-class anxiety about life in the continually expanding city that already went back at least a hundred years. Designated as 'citephobia' by Julian Wolfreys, this anxiety took the form of a belief that the city was the site of a separate society or *civitas* that was no longer fulfilling its etymological purpose of 'being civil', and it became commonplace in art and literature, for instance in the nineteenth-century realist depictions of authors such as De Quincey and Dickens, to set up London as a 'location-as-premise' for narratives of moral corruption.[1] In the avant-garde of the mid-1890s two extremes can be discerned in the response to these widespread misgivings about urban life: a Decadent position that is toyed with in the *Yellow Book* and the *Savoy* that provocatively implies a celebration of the supposed urban destitution, and its diametrical opposite that hoped to put Aestheticist principles to use to remedy such social ills, and which is showcased in its purest form in the two little magazines under scrutiny in this chapter: the *Quest* and the *Evergreen*.

As Nicholas Freeman has noted,

> what was new in the late nineteenth century was a sustained, albeit haphazard, interest in developing a specialised language of urban life. This was not the political and economic critique of Marx and Engels but an attempt to articulate a condition of 'cityness' that seemed of urgent importance in an era of unprecedented metropolitan expansion.[2]

Arthur Symons wrote several books of impressionistic character studies of the major cities of Europe, and in his poetry too delighted in showing off how much he felt at home in the urban hubbub. However, like so many aspects of Aestheticism, such urbanite personae were frequently ambiguous. Symons, who temporarily at least seemed comfortable with being pigeonholed as a Decadent, collected his most controversial lyrics in his *London Nights* (1896). In this collection, as Kostas Boyiopoulos suggests, 'the metropolis not only confirms the triumph of artifice over nature, but serves as a metaphor for Decadent style itself: its divisions, streets and blocks, its prismatic splits in light and shadow, serve to partition and fragment space *ipso facto*'.[3] Approval of this fragmented social life has been seen as a clear symptom of supposed 'Decadence' since the term became current in the late nineteenth century. Nevertheless, squarely in the middle of *London Nights* there is a section entitled 'Intermezzo: Pastoral' in which the lyrical subject escapes to the Welsh countryside in search of 'the green cool song' that he 'long[s] to hear'.[4] Switching back and forth between approval and condemnation, justifying amoral practices but also treating them as dangerous addictions, was after all a Decadent commonplace too.

Less invested in the image of the *poète maudit*, Symons's friend Yeats had also longingly heard 'lake water lapping [. . .] in the deep heart's core' in the middle of the city.[5] To him, London was stimulating as well, but what appeal it had came out of an ultimately jarring disharmony. Yeats recalled later that as a young man in 'abhorred London' he had objected to the fragmentation of modern life that informs the very architecture and social interaction of the modern metropolis. He sought a way to piece together a long-lost 'Unity of Being', believing that the activities and aspirations of all trades and classes in the past had completed each other instead of clashing as they did in the modern age, and hoping that this could be approached through forms of artistic production that would be appreciated across the social strata. 'Had not Europe shared one mind and heart, until both mind and heart began to break into fragments[. . .]?'[6] To fit the fragments of society together again was the business of the social reformer, in the same way as reuniting the estranged Sister Arts was the mission of the artist. The belief that the artistic and the political vocations belong together was, as we have seen, advocated by Ruskin and his major disciple William Morris, whose relationship to city life is just as complex as those of their younger followers, and who inspired some highly ambitious groups in the Aesthetic avant-garde to adopt the urban space into their Total Art projects.

Fin-de-Siècle London could not be spoken of 'as a whole', but only as 'a collection of many wholes', Henry James eloquently found, and this is a view that appeared time and again in the period.[7] Much writing about London throughout the nineteenth century was characterised by what Wolfreys calls an 'over-reaction in the face of the multiple, mobile and fragmentary phenomena of the city' that 'serves to point to the fragmentation of identity' in the late-Victorian era.[8] The heterogeneous metropolis reflected the increasingly visible social, gender-political and ethnic diversity of British society, and posed a challenge to any author or artist who wished to capture the city in a totalising concept. This was all the more problematic for consciously political thinkers whose attempt at unification had a social as well as an artistic purpose. Ruskin, who had lived in and around London for most of his life, returned to this issue constantly throughout his career, as he propagated the principle that the improvement of the city as a living and working environment would be indispensable if any progress was to be made in the morale and labour conditions of its inhabitants. As Phillip Mallett put it, Ruskin believed that the problems of the modern city, of which London would be the most extreme instance, 'can be directly related to the idea of society as a huge market place in which individuals and groups compete with each other for gain', instead of being united through cooperation.[9] This belief was adopted by groups within the internally diverse Arts and Crafts Movement who sought to develop a form of local, politically militant Aestheticism that in its very production methods aimed to exemplify a constructive alternative to institutionalised power relations based on Victorian capitalism. Such militant Aesthetes often considered those members of the contemporaneous avant-garde who flirted with Decadence as narcissistic individualists, and their alienation from society a result of the bourgeois ideology that they themselves claimed to combat through their refusal to comply with its moral precepts. To emphasise that the alleged Decadents were not to be considered fellow travellers of theirs, these groups frequently resorted to a strategy of stern anti-Decadent rhetoric that was often equally as vehement as that of the Victorian moral orthodoxy, and that was part and parcel of their critique of the modern city and its primary example, the British capital. Because the Arts and Crafts view on the Total Work of Art was that of an expansive venture that would emanate from a core group of art workers operating in one specific location, the concrete situation of each group becomes important. Up and down the British Isles, local and politicised communitarian Aestheticisms were developed by participating groups in order to root themselves in their respective communities. The two understudied little magazines that will be the focus of this chapter belonged to this communitarian party and were to a great extent shaped by their explicitly *not* being based in London: the Arts and Crafts journal the *Quest* from Birmingham, and the *Evergreen* produced by the Edinburgh Ramsay Garden initiative around Patrick Geddes.

Arts and Crafts in the Midlands: the *Quest*

Although the Arts and Crafts Movement spread across Britain during the 1890s, influencing the formation of sympathetic causes throughout, its political strategy was always primarily localist. It consisted of groups of artist-artisans assembled in local associations that styled themselves as 'guilds' and that aimed to function in collaboration with other civil society institutions within their immediate communities. These guilds were diverse and ranged from loosely associated professional networks, such as the London-based Century Guild of *Hobby Horse* fame, to cooperative businesses that operated from a shared workshop (see Chapter 2). In most cases, the deliberately small scale of the guilds' production necessitated that they focus on their immediate environs for their target audience. As a leader in grassroots left-wing politics, Morris enjoyed nationwide recognition, and in his later years he identified as a communist, but his views had more in common with the downscaled anarcho-communism of his close friend Kropotkin than with the centralised state socialism of Marx and Engels, who counted on the revolutionary force latent in the industrial proletariat. Like Ruskin, Morris held that society should be a sum of inclusive yet autonomous communities that fulfil as much as possible their own material and cultural needs. By striving towards this goal, they would be investing in what he referred to as 'municipal life' in an address that he delivered at the Municipal School of Art of Birmingham in 1894, in which he also stated that '[w]ithout flattery, I can say that of course I know how this city has for long taken a leading part in this development'.[10]

Morris's praise may come as a surprise, as Birmingham at the time was one of the major industrial towns of Europe, and then already the second largest city in Britain. This might suggest that it, like London, would have suffered from the undesirable side-effects of Victorian industrialism's blinkered obsession with cost-efficiency, referred to by Morris in the same speech as the bleakest manifestation of the prevalent ideology of 'stupid utilitarianism'.[11] In an essay on the desired 'Revival of Handicraft', he later would lament that

> [d]uring the first or medieval period [. . .] what machinery was used was simply of the nature of a multiplied tool, a help to the workman's hand-labour and not a supplanter of it. The workman worked for himself and not for any capitalistic employer, and he was accordingly master of his work and his time; this was the period of pure handicraft. [. . .] The latter half of the eighteenth century saw the beginning of the last epoch of production that the world has known, that of the automatic machine which supersedes hand-labour, and turns the workman who was once a handicraftsman helped by tools, [. . .] into a tender of machines.[12]

Birmingham had been at the forefront of industrial innovation since Boulton and Watt pioneered steam technology there in the late eighteenth century; the very period that was anathema to Morris as the beginning of the end for craftsmanship.[13] However, its particular socio-economic situation allowed this city to avoid some of the undesired side-effects of industrialisation. In contrast to the surrounding Black Country where iron forgeries and coal pits predominated, or the cotton mills of nearby Manchester, Birmingham mainly had smaller manufactories that employed a less proletarianised workforce. These excelled in industries that required definite skills, such as the production of decorated metalwork and so-called 'Brummagem toys': items such as cheap jewellery, snuff boxes and belt buckles that were sold around the world. While these were not up to the standards exacted by Morris and his followers, they did require a mastery of 'handicraft'. According to social historians such as Asa Briggs, this predominance of skilled labour in Birmingham caused the social gap between employer and labourer to be smaller than in the other industrial centres of Britain. Of course, Birmingham had not been impervious to the negative social repercussions of industrialism, but living conditions and education for the most affected poorer inhabitants were further improved during and after the mayoralty of the populist Joseph Chamberlain in the 1870s. 'Radical Joe' appealed to the particular social relations of his town to generate the necessary communal spirit and financial backing for modernising public sanitation and establishing an array of new municipal cultural institutions.[14] In Chamberlainian rhetoric, the formerly administrative term 'municipal' became ideologically invested with what the mayor called his 'abiding sense of the value and the importance of self-government', and the new institutions it was applied to were presented to the town's populace as their collective property and as symbols of solidarity between the classes.[15] Examples close to our purpose include the Birmingham Museum and Art Gallery (1881) that among other treasures would amass an unparalleled collection of Pre-Raphaelite and other recent British painting, and the aforementioned Municipal School of Art (1885), one of the first art schools to teach applied arts such as metalwork and embroidery on the same level as fine-art skills like drawing and sculpture. Victorian businessmen, especially in the industrial towns of Northern England and the Midlands, were prone to investing in new art to acquire cultural distinction, and in Birmingham they could be persuaded to show their 'municipal' spirit by supporting local artists and initiatives. All of these elements together made fertile soil for Arts and Crafts associations to take root.

Morris speculated that the movement of which he was perceived to be the leader had the largest number of supporters, after London, in Birmingham.[16] The city was home to several groups that were dedicated to artisanal aesthetics – for instance, the later and more business-minded Bromsgrove Guild of Applied Arts that lasted from 1898 to 1966 and managed to obtain commissions for such landmarks as the ornamental gates of Buckingham Palace and the Liver Bird perched on the Liverpool Royal Liver Building – but the earliest, and during the early 1890s most renowned, group was the Birmingham Guild of Handicraft.[17] This organisation grew out of the Birmingham chapter of the Kyrle Society, a nationwide charity set up in 1876 to provide educational and artistic courses to the working classes, securing the involvement of leading artists associated with Aestheticism.[18] Perhaps out of frustration with the Kyrle Society's often criticised patronising attitude towards the beneficiaries of its schemes and inefficiency in achieving genuine improvement, which has been jokingly referred to as 'missionary aestheticism' in scholarship,[19] the Birmingham chapter reformed itself into an Arts and Crafts guild in 1890, shortly after an exhibition of applied art was held in its home town. There the future Birmingham Guild members established contact with other represented organisations such as the Century Guild, and especially Charles Ashbee's Guild of Handicraft based in the London East End, which was declared by its first director Arthur Dixon to be the 'prototype' of the Birmingham Guild.[20]

As discussed before, book production offers opportunities for collective artistic practice and was one of the most popular applied arts among Arts and Crafts practitioners. The Birmingham Guild was no exception. Several members worked in printing and book illustration, both of which were also taught at the Municipal School. The Guild and the School were seen as complimentary ventures, as

> the Guild [. . .] strives to familiarise the craftsman with the principles of design and to give him as well as the designer the opportunity of carrying out those principles to a commercial result as far as possible from the disabilities which attend the modern industrial system.[21]

It therefore subscribed to the Arts and Crafts Movement's views on print, which, as Elizabeth Carolyn Miller has shown, developed in the late nineteenth century as an alternative to mass-produced texts that could escape being relegated to the status of mere commodity in a capitalist market. Whereas earlier reformist movements had welcomed new printing technologies because these enabled the cheap and efficient dissemination of their message across a wider audience, 'artworkers' such as Morris believed that adopting the production methods of industrialism amounted to tacitly supporting the socio-economic effects of the capitalist and utilitarian ideology which it represented.[22]

Bill Waters has argued that the buzzing interest in Fine Printing of the early 1890s 'was an important development' for the Birmingham Guild, 'since even the most modest of talents could reach a certain level of proficiency; a number of newly-emerged publishers were ready to take them up and it was an effective means of disseminating their works'.[23] No print form is more suited to such dissemination of both message and palpable material workmanship than the periodical, and inspired directly by the (*Century Guild*) *Hobby Horse*, the Birmingham Guild decided that it needed a magazine of its own. It is obvious that the resulting *Quest* (1894–6) wanted to outdo its less political model in the ideological consistency of its contents and the stringent anachronism of its production methods. The links between the Birmingham journal and the older magazine, in both its series, is immediately apparent when the respective wrappers are compared. Both feature knights to indicate the medievalist inspiration of the journals, but whereas the *Hobby Horse*'s are mounted on the eponymous folkloric stick-horses to indicate a relativist awareness of its own anachronism, the consistently serious *Quest* never breaks character (Figures 5, 6 and 27). Officially at least, no editor was assigned, no doubt to further bring home the cohesion of the 'Brotherhood of the Quest', the slightly bathetic name that the Guild members involved with the periodical used for themselves in the *Quest*, thereby declaring themselves the inheritors of the legacy of *The Germ*'s Pre-Raphaelite Brotherhood and perhaps the *OCM*'s Set or Brotherhood as well. Six four-monthly issues were published, each at the price of a half-crown (2s. 6d), or 7s. 6d for a yearly subscription. This rather low price indicates the purpose of the journal as a publicity scheme and collective portfolio for the Guild. It was the same price as the *CGHH*, while the *Hobby Horse* after the Century Guild's disbanding, and the bestselling Aestheticist periodical at the time the *Yellow Book*, at 5 shillings were twice as expensive.

The first three numbers of the *Quest* (November 1894–July 1895), later assembled as its first volume, were published by the Cornish Brothers, booksellers from Birmingham who decades before had changed the life of an undergraduate Morris by selling him a copy of Mallory's *Morte d'Arthur*.[24] The final three numbers (November 1895–July 1896) or second volume appeared under the imprint of G. Napier & Co., perhaps a family connection of later Guild Director Claude

Napier-Clavering.[25] Birmingham Guild members were involved in most of the few books published with this firm, likely a spin-off of the Guild, as an advert in the third number announces

> the publication, at an early date, of a series of books in which the chief aim will be to produce work in accord with the best ideal of the Craft of bookmaking, without falling into the mannerisms which result from a slavish imitation of archaic models. In these books, the best materials will be used, and care will be given to the choice and arrangement of both type and decoration.[26]

The six numbers of the *Quest* demonstrate the same unwavering dedication to the principles of Fine Printing, and appeared in a small edition of 300 copies hand-printed at Kyrle Hall. This most literal 'handicraft' is an important statement that the magazine made much of, because it was 'the aim of the Guild to supply handmade articles superior in beauty of design and soundness of workmanship to those made by machinery; and to make only such as shall give just pleasure both to the craftsman and the buyer of them'.[27] For the last three numbers, a London edition was issued through G. Napier's agents Tylston, Edwards and Marsden, and an American edition by the Boston-based Daniel Berkeley Updike of the Merrymount Press, one of the leading purveyors of Fine Printing on the other side of the Atlantic.

Each number of the *Quest* contains adverts at the back of the magazine, most having a clear connection to the Birmingham Guild, or to the broader Arts and Crafts Movement and its allies in Birmingham. Except for Updike, the involved publishing partners always get an advert for their list, in the case of the Cornish Brothers and G. Napier featuring books which have some connection to the magazine, for instance illustrated or written by *Quest* contributors. Like the *CGHH* before it, the *Quest* follows the familiar strategy of integrating advertisements into the artistic concept of the magazine. Adverts are conspicuously designed and illustrated in the style upheld throughout the body text of the journal, usually by Guild members, and their medievalist decorations are in accordance with the concept of the magazine. There is also a recurring advert for the Chaucer's Head Library, like the Cornish Brothers a Birmingham-based 'dealer in rare, curious and out-of-way books'. Chamberlain, King and Jones, 'sole agents in the Midlands for the sale of the far-famed Morris fabrics', advertise here as well. 'Stickphast Paste Sticks', an adhesive that was for instance used by book binders and that would later be advertised in the *Savoy*, and 'Reeves & Sons artist's black for decorative work' are loyal to the magazine too, advertising in every number. While the latter two companies were obviously not run on Arts and Crafts principles, it was no doubt surmised that the *Quest* would be read by practising artists who would require their wares, bringing business for the advertisers and cementing the reputation of the magazine as read by practitioners. Finally, just like the Century Guild in their *CGHH* had included a list of members and associates to advertise their services and draw work for them, the *Quest* in each number has an advertisement for the Birmingham Guild. The page-long notice, illustrated with a view of the workshops at Kyrle Hall, states that '[t]he Guild are prepared to undertake work in the following departments: metalwork, furniture, woodcarving, bookbinding, wood engraving and printing: not just books, but also cards for Christmas, bookplates'. After the *Quest*, the Guild would also be commissioned with the first three volumes of *Saint George* (1898–1904), a quarterly journal issued by the Ruskin Society of Birmingham, yet another Arts and Crafts-inflected initiative in their hometown, which especially in these early numbers, as Brian Maidment has argued, also embraced anachronistic design principles in order to signal its hostility to contemporaneous modes of production.[28]

London publisher David Nutt, who issued books by Aestheticist writers such as Wilde as well as books of a medievalist interest such as reprints of old texts and early studies of Arthurian lore by Jessie Weston, advertises only once, in the first issue. This is not surprising, as in the second number Count Stenbock's *Studies of Death* (1894), published by Nutt, is disapproved of by Napier-Clavering in the review section entitled 'Fine Feathers and Fine Birds'. The section's title can be interpreted as a reference to the core principle of the Revival of Fine Printing that a conceptual discrepancy between presentation ('feathers') and content ('birds') would result in a flawed book. According to the reviewer, this was the case with Stenbock's book:

> We have of late become too well accustomed to the empty work of the stylist who is nothing more; the graceful phrasemonger in prose or verse who has nothing to say, and who says it in periods of varying degrees of perfectness. [. . .] But now with the revival of an interest in that which, however good and desirable in its way, is more an external of the book even than its style – the interest I mean, in its printing, binding and general arrangement – we are, it seems, to have a worse evil.[29]

While the design of Stenbock's book viewed separately would be exquisite, '[i]t is surely to be regretted that the newly awakened interest of the book-buying public should be attracted by such outward signs, only to find such a lack of inward virtue'.[30] Stenbock's tales of supernatural horror and moral degeneration were commonly associated with Decadence, and significantly the *Quest* hereby explicitly distances itself from this entire phenomenon. Similarly, in the first issue, the illustrations in Laurence Housman's *A Farm in Fairyland* (1894) are praised for their technical mastery, but they are also said to suffer from a 'weirdness of conception'.[31] In all reviews, more attention goes to the paratext than to the content of the books, and what is frowned upon in this case seems to have been Housman's ongoing development towards a more Symbolist style, with all its controversial moral connotations, away from Arts and Crafts' medievalist conventions. This anti-Decadent stance is typical of the Arts and Crafts Movement in the period. Conversely, in another review, Napier-Clavering remarks of C. R. Ashbee's work of Arts and Crafts theory on the potential of artistic production for the improvement of society, *A Few Chapters in Workshop Reconstruction and Citizenship* (1894), that 'it is to be regretted that the printer has not done the book justice either in the quality of the ink used or in the evenness of the impressions'.[32] Theorists must be practitioners, and vice versa. By means of such insistence on the design and materiality of the reviewed books, the Birmingham Guild can through the review items in the *Quest* additionally showcase their own expertise and invite favourable notices of their own publications.

Periodicals such as the *Quest* seem to be aimed at an audience of practitioners rather than passive consumers of applied art, and favoured the demonstration of practical production principles over the mere palaver of the outsider critic. The *Quest* shared the views of Ruskin and Morris, as described by Walter Adamson, who 'saw production rather than consumption as the main locus of cultural taste and value'.[33] This emphasis on production has important repercussion for the late-Victorian philosophy of art. In the first issue of the *CGHH*, Selwyn Image had taken issue with the realist notion that art should be a 'facsimile' of 'what we all know', contending that a one-on-one correspondence should not be the ultimate goal of artistic representation. 'Fine art is not imitation, but invention: it is not reflection, but creation: it is not the counterfeit of Nature, but another world of imaginative creation out of the raw material of Nature supplying it with symbols.'[34] The first issue of the *Quest* contains an aesthetic mission statement that is unusual for the little magazines of the 1890s in its philosophical density, in the form of an essay on 'The Platonic Theory of Art' by Edward Adolf Sonnenschein, professor of Classics at Josiah Mason College (now the University of Birmingham). Like Image, Sonnenschein is hostile to mimetic naturalism, believing that rather than copy the appearances of the world, artists should improve on sensory observations so that these can suggest Ideal manifestations of Beauty. He argues that Plato's much-discussed dislike for the arts is the result of a common misreading, claiming that the Greek philosopher only meant to prove that the accuracy of correspondence between object and mimetic representation, contrary to doctrines of pictorial realism, cannot be the highest goal for artists, because by copying the (in comparison with the Platonic Ideal) inevitably debased phenomenal reality, the viewer is not provided with a higher model to aspire to.[35] Plato wished all aspects of social life to contribute to the improvement of the polity, and that artists should aim to make their art a means for 'the rounding and perfecting of human life'.[36] This moral theory also provides a useful context for the *Quest*'s hostility to Decadence, as suggested by its dismissal of seductively designed works of immoral literature, like Stenbock's. Sonnenschein makes sure his argument is understood by a readership well versed in Arts and Crafts rhetoric by quoting Ruskin:

> I may shelter myself behind the name of Mr. Ruskin, who here as much as elsewhere is a modern exponent of much of the wisdom of the ancients: 'that art is the greatest', he teaches, 'which conveys to the mind of the spectator, by any means whatsoever, the greatest number of the greatest ideas'.[37]

Within the *Quest*, the consistency of design and content demanded in the reviews was achieved by means of collaborations between the 'Brothers of the Quest', who worked together to mobilise individual leanings towards one, coherent, collective achievement. As was the case in the *CGHH* and the *Dial*, articles in the *Quest* occasionally receive tailored decorations that in shape or reference are linked to the textual items with which they appear. Sonnenschein's essay comes with an intriguing tailpiece by Sidney Meteyard that features the inscription 'Truth is Beauty, Beauty is Truth', above a long-haired youth gazing down at a flower (Figure 28). We know that we have Meteyard to thank for this decorative feature because the *Quest*, like other little magazines invested in the valorisation of artistic crafts, always specifies that the role of every participant in the collective enterprise of the magazine be duly stated to once again emphasise the horizontal hierarchy in the production process, whether they be authors, editors of republished texts, engravers, illustrators or designers of decorative features. This ornament is thereby not a mute piece of decoration; it is a cross-medial (visual and verbal) comment on the article with which it appears, and a perfect instance of collaboration between magazine contributors. Meteyard's depiction of the youth and the flower have obvious echoes of D. G. Rossetti's poem 'The Woodspurge', but the key to understanding the meaning of the tailpiece is its use of the gnomic closing lines from Keats's 'Ode to a Grecian Urn', which were then, as now, usually read as an affirmation of the primacy of affect in the evaluation of art, emotion over reason, but with an additional ethical dimension that manages to recuperate Keats at once for Aestheticism and for Victorian moralism. In a recent study of Keats, William Michael Rossetti had given the following paraphrase:

> [a]ny beauty which is not truthful (if any such there be), and any truth which is not beautiful (if any such there be), are of no practical importance to mankind in their mundane condition, but in in fact there are no such, for, to the human mind, beauty and truth are one and the same thing.[38]

By demonstrating its message in its visual and textual contents as well as in the palpable proof of its material production, the *Quest* too would have worked out Keats's equation.

As stated above, despite the ubiquity of the core issues in the *Quest*'s ideological programme, most contributions are rather a practical demonstration of their principles than polemics or explicit propaganda. Arthur Dixon elaborates on the mission of the Birmingham Guild in No. 2, but says little more than what is already stated in their recurrent advertisement. In No. 6, there is a guest contribution by William Lethaby, cofounder of the London-based Art Workers' Guild, which is a further explanation of the political aims of the Arts and Crafts Movement. He hopes that the artistic guilds may become a source of inspiration for the then developing trade unions, with whom he seems to differ in opinion because of his greater emphasis on meritocracy over prescriptive egalitarianism, as 'only the properly proficient must become master-craftsmen',[39] an argument that echoes Mackmurdo's doubts about socialism in the early numbers of the *CGHH*. The medieval interest of the *Quest* is combined with a nostalgia for the calm bliss of rural communities in a series of three illustrated causeries on old towns. It is probably no coincidence that all three are quite remote from London, two like Birmingham being in the West Midlands area (Evesham – No. 3, Warwick – No. 6) and one in Northumberland (Warkworth – No. 2). These articles were probably as much a boost to local morale as they were treatments of architectural issues, despite some attention to what was being done in these towns in the way of anti-scrape restoration work that preserves the changes that have happened to centuries-old buildings over the course of history without returning them to an idealised, supposedly original state. Bertram Tennyson, cousin to the late poet laureate, contributes a poem on 'Cumbrian Vales and Fells' to No. 3, another contribution with strong local colour.

It is fair to say that the *Quest* is the most faithful application of Morrisian Arts and Crafts ideology as well as the Kelmscott printing aesthetic of any little magazine of the 1890s. The Birmingham Guild deferred to their more experienced colleagues in several instances, to the extent that the *Quest*, in guild terminology, may be seen as a 'masterpiece' submitted in completion of their apprenticeship in Fine Printing. Wood engraver and short-time Birmingham Guild associate Bernard Sleigh tells us that their hand-printing press had been bought from Morris, and that the editors were advised by Kelmscott (and former *CGHH*) image printing specialist Emery Walker.[40] The *Quest*'s dense block of text surrounded by wide margins and occasionally decorative borders looks distinctly Morrisian, and several engravings take after the work of Kelmscott house illustrator Burne-Jones. Furthermore, the magazine includes two newly edited and illustrated lives from Caxton's *Golden Legend* (1438), of which Kelmscott had produced an edition in 1892. The 'Life of Saint Silvester' (No. 1) and 'Life of Saint Kenelm' (No. 6) are especially impressive as group endeavours, as up to three different illustrators worked together here, and obviously took care to work in a uniform style (Figure 29). Some Brothers of the Quest received commissions from Kelmscott too. During the run of the *Quest*, Arthur Gaskin had furnished illustrations for their edition of Spenser's *Shepheardes Calendar* (1896), and Charles Gere delivered the frontispiece to Morris's *News from Nowhere* (1892). The latter is a well-known engraved depiction of Kelmscott Manor that has often been reprinted in studies of Arts and Crafts architecture, and it appears in the fourth number of the *Quest* (November 1895) with an architectural causerie by Morris entitled 'Gossip About an Old House on the Upper Thames', a guided tour of the manor that focuses on its architecture and interior decoration. It is worthy of note that this is the only instance of Morris contributing to a little magazine, apart from his less committal permission to publish a transcribed lecture in the *Hobby Horse* (January 1892). As a final token of his support of and trust in the Birmingham Guild,

Morris allowed them to use the original blocks for the printing of this engraving, a boon he normally refused.[41] Charles Ricketts, who in the *Dial* had been drawing attention to the engraver's art, also recognised the valuable contribution of the 'School' of Birmingham, and would single them out for praise in an article in the *Pageant* as one of the few in England that was 'conscious of the desirability of a revival'.[42]

Although such peer recognition must have been gratifying, the ultimate precariousness of their success was acknowledged by the artistic craftsmen themselves from the very first contribution in the *Quest*. This poem, entitled 'The Quest: A Sonnet', is the only contribution throughout the six issues to be printed in italics, as one often sees in peritextual items such as epigraphs, and it appears next to the frontispiece for that number, entitled 'The Quest of the Soul's Desire' (Figure 30). The frontispiece is credited in the table of contents to Ernest Treglown, but the poem is left unsigned – a rarity in this periodical, which attributes nearly all content items because of the previously discussed ideological obligation to acknowledge every individual contribution to the collective enterprise. This anonymous poem, therefore, should arguably be read as a mission statement for the entire Guild:

> He follows her for ever, leaving all
> Led on by sudden glimpses of her face,
> Each fairer than the last, and with a grace
> Of welcome, and sweet lips that seem to call,
> But weary is the knight who is her thrall,
> And well for him that love is here to brace
> His strength, and will not let him slack his pace,
> Nor stay to take the apples as they fall.
> And though he never win his shadowy Best,
> Winning or losing, it is his to live
> Forever weary in a noble quest
> With hope throned high and pleasure fugitive
> And not to linger in an unearned rest,
> Tasting the soulless sweets that the world can give.

In this allegorical sonnet, the Brothers of the Quest are collectively personified as a knight in pursuit of his 'shadowy Best', or ideal, adored faithfully in a courtly *amour lointain*. The knight will not waiver from his final goal, but the poem acknowledges the importance of 'each fairer' 'sudden glimpses', that may stand for the realisations of Guild projects. The imagery fits the Victorian trend for Arthurian verse romances and ballads instigated by the immensely popular Malory adaptations of Tennyson – for example, the opening poems of Morris's debut collection *The Defence of Guenevere, and Other Poems* (1858) and Swinburne's *Tristram of Lyonesse* (1882). Morris's collection would be more explicitly honoured in the pages of the *Quest*, with two illustrations respectively depicting scenes from Morris's 'Rapunzel' (by Meteyard) and from the title poem (by Arthur Gaskin) in No. 3 (July 1895), both furthermore obviously influenced by Kelmscott's house illustrator Edward Burne-Jones. The characterisation of the questing hero in the 'Sonnet' above all recalls the chaste Grail knight Galahad, who in the medieval romances alone can secure the divine blessings necessary to fulfil the will of God, and whose purity in the face of worldly temptation is the theme not only of Morris's poem 'Sir Galahad: A Christmas Mystery', but also of Tennyson's earlier 'Sir Galahad' (1842) that had been such a favourite with the group behind the *OCM* that they recited it at meetings.[43] The accompanying frontispiece illustration substantiates this visually by showing a yearning youth in armour reaching out to a fleeing woman who looks back at him with an equally longing glance. The angel represents the Guild's quest, traditionally symbolising the link between the earthly and the heavenly planes, or between imperfect reality and perfect ideal, and the relationship between the knight and his leman indicates a pure desire that validates every failed attempt at union. The 'quest' itself is more important than its completion.

In Arthurian lore, quests only come to a successful end – if they ever do – after a spiritual redemption through the perseverance of the knight to keep pure along the way, and this trait is shared by the myth, if not the reality, of the Aestheticist little magazine. By attempting to provide through the easily circulated periodical a utopian and largely untainted view of their envisaged ideal, the Birmingham Guild hoped to inspire change in the outside world. We might forgive them if along the way they also publicised services and wares offered by themselves and friends. Even the proudest paladins have overheads to cover.

Community, nature and art in the *Evergreen*

It is a somewhat vexed question whether the Arts and Crafts Movement ever established itself across Britain, or instead remained based in England while attracting some admittedly notable fellow travellers elsewhere. One the one hand, Irish and Scottish artists and activists in the 1880s and 1890s took part enthusiastically in an international debate on the relationship between art and social politics, their ideological positions were often informed by the same thinkers as those of English artworkers, and there was a definite solidarity between practitioners of different British nations. On the other hand, political activism and artistic output across Britain differs considerably, with discernible trends particular to each specific nation.

Obviously, this very difference in styles, political tactics and political emphases between English, Irish and Scottish initiatives can be argued to be true to an important principle of Arts and Crafts described above, namely the conscious rooting of the artistic project in the community from whence it sprung. In late-Victorian Ireland and Scotland, followed in the early twentieth century by Wales, Cornwall and the Isle of Man, a resurgent identity politics reinforced by Ruskinian nostalgic anti-capitalism came to fulfil in these Celtic territories much the same function as the Arts and Crafts Movement had done in England. This radical revaluation of non-English British culture came to be known as the 'Celtic Revival'. As Murray Pittock and Isla Jack explain, the early Celtic Revival in Ireland is likely better remembered because 'it alone was combined with an effective political nationalism, [. . .] but at the time its Scottish equivalent seemed almost as important, and it remains sadly neglected today'.[44] While the Irish branch, with the likes of Yeats and Lady Gregory, issued several important periodicals, the first little magazine of the Celtic Revival was arguably the Scottish *Evergreen* (1895–6), spearheaded by the indefatigable scholar and activist Patrick Geddes.

In 1887, the National Association for the Advancement of Art and its Application to Industry (NAAAI) was founded under the auspices of English Arts and Crafts leaders such as the then master of the Art Workers' Guild Walter Crane and the Century Guild's Arthur Mackmurdo, with the intention of improving the standards of design, and with them the position of skilled labourers, across the United Kingdom. While the majority of its founding members were based in London, it purposely held its three national conferences elsewhere. The choices of Liverpool (1888) and Birmingham (1890) were no doubt motivated by the fact that the elite of both cities not only had patronised new art since before the days of the Pre-Raphaelite Brotherhood, but also mostly had a commercial and manufacturing background themselves, and therefore were well placed to further the ideas of the Arts and Crafts Movement beyond their own small workshops. It is likely that the specific theme of the Birmingham conference, art education, was additionally inspired by the backing that the above-mentioned Birmingham School of Art had received from municipal authorities and by the public commissions that it had begun to secure. Unfortunately, the NAAAI disbanded in the early 1890s because its conferences failed to attract delegates outside an already convinced in-crowd and did not win over sufficiently high-ranking backers, but also, it would seem, because the three conferences had ironically brought out the disparity in artistic interests and political opinion among the delegates.[45] In 1889, an NAAAI delegation consisting among others of Crane, Morris and Emery Walker organised a meeting in Edinburgh. The Glaswegian economist and magazine editor James Mavor, one of the chairs, noted that his fellow Scottish delegates 'were critical rather than sympathetic'. This created tensions, and especially 'Morris was clearly not quite at home', getting involved in heated arguments with the unofficial leader of the Scottish artistic reformers, Patrick Geddes.[46]

During the 1880s, the Scots had already set up several groups of their own who, like the English guilds, were reviving traditional crafts, and Scottish public intellectuals had propagated a role for art in social reform. The so-called 'Glasgow Boys' (several of whom were actually 'Girls') associated with the Glasgow School of Art after its foundation in 1885 were instrumental in popularising French Symbolist and Art Nouveau styles in Britain, weaving these influences into Celtic knotwork patterns, and generally favouring Celtic mythical themes over the Gothic medieval inspirations of the Ruskinian/Pre-Raphaelite legacy that at the same time was captivating their English counterparts. In the same city, Mavor at the time edited the *Scottish Art Review* (1888–9); this was not a little magazine but an attempt at an artistic trade journal of wide appeal along the lines of the London-based *Magazine of Art* or *Art Journal*, which, however, did prominently feature local artists.[47] The Scottish capital had at that point no strictly artistic institutions that could vie with those of Glasgow, but it could pride itself on a more politicised artistic practice through the efforts of the Edinburgh Social Union (also founded in 1885), initially led by Geddes, which campaigned for sanitary improvements in the run-down Old Town and facilitated opportunities for local artists to decorate newly erected and renovated public buildings. Morris could have had no objections to the motivations behind the initiatives in either Scottish city, but he generally had little sympathy for the practical artistic output of the Scottish artists or their approach to political activities. Mavor suggests that while both

Morris and Geddes, arguably of equal status as theorists of the interactions of art and social politics, wanted 'to bring back the surroundings of the period before the factory system had divorced the fine arts from production', Geddes did not draw so much from medieval precedents as from 'the hard experience of direct social experiment'.[48]

Now most famous as a pioneer in sociology and urban planning, Geddes started his formal scientific education as a student of 'Darwin's Bulldog' T. H. Huxley. Studying evolutionary biology, he became fascinated by the Darwinian principle that animal and plant species evolve by adapting to their natural surroundings. Although he succeeded to the chair of Professor of Botany at the University of Dundee, he would soon transfer his evolutionary insights to the study of society, further inspired by related upcoming currents of thought such as social geography and the positivist determinism of the French thinker Auguste Comte. Geddes's sociological views can be summarised as the belief that communities historically develop identities from their collective engagement with their specific habitats. To improve their welfare, we therefore first need to look to the spatial organisation and the sanitary as well as aesthetic conditions of these habitats. For Geddes, this theory was not a purely academic concern, but the basis for the socio-political practice of an 'applied sociology' that he would later refer to by the name of 'Civics'. According to his biographer Helen Meller, Civics 'was to be a crusade with the humanitarian object of cultural evolution which would be produced by an interaction of environment, modern knowledge and the historically determined values of the people'.[49] There are distinct similarities between the organisations set up to this end by Geddes and the Arts and Crafts associations of England, the *Quest*'s Birmingham Guild of Handicraft being a good example. All of these professed equal disdain for mainstream, market-oriented art and literature as for the Decadent tendency in the contemporaneous avant-garde, and both placed artistic production at the service to the local communities of which they considered themselves part, and which they saw as the priority of their social mission and the first interpretative context for their output. However, as Mavor suggested, the strategy of seeking scholarly legitimacy sets Civics apart as a distinctly different tradition from the historical inspirations and grassroots-political backgrounds of the Arts and Crafts rationale of the *Quest* group. As Geddes would explain in his later study *Cities in Evolution* (1915), he viewed history as an ongoing process, and subscribed neither to the deliberate anachronism evinced by Arts and

Crafts, nor to the utilitarian ideology of maximising profit only with a view to the present:

> The study of human evolution is not merely a retrospect of origins in the past. That is but a paleontology [sic] of man – his Archaeology and History. It is not even the analysis of actual social processes in the present – that physiology of social man is, or should be, Economics. [. . .] For it is surely of the essence of the evolution concept [. . .] that it should not only inquire how this of to-day may have come out of that of yesterday, but be foreseeing and preparing for what the morrow is even now in its turn bringing towards birth.[50]

Geddes considered art primarily as a record of the affective response of artists to their environment that would always be rooted in cultural history, which, when combined with the scientific study of society that would deliver the hard facts, could counterbalance the tendency of detached scientists to abstraction, allowing us to learn how to function more happily as one of its components. From December 1894 to December 1896, Geddes and his associates defended these eclectic views through a remarkable little magazine entitled the *Evergreen*. In an article in this journal on the application of science to everyday life, Geddes explains that any assessment of life in its manifold aspects, scientific or otherwise, should above all contribute to a heightened awareness and appreciation of the living organism that is nature, and not solely assign an abstracted natural phenomenon to 'its index letter or reference mark in that great nature-catalogue, which so few consult at all', as do 'our specialist societies with their Proceedings and Transactions, their Microscopical Journals and the rest'.[51] The *Evergreen*, by contrast, was to prove the relevance of science, art and folklore to a comprehensive appreciation of life in all its aspects. For its integration of social politics, science and art into one overarching project, represented conceptually in the integrated ordering of its contents and the cohesion of its design aesthetic, the *Evergreen* may of all little magazines of the 1890s be the most invested in the Total Work of Art ideal. As the mission statement of the first number declares, the purpose of the magazine was 'to bring the most diverse interests under the dominance of a common civic ideal, in what to naturalists is known as a Symbiosis, in which the strength of one shall call forth, instead of cancelling the strength of the other'.[52]

The *Evergreen* was printed by Constable, stalwarts of the Edinburgh printing trade since the early nineteenth century, and a frequent partner of publishing houses with Fine Printing credentials, including the Bodley Head. A London edition was licensed to T. Fisher Unwin, and from the second number the transatlantic firm of J. B. Lippincott acted as publisher for America, both commercial trade publishers which, however, championed new authors and did not shy away from potentially contentious material. All issues of the *Evergreen* were part of the list of the modest publishing business Patrick Geddes and Colleagues. Their most acclaimed author was our old acquaintance William Sharp, albeit under his popular persona 'Fiona Macleod'. Sharp supported Geddes's mission to promote by way of literary publication the justified confidence of Scotland to reclaim its position as an equal among the other national cultures of Western Europe, and accepted the responsibility for the 'Celtic Library' series of new Celtic Revival literature, mainly by Scottish authors, but also containing less obvious titles such as the pan-Celtic 'anthology of representative Celtic Poetry' from the earliest records to the present entitled *Lyra Celtica* (1896), and the novel *The Fiddler of Carne* (1896) by Anglo-Welshman Ernest Rhys. Sharp also became the editor-in-chief for the *Evergreen*, despite the claim in the 'Envoy' closing the final issue that nobody had been officially assigned this post, likely to inflate the collectivist set-up of the journal.[53] Sharp could draw on previous experience for both tasks, as he was already in charge of the 'Canterbury Poets' series for the publisher Walter Scott and had of course published a little magazine before, the *Pagan Review* (see Chapter 3). At 5 shillings (or £1 for the full set), the *Evergreen* cost the same as the post-Century Guild *Hobby Horse* and notably the *Yellow Book*, with which its run overlapped. As we have discussed, with the *Yellow Book* this price was roughly the same as for the trade editions of the books issued by its publisher the Bodley Head, in order to claim for the periodical the prestige of that firm's book publications, for which the more widely circulated magazine in turn functioned as an indirect advertisement. The *Evergreen* too was published in book format, and it too was meant to be seen as representative of the list of its own publisher. Correspondence between Sharp and Geddes indicates that the former saw the *Evergreen* as a 'splendid adv[er]t' for the publishing firm, whereby he, as before with the *Pagan Review*, proves his willingness to consider the dissemination of avant-garde publications in commercial terms, and at least so far play by the rules of the literary marketplace.[54]

The contributors are said in the magazine to have been 'an open and growing group' with 'guests'.[55] A clue as to the background of this 'group' can be found in a rarely studied one-off publication that preceded the *Evergreen* proper. Before it would truly set off in the springtime of 1895, one small number appeared that in several respects falls outside the series. This *New Evergreen* (December 1894), subtitled *The Christmas book of University Hall*, features several of the regular contributors to the later *Evergreen* proper, and nearly all of these have connections to University Hall. This institution had been founded in 1887 at Ramsay Garden, a development started by Geddes in Edinburgh's Castlehill quarter, to enable students of Edinburgh University to 'enjoy social intercourse and free exchange of opinions combined with various other advantages not usually attainable in lodgings, the idea being to carry on an institution much on the lines of residence in English universities without the restrictions enforced there', as one resident put it.[56] As well as furthering the general purpose of Ramsay Garden to turn the tide in this dilapidated neighbourhood, which since the construction of the New Town in the late eighteenth century had lost its economic and cultural importance and in places had receded to little better than a slum, the Hall was intended to allow students to educate each other in the principles of Geddesian Civics, and to encourage and facilitate activism. *Evergreen* contributors such as John Arthur Thomson and Victor Branford were residents, and conveniently, the development also housed the Old Edinburgh School of Art set up by Geddes, where the *Evergreen*'s most prominent art contributor John Duncan taught courses on design, modelling and ornament, and coordinated public decoration schemes.[57] The *New Evergreen* and the *Evergreen* proper can therefore be seen as the house journals of Ramsay Garden, which becomes all the more clear when we take its namesake into account. As the second number of the *Evergreen* proper explains, '[i]n 1724 Allan Ramsay published his "Evergreen", desiring thereby to stimulate the return to local and national tradition and living nature'.[58] The reference is to this Scottish poet and editor's *The Ever Green: being a collection of Scots Poems, Wrote by the Ingenious before 1600*, an anthology that upon its original publication formed part of a cultural-political strategy to reinstate Scottish literary culture after Scotland lost its independence with the 1707 Act of Union, and, given its historical scope, even before the personal union of the Scottish and English kingdoms under their joint monarch James VI and I, and that therefore can be seen as a precursor to the 'Scottish Renascence' that this Fin-de-Siècle magazine wanted to instigate. As Elizabeth Elliot has argued, the reference to this historical precursor is significant, as Ramsay too had presented the Scottish literary culture collected in his anthology as rooted in its national setting and in an 'ever-green' state of development.[59]

Unlike the *Evergreen* proper, the *New Evergreen* (December 1894) presented itself as a student publication, a likely inspiration for which could be sought in Lord Alfred Douglas's irreverent Oxford journal the *Spirit-Lamp* (1892–3), this too having been a student periodical intended for a discriminating elite. The *New Evergreen* also appears in the same month as Douglas's notorious second periodical, the single-issue *Chameleon* (1894), which like the final issues of the *Spirit-Lamp* before it featured several explicitly 'Uranian' (i.e. male-homosexual) contributions, including by Wilde and Douglas himself, that only a few months later would be used as particularly damning evidence against them during the Wilde trial. While never seeking out controversy like these two Oxonian student magazines, the contributors to the *New Evergreen* do wear their allegiance to Aestheticism and to topical controversies on their sleeves as well. The concluding contribution is a set of epigrams by Branford that seems to have been intended as a crude first manifesto for the student associates of the Ramsay Garden initiative. This 'A Series of Remarks' is on the surface reminiscent of the provocative preface that had opened the 1891 version of Wilde's *Dorian Gray*, but Branford immediately makes it clear that no celebration of Art for Art's Sake is to be expected, for 'the separation of Arts and Crafts is the root of all evil', and 'the Aesthetic is the best Anaesthetic'. Another 'Remark' states that 'When the New Woman has cast forth the Old Adam, the Utopia may be found out', showing again that the magazine was explicit in its endorsement of causes.[60] The *New Evergreen* acquires a character all of its own through its repeated references to the scientific backgrounds of the writers. The most curious contribution in this issue, and this too a crude version of things to come, is a bizarre causerie by Thomson on the lifecycle of salmon, as much a parable extoling the wonders of a prevalent organic order as an article of scientific interest. Though generally written in a style accessible to the lay reader, this item occasionally trails off into scholarly jargon, and even contains a physics equation to explain the physiology of the fish. Visually and materially, this extraneous issue is nothing out of the ordinary. Unlike the later volumes, it has plain paper boards, and despite some roughly drawn ornaments in the Glaswegian Art Nouveau style, there is not much to announce the design aesthetic that would make the coming numbers of the *Evergreen* proper stand out.

The difference from the first issue in the actual series, published in March 1895, could not be greater. The *Quest* and the *Evergreen* could both have contested the title for the little magazine of the 1890s least willing to compromise with the profit-focused publishing of the mainstream market, but whereas the *Quest*'s conspicuous inefficiency mainly lies in its production methods, the *Evergreen* is characterised by its incautious material opulence. Its luxurious features raised the production expenses of the *Evergreen* to such a level that the magazine's small run, and the unwillingness of Geddes and his associates to include advertisements and charge more than 5 shillings per issue, never allowed the *Evergreen* to cover its own expenses; small wonder that the magazine never made it past its fourth number and that the ambition to pay its contributors had to be abandoned after the first.[61] Its boards are covered in morocco leather, containing green notes that conceptually refer to its title in the same way that the *Yellow Book* was yellow, and there are new embossed ornaments for each number. For Nos. 2–4, the title pages include ornaments in red ink. The recent success of the *Yellow Book* in securing a wider readership than any other little magazine, and in the branding of its publisher Lane as a supplier of cutting-edge publications, must have been an incentive. Of course, the *Yellow Book* had been a more commercially planned publication, and while it contained innovative art and literature, it did not have the same high intellectuall level, nor the conspicuous local element of the *Evergreen* to hold it back commercially. However, unlike the *Yellow Book*'s, the *Evergreen*'s design not only serves to catch the reader's eye, but also to demonstrate the potential of craftsmanship for the book arts. All four issues also contain a large number of detailed head- and tailpieces, and just like the magazine informs us that the different covers were designed by Charles Mackie, these are always attributed to the artist in the table of contents, true to what by now had become an unwritten law of Aestheticism. Many of these involve abstract knotwork designs and decorated initials that often include miniatures referring to a topic or theme of the decorated text. For instance, the Celtic hounds known from Old Gaelic sacred manuscripts feature in the headpiece to a story by William Sharp under the guise of 'Fiona Macleod' about the early-medieval Saint Bridget, whose legend would originally have been passed down through such manuscripts (Figure 31). As Lorraine Janzen Kooistra finds,

> [m]aterially, the textual ornaments effect a visual coherence, weaving the title's various items together into an expressive community. More abstractly, the decorations model a way of reimagining and regenerating the built environment of cities, books, and social relations by remediating historical design with the tools and knowledge of the present.[62]

This metaphorical potential of the title *Evergreen* is repeatedly explored along such lines in the contents as well. In the 'Proem' to the first issue that serves as a preface for the whole series, William Macdonald and J. A. Thomson refer to the rhythmic constancy of nature, that is presented as an analogue for the role of our cultural-evolutionary background in our individual and collective lives. 'The old memories and the old ménage of the race' ought to be kept alive, 'unless ourselves be lost altogether', because the 'desire of them is an organic inheritance of the heart'.[63] This inheritance is as such allied with natural cycles, and in this springtime of the budding Celtic Revival, 'it now shares in the fullness of sap that is given to all things living'.[64] This enduring background is the common evolutionary basis from which a particular society sprang that will continue giving its existence meaning and substance: 'Truth and evergreens alone are perpetual.'[65] Another essay by Thomson on the theme of cyclical regeneration in myth and folktale ends with a call to 'light the Beltane fire, and keep the Floralia [. . .] for while Biology is well, to enjoy the Spring is better'.[66] Our ancestors would have made sense of the world by adapting their activities to the passing seasons, and we would be happier if we still did so today, and if we realised that both our own individual lives and the histories of the society to which we belong may be divided into such phases as well. Each number also has a frontispiece, referred to as an 'Almanac', that incorporates zodiac signs and other images referring to the season in question. Throughout its run, the magazine adopted the yearly cycle as a motif to organise its contents consistently throughout the series. The *Evergreen*'s subtitle is in fact *A Northern Seasonal*. An epigraph opening the first issue and thereby the series quotes John Keats's sonnet 'The Human Seasons', containing the lines '[f]our seasons fill the measure of the year, / there are four seasons in the mind of man'. The *Evergreen*'s seasonality is conceptual and does not refer to a quarterly frequency; it does not complete its first and only cycle until after its second year, and due to constant delays in production the magazine failed to establish a consistent publication rate.[67] Its four issues are referred to consecutively as 'The Book of Spring' (March 1895), '. . . Autumn' (September 1895), '. . . Summer' (May 1896) and '. . . Winter' (November 1896), and when Geddes in the 'Book of Summer' anticipates an article in a coming issue, he does not speak of 'another issue' or 'number', or any other current term, but of 'another season', once again emphasising the centrality of the concept.[68]

In a second instance of conceptual organisation, the contents of the *Evergreen* are divided into four recurring categories, which in every issue are consistently categorised in four corresponding sections: 'I. [Autumn] in Nature', 'II. . . . in Life', 'III. . . . in the World' and 'IV. . . . in the North'. All four categories contain literary contributions, consisting of poems and short stories, as well as essays that popularise scientific subjects, the latter often with an abstract in the headnote, and ornaments and illustrations. The order of the recurrent sections is not arbitrary, but obviously intended to descend level by level from the most abstract forces that shape natural life and cultural history at large, to the concrete location where the *Evergreen* was based. The magazine waits until the final issue to explain that

> [t]o see the world, to see life truly, one must see these as a whole [. . .] Our arts and sciences are but so many specialised and technical ways of showing the many scenes and aspects of this great unity, this mighty drama of cosmic and human evolution.[69]

The contents of the magazine are organised so as to reflect this systematic harmony, with all the contributions that form its content meant to add together to one unified representation of this 'whole'.

'I. Nature' contains all treatments of the seasons as a fact of biology, though literary and artistic treatments of the experience of nature are as much at home here as scientific exposition. While articles can be found in this section that have titles such as 'Biology of Autumn' (No. 2) and 'Biology of Winter' (No. 4), both by Thomson, there is also poetry descriptive of the seasons in weather and wildlife. Nature and its human subjects are often linked through analogy: '[t]he life of plants and animals – and of man himself – is rhythmic. Rest alternates with work, repair with waste, and periods of hunger and self-increase are followed by periods of love and species-continuing.'[70] This statement is not merely descriptive, it sets out an ideological programme too. As the relationship between man and nature is stated as an objective scientific fact, the implication is that this inescapable organic bond is to be embraced before we can develop healthful societies and live fulfilling lives. To this end, impressionistic poetry such as that of that 'Fiona Macleod', celebrating the moment of daybreak when '[f]rom grey and dusk, the veils unfold, / to pearl and amethyst and gold', is also included here, serving the same purpose as the biological studies.[71] In this section, we also find the most often reproduced illustration from the magazine, the Art Nouveau artist (obviously not to be confused with the eighteenth-century poet) Robert Burns's 'Natura Naturans' (Figure 32). A naked mythical Mother Nature is depicted in the act of 'naturing', surrounded by a swirling wave pattern teeming with fish and birds, symbolising the continuous flow of life governed by nature. This image additionally offers a perfect visualisation of the *Evergreen*'s idea of cultural history as an ongoing movement in which enduring ancient values are renewed throughout the ages, notably in the case of Scotland engaging with the cultures of other nations in a relationship of parity. As in the style popularised by the Glasgow School, motifs borrowed from ancient Celtic manuscripts and from architectural features are combined with the long swirling lines of Continental Art Nouveau, and citations from then fashionable Japanese print artists such as Hiroshige and Hokusai (see Chapter 3). Placed between two essays to which it could equally pertain, it is not so much an illustration of a specific textual contribution as directly illustrative of the general principle of the series itself. In the table of contents, the magazine consistently refers to its pictorial items as 'Decorations', instead of the more intuitive 'illustrations' which could suggest a hierarchy in which the pictorial artist is subordinated to the author. The term furthermore has the faux-naïve connotations of craftsmanship, which is one element that the *Evergreen* clearly borrows from the English Arts and Crafts Movement, and it shows that the magazine participated in the campaign to emancipate the book and periodical artist that can be attested to in nearly all the little magazines of the 1890s.

The next section, 'II. Life', pertains to how mankind deals with the season presently under scrutiny. There are articles based on anthropological and sociological scholarship such as Geddes's 'Sociology of Autumn' (No. 2), but here too we find pieces that seem to focus on broadly affective responses to the seasons that are not particular to specific cultures. Irish Celtic Revivalist Katherine Tynan, for instance, contributes the short story 'The Mother of Jesus' (No. 4), dealing with a young woman who loses her child to illness, but who learns how to face this bereavement with equanimity because of her faith in Providence, getting through this trying 'winter' because she knows that her family is part of an all-encompassing order that eventually will bring about the 'spring' of an ultimate good. Despite this and other Christian statements that are inevitable in a periodical on these Celtic territories, where religion had always played such a large role in folk culture, the *Evergreen* recurrently shows an interest in paganism. This of course fits the magazine's nature worship as well as its cultural-evolutionary ideology, where the atavistic resurgence of types is a common interest. In the same number, Nimmo Christie assumes the persona of a pre-Christian Celt to declare that it is 'better to die than to yield / to a Child-king of peace'.[72] Like much of nineteenth-century cultural nationalism, the *Evergreen* values what

Raymond Williams would later refer to as 'residual culture' in order to inspire an empowering counter-tradition to the nineteenth-century British perspectives on Scottish national history. By claiming that the Christian and even the pre-Christian past have left residues in attitudes and institutions that are key to understanding the dispositions of the people, the magazine suggests a 'predisposed continuity' for the reforms it proposes for the present and future.[73]

Section 'III. World' deals with sociology, folklore, literature and historical topics either from outside of Scotland, or related to direct links between Scotland and other nations. This section contains most of the French items that appear with notable regularity throughout the magazine. Including contributions in a foreign language was meant to indicate that the Ramsay Garden group, next to their efforts for a stronger Scottish identity, 'would also share in that wider culture-movement which knows neither nationality nor race',[74] although their neighbourliness does not seem to extend beyond the Celtic nations and French-speaking Europe. According to Siân Reynolds, to Geddes 'France *was* Europe'.[75] The *Evergreen* would also publish an etching by the Nabis artist Paul Sérusier in its opening number, probably procured through his friend Charles Mackie, a bridge-builder between the artists of Scotland and France.[76] We are told that 'Magna Scotia' had maintained strong ties with the Continent since the Middle Ages, and that the 'Ancient League with France' could safeguard a revived Scotland against becoming mired in provincialism.[77] Not coincidentally, the only title published by the firm of Patrick Geddes and Colleagues that is not Celtic themed or related to the Ramsay Garden initiative was an account of *The Dreyfus Case* (1898) by the French Anarchist Paul Reclus (under the pseudonym 'George Guyou'), whose brother Élisée was an *Evergreen* contributor. More nostalgically, this Auld Alliance is honoured by means of a depiction by John Duncan of Jeanne d'Arc and her Scottish guard (No. 3) to commemorate the recent foundation of the Franco-Scottish Society, yet another initiative coordinated from Ramsay Garden, which in fact is still active across Scotland today. We also find here translations and adaptations from the Breton by Edith Wingate Rinder (Nos. 1, 2 and 4), and a few contributions either Irish (as by Gaelic language activists Douglas Hyde and Standish O'Grady in No. 4) or pan-Celtic in theme. There is criticism of contemporary French literature (in French) by the Abbé Félix Klein, a follower of the Catholic sociologist Frédéric Le Play whose thought bore similarities to that of Geddes, and Edinburgh University French professor Charles

Saroléa. Sharp too had many contacts in Paris and was interested in French-language Flemish literature, supplying his translation of a play by Charles Van Lerberghe (although this appears in section 'II. Autumn in Life' of No. 2). He considered Flemish literature in French a possible inspiration – or perhaps rather a justification – for Scottish writers writing in English rather than in Scottish Gaelic, which due to the particular history of the Scottish people was less prominent than the Celtic languages in other national movements within the Celtic Revival. The Flemish cultural background of such writers would be apparent in the spirit of their work even though they were expressing themselves in French instead of Dutch, the language of their forebears.[78]

Only in the final section, 'IV. North', does the *Evergreen* specifically address its local aspirations, mainly in the form of tales, poems and plates by Scottish authors and artists. The fact that they would opt for the term 'North' is remarkable, given the use of the adjectives 'Scottish' or 'Scots' throughout the run of the magazine, and because the appellation 'North Britain' for Scotland has eighteenth-century unionist origins that their hero Ramsay may not have appreciated. In the context of larger Britain, there have of course been instances of a 'Northern' solidarity against the more privileged 'South' that on occasion leaps Hadrian's Wall. In those cases, Scotland and the North of England find a common foe in the perceived centralisation of investment in Southern England and of political power in London. The editorial opening the first number declares that we must change into 'Cities Beautiful'

> the granite city of the north, cold and clear, defined into dignity, softened into music. Upon them all is the flying shadow of a regret, the breaking light of a promise. We see them with Durham, York and Liverpool, Manchester, Bristol, Dundee and Perth all with a struggling sublimity, all dishevelled and disgraced, all alive and full of hope![79]

Elizabeth Sharp, who besides being wife to the *Evergreen* editor was also a contributor and author for Patrick Geddes and Colleagues herself, wrote of Geddes that it was his mission to 'arrest the tremendous centralising power of the metropolis of London'.[80] The magazine's understanding of 'the North', of which Bristol is not usually considered part anyway, may perhaps be 'not-London'. This would link the *Evergreen* to the mission of the by then already defunct NAAAI, which had tried to give a voice to craftsmen and social thinkers in centres of industry and artistic innovation throughout the United Kingdom.

Nevertheless, although the critical consensus has it that few contributors delivered their best work, this final section is a valuable resource on the often overlooked specifically Scottish literary contributions to the Celtic Revival. The *Evergreen* offers a representative survey of Scottish literature at the end of the Victorian era, ranging from the Gaelic-inflected Symbolist haze of 'Fiona Macleod' to the mild realist fiction of authors such as 'Gabriel Setoun' (pseudonym of Thomas Nicoll Hepburn). At the time of publication of the *Evergreen*, the latter strand of writing was coming under attack as 'the Kailyard School', considered by some critics to present a sentimentalised image of Scottish society.[81] Geddes in his causerie on 'The Scots Renascence' (No. 1) hoped to add with the new magazine

> a fresh page to the wide reviving Literature of Locality to which the kindly firesides of Thrums and Zummerzet, the wilder dreamlands of Galway and Cader Idris, of Man and Arran and Galloway are ever adding their individual tinge and glow.[82]

The mention of the fictional village of Thrums can only be a reference to the setting of J. M. Barrie's highly successful book series consisting of the *Auld Licht Idylls* (1888), *A Window in Thrums* (1889) and *The Little Minister* (1891), which had been damned by faint praise during the Kailyard debate as the best work of its supposedly insipid kind. Geddes uses the phrase 'Literature of Locality' a second time in the same piece, stating that this proposed subgenre,

> we are told by many reviewers, has had its little day, and is subsiding into mere clash o' kirkside, mere havers o' kailyard; so doubtless the renewal of locality may polarise into slum and respectability once more. Be it so; this season will have its term.[83]

This coexistence of avant-garde and unabashedly popular literary styles in the *Evergreen* is striking, and the rejection of cultural elitism in Geddes's description of the aims for the Scottish branch of the Celtic Revival is one of several features that complicates the relationship of the *Evergreen* to the rest of the British avant-garde of the 1890s.

As said, the *Evergreen*'s run overlapped with that of the *Yellow Book*, and also with that of the *Savoy*, so the controversy surrounding these little magazines is part of its publication context. The press coverage of the *Yellow Book* temporarily presented a frame for the reception of all literary production that critics saw as sharing its themes and styles, but also design and material presentation, and critics often compared the *Evergreen* and its contributors with the firebrands at the Bodley Head. As Sharp had actually anticipated, this comparison was generally unfavourable to the *Evergreen* as far as their respective artistic and literary merits were concerned.[84] Several reviewers associated the *Evergreen* with the *Yellow Book* because of the similarity of some of the illustrations, spotting the Art Nouveau influence in the drawings of Beardsley and in those of the Glasgow School-inspired *Evergreen* artists alike, but primarily because both periodicals were designed to look like books. This sheds further light on the *Savoy*'s decision against the book format that was seen as its older rival's trademark (see Chapter 4). *Evergreen* regulars 'Fiona Macleod' and Parisian-American illustrator Andrew K. Womrath would also contribute to the *Savoy*, but besides this, there are few overlaps in contributors. When critics addressed the differences between these journals, they often noticed their diverse cultural backgrounds. For instance, the topic of this chapter was anticipated by the anonymous critic of the minor newspaper *London*: 'London has its *Yellow Book*, Birmingham has its *Quest*, and now comes Edinburgh with its *Evergreen* [. . .] The *Evergreen* differs very materially from the other two publications, which it somewhat resembles in style.'[85] Critic and novelist Israel Zangwill too stated that until he had visited Edinburgh, he

> did not know what 'The Evergreen' was. Newspaper criticism had given me vague misrepresentations of a Scottish 'Yellow Book' calling itself a 'Northern Seasonal'. But even had I seen a copy myself I doubt if I should have understood it without going to Edinburgh [. . .] 'The Evergreen' was not established as an antidote to the 'Yellow Book' though it might well be seen as a counter-symbol – the green of spring set against the yellow of decadent leaves.[86]

An anonymous but enthusiastic reviewer for the *Sunday Times* did go as far as styling the *Evergreen* 'the anti-decadent *Yellow Book*', rejoicing that it was calculated to 'combat avowedly and persistently the decadent spirit which we have felt to be over aggressive of late'.[87] However, as Michael Shaw has demonstrated, several items suggest that for Geddes, 'aestheticism and decadence could be key cultural *phases* in a process towards rejecting this [. . .] economy [of Victorian industrialism] and embracing synthesis and "Renascence"'.[88] It is, again, a 'season' in the cultural-historical cycle of Scotland that eventually will pass, to be followed by the rejuvenation of a new spring: '[t]hanks then, and even honour, to the art and science of the Decadence, since from it we have learned to see the thing as it is'.[89] Moralism in the High Victorian vein would be a contradiction in this publication, which with its pagan sincerity aims to refute petty dualism and assess humankind's place in the world frankly, but its studied philosophical indifference to philistine outrage should not be mistaken for approval of Decadent attitudes either. In the 'Proem' to the first issue, the group's belief in an eminent springtime of cultural rebirth is placed in context with the current debates on the supposed degeneracy of Western civilisation:

> At first we would say that we do not ignore the Decadence around us, so much spoken of. If we wished, we could not. For while at one social level, all the land over, it fills the gaze with a vision of slums and the hearing with outcries of coarseness and cretinous insanity – at another it is trumpeted as a boast and worn as a badge and studied as the ultimate syllable of this world's wisdom. So many writers emulously working in a rotten vineyard, so many healthy young men eager for the distinction of decay![90]

Macdonald and Thomson consider Decadence from a sociological rather than a moralistic point of view, attributing the phenomenon to a broader social illness. All classes and vocations are faced with unsuitable living and working environments, and warped social relations, that disrupt their worldview: '[a] literature of distinguished style and moral vulgarity is indeed a misproduct of the same process that gives us in our meaner streets a degeneration of human type worse than what follows famine'.[91] Neither the destitute working classes nor the misguided upper-class harbingers of culture are to blame for the current situation, because both suffer from the repercussions of the utilitarianism of Victorian Britain. Its approach to labour, namely industrialisation, condemned the worker to mind-numbing wage slavery, and the leisurely classes to a debilitating idleness.

Appropriately in the second number dedicated to autumn, Félix Klein addresses the topic of 'Le Dilèttantisme' in French literature, identified with one of the often perceived tenets of literary Decadence: an overwrought literary style that in its self-centredness would reflect an egotistical shirking of the responsibility on the author's part to make a constructive contribution to the development of society. The critic does not explicitly call out any authors who were commonly perceived to be 'Décadents', arguably with the exception of Maurice Barrès, but focuses on anti-religious authors like Anatole France and Jules Lemaître, who not only display an unhealthy fixation on style, but also treat the human condition all too pessimistically. If that is all they have to say, keeping silent would have been preferable to 'applying oneself, as they do, to ruin the little conscientiousness that the rich have kept, and the little hope that comforts the poor'.[92] A similar point is made by Saroléa in the first number, who is equally unhappy about the current state of literature in France. He judges that French literature in the Fin de Siècle demonstrates an obscurantist reaction against the 'bankruptcy of pseudo-scientific philosophy' (often mistaken for true science) and a subsequent 'bankruptcy of Naturalism' in the arts.[93] Earlier Naturalist literature would have subscribed to a coercive determinism instead of addressing the opportunities that our sociocultural backgrounds can provide to get out of the current crisis. The recent generation of Decadent Symbolists, with their deliberate opacity and escapism, simply reacted against this, and might be corrected if directed to a way out of this impasse. This interesting perspective is echoed by Geddes and Thomson in the next number, when they state that the misguided 'decadent novelists [are] bemired halfway between old ideals and new'.[94]

Meller states that Geddes's default position in moral issues was 'at once radical and conservative', a case in point being his opinion on the Women Question, another then hotly debated issue.[95] In their collaborative work *The Evolution of Sex* (1889), he and Thomson made a case for a better understanding between the sexes, though with a singular qualification. They concluded from relating human biology to social history that '[w]omen were the nurturers, the conservers of tradition and moral values, their biological roles as wives and mothers keeping them untainted by the artificial machinations of the world'.[96] Although cast in scientific terminology, this statement follows Victorian orthodoxy in welding together biological sex and social gender. The authors find a basis for their argument in Geddes's previous work on biological cell theory, where he explains the developments of cells as resulting from the interaction of anabolic/constructive 'female' and katabolic/destructive 'male' processes. To the detriment of Geddes's posthumous reputation, their pithy remark on the call for women's suffrage is often quoted: 'what was decided among prehistoric protozoa cannot be annulled by acts of parliament'.[97] While this reference to the most fundamental issues of biology in cultural matters might seem disconcerting to us, as Regenia Gagnier has noted, in the second half of the nineteenth century many scholars believed that 'the interface between nature and culture goes all the way down to the development of the gene itself and that only human and natural science together can answer the most pressing problems of our day'.[98] A similar attitude is found in the *Evergreen*, which despite its spirited critiques of other forms of perceived social injustice, does not contain any hints at the proto-feminism that an attentive reader can find in some items in the *Yellow Book* and the *Savoy*. Its social mission too, however strong, had always been distinguished from that of the 'desperadoes of chimerical reform' which they appear to have seen in contemporary socialist movements, and they are equally prudent in their gender politics.[99] The *Evergreen*'s hints at a need for women's emancipation are restricted to an improvement of the prestige of roles already accessible to women, and do not extend to access to a wider range of vocational roles or to political equality, as was demanded by the New Women and the women's suffrage movement.

The point of *The Evolution of Sex* is taken up again, though with less recourse to science, in the third number of the *Evergreen*, in the article 'The Moral Evolution of Sex', significantly attributed to 'the authors of *The Evolution of Sex*'. For a periodical that otherwise stresses that the laws of cultural evolution are not a straitjacket but rather a guiding line that leaves much freedom to its subjects, the order of society is presented here as quite restrictive. Maternity and the corresponding duty to raise children would for women be the highest attainable bliss and responsibility, near-synonyms in such a thoroughly organicist ideology as the *Evergreen*'s . However, this article does not prescribe such a domestic role as strongly as the book on which it elaborates, and it takes into consideration the fact that many women were forced to find additional employment outside their homes, and furthermore found therein a source of personal fulfilment as well as (additional) income. The authors do not wish to see the entire sex limited to either caring housewife or worldly-wise New Woman, and are convinced that both types have been part of the female psyche since the dawn of humanity, and would need to be acknowledged by society in order for women not to become either frustrated or cynical. A needed 'remoralisation of the sexes' would come about through changes in education. Surprisingly, it is suggested that girls and boys should have the same schooling, or at least 'mutual education'. Ideally, men and women should hold to the same basic, reciprocally corrective virtues of 'Courage' and 'Kindness', and adapt them to their respective desired moral profiles of 'Chivalry' and 'Purity', sharing steadfastness in their own social roles and complementary attitudes that (again) help them to shape a harmonious society together.[100] The *New Evergreen*'s aforementioned maxim that called for the 'New Woman [to] cast forth the Old Adam', should be likely interpreted in this light as well. 'Just as civilization grows richer and softer, there is increasing need of a hardy upbringing for girl as well as boy.'[101] Education should be integrated into a grander scheme or 'practical life-drama', with the teaching of natural sciences taking place in nature, while history and culture should be introduced as a communal narrative in which all may find their place. Typical of the *Evergreen*, this educational programme always refers back to the integrated view of society which the structure and design of the magazine perpetuates conceptually.

The *Evergreen*'s prominent utopian outlook greatly annoyed H. G. Wells, who reviewed the first number of the *Evergreen* for the enduringly prestigious scientific journal *Nature* (1869–) in August 1895, under the telling title 'Bio-Optimism'. A certain sympathy could have been expected, as the Fabian socialist Wells had explored the interstices of science and literature in his novels, and his later contribution to the *Yellow Book* implies that he did not object too strongly to the rhetoric and prose styles particular to the little magazines of the 1890s. Wells had authored an essay on 'Zoological Retrogression' as early as 1891, to inform the lay reader of there having been 'almost always associated with the suggestion of advance in biological phenomena an opposite idea', that, if duly acknowledged, would counterbalance 'the monotonous reiteration of "Excelsior" [. . .]; the too sweet harmony of the spheres would be enhanced by a discord, this evolutionary antithesis-degradation'.[102] This too had been a scientific, early intervention in the debates on decadence and social degeneration, but from a different and less optimistic perspective than the *Evergreen*'s. In his review, Wells finds that the literary content consists of 'amateurish short stories about spring' and '"descriptive articles" of the High School Essay type', and disparages the illustrations with the verdict that 'his training should render the genuine biologist more acutely sensitive to these ugly and unmeaning distortions than the average educated man'.[103] Wells expected that the *Evergreen* was the work of scientists dabbling in the arts and artists in science, and presenting here their first dilettante trials. His main complaint about the publication does, however, seem to stem from a disagreement with its central message, taking issue with the way Geddes, Macdonald and Thomson – at whom he primarily directs his attack because as reputable men of science they should know better – appropriate the theory of evolution for their aesthetic-ideological project. Even though Geddes and his followers believed that the community is defined by its cultural history and interaction with its environment, and that these lay out a course of development which will allow it to continue evolving in the future, they denied that the outcome would be, in the often misused phrase of Herbert Spencer, only the survival of the fittest. No doubt wishing to avoid their message being misconstrued as an advocacy of social Darwinism, they claim that 'the conception of the Struggle for Existence as Nature's sole method of progress [. . .] was to be sure a libel upon nature', as Wells paraphrased the argument of the 'Proem' in the second issue.[104] Their social project relies on the belief that we have to cooperate within our respective communities in order to fulfil the evolution of these collective entities and subsequently ourselves as members thereof, and one of the metaphorical links they find to the natural world is 'the dominance of one civic ideal, which to naturalists would be known as a Symbiosis'.[105] A symbiosis being a cooperative relationship of two separate organisms for the greater good of both, Wells replies that '[t]here is nothing in Symbiosis or any other group of phenomena to warrant the statement that the representation of all life as a Struggle for Existence is a libel on Nature'.[106] He sees such forms of cooperation as a regrouping of self-centred entities rather than a genuine regard for each other's well-being, the belief in which would be a projection of human sentiments onto animal and vegetable life. By first reproaching the rapprochement of artists and scientists, and later by refuting the magazine's ideology of an all-pervading natural order beneficial to all that works as both a metaphor for cultural production and a principle for social organisation, Wells in fact rejects the central concept behind the *Evergreen* that made it perhaps the most integrated periodical Total Work of Art of the British Fin de Siècle.

Overall, the *Evergreen*, unlike other ventures by its producers and contributors, made only a small impression on both the artistic avant-garde of the day and the scientific world, and did not succeed at bringing these closer together. The magazine folded after its fourth number, but partnerships had been strengthened that would last a lifetime and that would exert a far greater influence on the history of Scotland, Britain and, through Geddes's innovations in urbanism, the entire world. The *Evergreen* itself, still optimistic, expressed its hopes as follows:

> There are certain elemental forms of life, whose way it is after some solitary wandering silently to flow together, uniting their microscopic forces into a vague semi-fluent mass. This at first shows only that apparent

> quiescence which in life is needed for internal rearrangement, or at most some of those external symptoms which express any internal clearing up, though they may superficially suggest the opposite. By and by these associating lives awaken to a world without; they arouse to new activities, they rise into new forms, protean yet individual. These die in their turn – that is, float into new young life; much it may be, to perish, but enough at least to germinate anew elsewhere.[107]

'Germinate anew' the *Evergreen* did, over a century later, and, rather than 'elsewhere', in the same soil from whence it had sprung, first in Allan Ramsay's day and then again in the 1890s. The *Evergreen: A New Season in the North* has been appearing annually since 2014 and is due to reach its conclusion in 2018, like its historical model, with its fourth number. The new publication is associated with the Edinburgh Old Town Development Trust, an organisation that has similar goals as the society at Ramsay Garden, which it explains with regular implicit and explicit references to Geddesian civics: 'as Scotland debates what kind of country it wants to be, the *Evergreen* prompts a shifting of the question to our neighbourhoods: what kind of places do we want to live in? And what are we prepared to do about it?'[108] Wisely avoiding the trappings of historical affectation by swapping the Art Nouveau style of the former germination for a fresh minimalist design, the green cloth covers of the magazine and its recurrent ornamental motifs still hint at the integrated design concept of the 1890s. Whereas the contents of the *Evergreen* proper were tied together by Celtic knotwork, the *New Season* features one rudimentary motif that is used both on the cover design and as an ornamental device on the title pages preceding every single content item (Figure 33).

This design too emphasises the coherence of the publication's discourse, but in contrast to the 1890s *Evergreen*, each separate item is literally allowed more of its own space, and therefore appears to be less constrained by its surroundings than the content items of the *Evergreen* proper. The contributions are as thematically diverse as they were before, but are also no longer organised in rigidly upheld categories, the table of contents listing everything in one continuous list. The *Evergreen* proper, as we have seen, welcomed contributions from outside of Scotland, and it never spoke disparagingly of people of other nations. Nevertheless, in the older magazine, national identity tends to be reduced to innate ethnicity, and the metaphorical rootedness that is fundamental to organicist ideologies does not combine well with recent realities of human migration. The *New Season* exchanges this implied nativism for a sense of place. For instance, in the 2014 number, Sudanese-born author Leila Aboulale addresses her experiences in Aberdeen, and in 2015 Brian McLaughlin relates his experiences of having lived in Barcelona for thirty years to living in Edinburgh. The conceptual as well as ideological distinctions between the two germinations are informed by lessons learned in the intervening twentieth century. Geddes, Sharp and their associates cannot be blamed for the crimes of later political movements, but their exceptionally thorough adherence to the Total Work of Art ideal, at the service of its socio-political creed, is now viewed with suspicion as a potential sign of class or ethnic determinism, and suppression of the individual.[109] In their own time, these associations did not exist, and therefore cannot be held against these ambitious artists and thinkers.

The *Evergreen* and the *Quest* both managed to demonstrate that avant-garde art and literature, combined with new strategies for social activism, were to be found outside of London as well. While they both had little in common with the Decadence supposedly found in the leading London little magazine, and even to some extent combated it, they were doomed to go down along with it. By 1896, the Aestheticist little magazine had peaked, and its history – like this book – reached its final chapter.

Notes

1. Wolfreys, *Writing London*, p. 102.
2. Freeman, *Conceiving the City*, p. 3.
3. Boyiopoulos, *Decadent Image*, p. 84.
4. Symons, 'Vale of Llangollen', p. 29.
5. Yeats, 'Lake Isle of Innisfree', p. 121.
6. Yeats, 'Trembling of the Veil', p. 193.
7. James, 'London', p. 30.
8. Wolfreys, *Writing London*, p. 98.
9. Mallett, 'City and the Self', p. 46.
10. Morris, *Address*, p. 3.
11. Ibid., p. 3.
12. Morris, 'Revival of Handicraft', pp. 605–6.
13. Jones, *Industrial Enlightenment*, pp. 48–60.
14. Briggs, *Victorian Cities*, p. 187.
15. Quoted in Coleman, *Idea of the City*, p. 159.
16. Morris, *Address*, p. 24.
17. Crawford, 'Birmingham Setting', pp. 30–2.
18. Maltz, *British Aestheticism and the Urban Working Classes*, p. 207.

19. Fletcher, 'Some Aspects of Aestheticism', p. 24.
20. Dixon, 'Manufacture and Handicraft', p. 26.
21. Ibid., pp. 26–7.
22. Miller, *Slow Print*, pp. 36–40.
23. Waters, 'Book Illustration', p. 85.
24. Mackail, *Life of William Morris*, p. 84.
25. No records have been retrieved to establish the name behind the initial. None of Napier-Clavering's parents, siblings, or parent's siblings appear to have had a first name starting with 'G'.
26. 'Messrs. G. Napier and Company', n.p.
27. 'The Birmingham Guild of Handicraft', p. iii.
28. Maidment, 'Influence, Presence, Appropriation', pp. 77–8.
29. Napier-Clavering, 'Fine Feathers and Fine Birds', p. 49.
30. Ibid., p. 50.
31. 'Some Illustrated Books', p. 43.
32. Ibid., p. 51.
33. Adamson, *Embattled Avant-Gardes*, p. 51.
34. Image, 'Three Notes on Art: III', pp. 17–18.
35. Sonnenschein, 'Platonic Theory of Art', p. 28.
36. Ibid., p. 28.
37. Ibid., p. 26, quoting from Ruskin's essay 'The Definition of Greatness in Art', included in *Modern Painters*, vol. 1 (1843).
38. Rossetti, *Life of John Keats*, p. 198.
39. Lethaby, 'Arts and the Function of Guilds', p. 99.
40. Sleigh, 'Memoirs of Bernard Sleigh', p. 248.
41. Peterson, *Kelmscott Press*, pp. 156–7.
42. Ricketts, 'Note on Original Wood Engraving', p. 266.
43. MacCarthy, *Last Pre-Raphaelite*, p. 37.
44. Pittock and Jack, 'Patrick Geddes and the Celtic Revival', p. 338.
45. Carruthers, *Arts and Crafts Movement in Scotland*, p. 67.
46. Mavor, *My Windows on the Street of the World*, p. 199.
47. Cumming, *Hand, Heart and Soul*, p. 7.
48. Mavor, *My Windows on the Street of the World*, pp. 215–16.
49. Meller, *Patrick Geddes*, p. 4.
50. Geddes, *Cities in Evolution*, pp. 3–4.
51. Geddes, 'Life and Its Science', pp. 29–30.
52. Macdonald and Thomson, 'Proem', p. 12.
53. Geddes and Macdonald, 'Envoy', p. 155.
54. Quoted in Grilli, 'Funding, Publishing, and the Making of Culture', p. 25.
55. Branford and Geddes, 'Prefatory Note', p. 8.
56. Salt, 'University Hall', p. 942.
57. Carruthers, *Arts and Crafts Movement in Scotland*, p. 95.
58. Branford and Geddes, 'Prefatory Note', p. 8.
59. Elliot, 'Old-World Verse & Scottish Renascence', *passim*.
60. Branford, 'Series of Remarks', p. 33.

61. Grilli, 'Funding, Publishing, and the Making of Culture', pp. 29–31.
62. Kooistra, 'Politics of Ornament', p. 108.
63. Macdonald and Thomson, 'Proem', p. 12.
64. Ibid., p. 9.
65. Ibid., p. 11.
66. Thomson, 'Germinal, Florial, Prairial', p. 25.
67. Grilli, 'Funding, Publishing, and the Making of Culture', p. 24.
68. Geddes, 'Flower of the Grass', p. 63.
69. Geddes and Macdonald, 'Envoy', p. 156.
70. Thomson, 'Biology of Autumn', p. 9.
71. Macleod [Sharp], 'Day and Night', p. 47.
72. Christie, 'Between the Ages', p. 62.
73. Williams, *Marxism and Literature*, p. 116.
74. Branford and Geddes, 'Prefatory Note', p. 8.
75. Reynolds, *Paris-Edinburgh*, p. 99. Emphasis original.
76. Ibid., p. 98.
77. Branford and Geddes, 'Prefatory Note', p. 8.
78. Alaya, *William Sharp – 'Fiona Macleod'*, p. 147.
79. Macdonald and Thomson, 'Proem', p. 12.
80. Sharp, *William Sharp (Fiona Macleod)*, p. 249.
81. See Nash, 'Kailyard: Problem or Illusion?', *passim*.
82. Geddes, 'Scots Renascence', pp. 136–7.
83. Ibid., p. 137.
84. Grilli, 'Funding, Publishing, and the Making of Culture', p. 27.
85. Quoted in ibid., p. 37.
86. Zangwill, 'Edinburgh', p. 289.
87. Quoted in Grilli, 'Funding, Publishing, and the Making of Culture', p. 35.
88. Shaw, 'Aestheticism and Decadence', p. 175. Emphasis original.
89. Geddes, 'Sociology of Autumn', p. 38.
90. Macdonald and Thomson, 'Proem', p. 10.
91. Ibid., p. 10.
92. 'Cela vaudrait mieux que s'appliquer, comme ils le font, à ruiner le peu de conscience qu'ont gardée les riches, et le peu d'espérance qui console les pauvres' (Klein, 'Diléttantisme', p. 88).
93. 'La banqueroute de la philosophie pseudo-scientifique'; 'La banqueroute du naturalisme' (Saroléa, 'Littérature Nouvelle en France', p. 92).
94. Authors of 'The Evolution of Sex' [Geddes and Thomson], 'Moral Evolution of Sex', p. 82.
95. Meller, *Patrick Geddes*, p. 82.
96. Ibid., p. 82.
97. Geddes and Thomson, *Evolution of Sex*, p. 267.
98. Gagnier, 'Twenty-First-Century and Victorian Ecosystems', p. 15.
99. Macdonald and Thomson, 'Proem', p. 12.

100. Authors of 'The Evolution of Sex' [Geddes and Thomson], 'Moral Evolution of Sex', pp. 83–4.
101. Ibid., p. 84.
102. Wells, 'Zoological Retrogression', p. 246.
103. Wells, 'Bio-Optimism', p. 206.
104. Ibid., p. 207.
105. Macdonald and Thomson, 'Proem', p. 12.
106. Wells, 'Bio-Optimism', p. 208.
107. Geddes and Macdonald, 'Envoy', p. 155.
108. Bradley, 'Introduction', p. 7.
109. For studies on the political function of the Total Work of Art in twentieth-century totalitarian regimes, see Boris Groys's *The Total Art of Stalinism* (1988, trans. 1992); Joachim Köhler's *Wagner's Hitler* (1997, trans. 2000).

Chapter 6

Little Excursions Outside the Avant-Garde: the *Pageant*, the *Parade* and the *Dome*

Throughout this book, the slippery terms 'avant-garde' and 'mainstream' have been applied to publications and their producers to distinguish positions in the market that do not lend themselves to essentialist definitions, but can only be understood as pragmatically defining each other in mutual opposition. On the one side, self-declared rebel alliances of variable internal cohesion insist on their fundamental differences with a vested interest that jealously guards its dominance. The heterodox challengers associate this dominance with either commercialist vulgarity, or with academic neophobia. On the other side, an equally diverse array of orthodox established or aspirational producers employ the rhetoric of common sense and consecration through institutionalized authority to ward of challenges to the status quo.

In reality, however, there are countless overlaps between the two purportedly opposite positions, and many artists and authors do not consistently stick with either side. Most will affiliate themselves with both avant-garde and mainstream at various stages of their careers or for various aspects of their output, and representatives of either position can share publication contexts such as the same publisher's list, or the same periodical. The authors and artists of the 1890s, as we have noted time and again, were no exception. Nevertheless, from the first attempts to historicise the avant-garde position, or 'vanguardism' as it was termed by Renato Poggioli in the 1960s, the many schools within the Aesthetic Movement have been considered as not actually part of this wider phenomenon, but rather the culmination of its 'prehistory'.[1] In his much-debated reply to Poggioli, Peter Bürger too emphasised the indispensable role of Aestheticism as a precursor that heralded a phase in cultural history in which 'the apartness from the praxis of life that had always constituted the institutional status of art in bourgeois society' had become 'the content of works'. This introduced the 'self-criticism of art' and its place in society maintained in this book as one of Aestheticism's most important characteristics, but that according to Bürger only fully developed in the early twentieth century.[2] Both theorists denied Aestheticism its avant-garde status because they narrowed it down to the clichéd formula of 'Art for Art's Sake', which according to their shared Marxist perspective meant a lack of engagement with society. Bürger, for one, saw Aestheticism as a creed in which 'reflection about the relationship between individual and society' is 'overshadowed by the ever-increasing concentration the makers of art bring to the medium itself', thereby making it impossible for its adherents to proceed to the next step and 'organise a new life praxis from a basis in art'.[3] Primarily interested in early-twentieth-century artistic and literary practice, both critics liked to believe that the world started afresh when their favoured artists and authors cast the magic spell of 'Make It New'.

Over the past half century, such linearly historicist narratives have been discredited, and the act of positioning oneself among the avant-garde is no longer situated within stages in one distinct teleological historical movement.[4] Rather, it is seen as a pragmatic strategy that enables certain forms of self-marketing and that facilitates the consolidation of cultural networks with their own channels of distribution. Yet, even if we were to go along with the demand for politicised artistic practice, scholarship in the past few decades has shown that even those doctrines associated with Aestheticism that were claimed to be apolitical were in fact far from socially disinterested. In her study of the influence of Aestheticism on late-Victorian philanthropy and social movements, Diane Maltz also draws attention to several contemporaneous functions, for instance its potential for the middle classes to acquire cultural capital, its challenge to the ideology of utilitarianism, and its interventions in gender politics and sexual emancipation by providing a context for female and queer subcultures.[5] As we have seen in the previous chapters, all of these causes featured in those calling cards of the Aesthetic Movement: the little magazines of the British Fin de Siècle. These periodicals met Bürger's demand for an engagement with the 'institutional status' of art, because they served as alternative mini-institutions for the consecration of art and literature themselves. Not only did they serve to propagate the heterodox beliefs mentioned above, but they also did not restrict themselves to conditions imposed by the mainstream market concerning production and distribution.

Three ways for a magazine to participate in the avant-garde could be (1) the dissemination of (as yet) heterodox content, (2) the adoption of funding and production methods that are not calculated to either cut costs or inversely inflate these for the purposes of marketability, and (3) the bypassing of existing distribution channels. We should allow for certain mitigating circumstances to partially redeem the misguided denigrators of Aestheticism as an avant-garde movement, as already during the 1890s, some innovative publications were willing to settle, at least on occasion, for compromises that involved giving up on one or two of those options. In so doing, they divested themselves of possibly contentious associations, allowed production methods that allowed the maximisation of profit, and circulated through the normal distribution frameworks of the regular market. By all definitions of little magazines, that makes such compromised publications problematic to classify as examples of this genre. The *Yellow Book* and the *Savoy* are the most obvious examples, as arguably options 2 and 3 do not apply to it (see Chapter 4).

There are a number of other periodicals earlier in the late-Victorian era that are often singled out for the high number of contributors now associated with Aestheticism or their adoption of design principles of the Revival of Fine Printing, without fulfilling the avant-garde obligations that we may expect of a little magazine. A few examples will suffice to show the diversity of such publications. The *Dark Blue* (1871–3) was a review periodical that aimed at a wide appeal while still offering occasionally heterodox content in the form of essays by Ruskin, and original illustrations and poetry by founding fathers and mothers of Aestheticism such as D. G. Rossetti, Simeon Solomon, Mathilde Blind and Swinburne.[6] The dark blue boards that gave it its title also anticipate the self-awareness and attention to material detail of several little magazines of the 1880s and 1890s. Later, the *Artist and Journal of Home Culture* (1880–1902) was an art magazine that in its early years is notable for its attention to applied as well as fine art and for its initial explicit appeal to a female readership, and in the 1890s because it contained several frank Uranian articles theorising queer culture.[7] In the 1890s, the journal came to suffer because it remained unillustrated to allow for a low cover price, while its competitors were not only illustrated but also invested further in new image printing technology, foremost among them the soon leading art magazine the *Studio* (1893–1964), to which we will return shortly. A third example is the *Butterfly* (first series 1893; second series 1899–1900), a satirical journal edited by Leonard Raven-Hill, illustrator and art editor of the satirical weekly *Pick-Me-Up* (1888–1909) that like its more famous counterpart *Punch* often ridiculed the 1890s avant-garde (see Chapter 4). It took its name from the butterfly device with which J. M. Whistler famously signed his letters and littered his collection of polemics and monument of book design *The Gentle Art of Making Enemies* (1890) (see Chapter 3). It combined guest contributions by the likes of Maurice Greiffenhagen, Max Beerbohm and Laurence Housman, but also satirists and detractors of Aestheticism such as Norman Gale and Barry Pain, and in its editorial line did not commit to any ideological principles or a consistent aesthetic agenda.

Of course, journals that are routinely classed as little magazines, such as the *Yellow Book*, also slyly subverted avant-garde rhetoric and production methods by putting them to the use of a publishing firm focused primarily on profits. After it had set this example, at the end of the 1890s, a number of periodical publications would appear that in form and content harked back to the previously discussed little magazines, but were marketed towards a mainstream audience without attesting a necessity for clever reverse psychology, and any signs of a consistently promoted artistic doctrine, political contention or moral controversy. Although some of these are still discussed as little magazines in scholarship, they can therefore only be considered such with major reservations. What they did do is import the more conspicuous conventions of the little magazine into other publication genres that belonged to the mainstream position to which the avant-garde claimed to posit an alternative, such as the gift book (the *Pageant* and the *Parade*) and the non-partisan artistic journal intended for a wide audience (the *Dome*). By adopting the contents and appearance of little magazines but largely abandoning the production and distribution principles that had characterised this genre before, they furthermore now abandoned entirely the limited circulation that according to all definitions constituted its namesake littleness. Additionally, in their contents they questioned some of the major tenets of earlier avant-garde periodicals, and thereby too indicated that the first, Victorian-era heyday of the little magazine genre was coming to an end.

The *Pageant* and the *Parade* as Aestheticist Christmas annuals

Wherever we draw the line between the avant-garde and the mainstream, surely few would dispute the vanguardism of the little magazine the *Dial* (see Chapter 3). Here was a publication filled by authors and artists from the same coterie, the deliberately inefficient house periodical of a small press that willingly doomed itself to limited circulation, conspicuously banning new technologies in order to foreground artistic crafts. By making a point of playing by their own rules, the Vale coterie only reached a small readership, but it allowed them to circulate a portfolio of their talents that could showcase their skills and vision to the best of their abilities, providing peer recognition and networking opportunities that would improve their chances of getting published elsewhere or help them secure more lucrative design commissions. Several years into the run of the *Dial*, they came to play a prominent role in a very different periodical, which eschewed all exclusivity. This annual publication entitled the *Pageant* ran for two numbers, published in the November months of 1895 and 1896 but confusingly each postdated to the following year. Contributor and Vale regular Will Rothenstein claimed that it was first conceived by Charles Ricketts and Charles Shannon, which is plausible given the prominence of both behind the scenes and as contributors, as well as that of several of their former collaborators.[8] Shannon acted as its official art editor and Ricketts appears to have coordinated the design, furnishing for instance the famous ornaments on the pink cloth bindings of these hardbound volumes (Figure 34). Both could draw for their tasks on past editorial and design experience. This, however, was no Vale Press production.

The *Pageant* was published by H. Henry & Co., a London publisher with a diverse list, issuing highbrow non-fiction books and some of the more accessible literary work by avant-garde authors. In the same year, for instance, they had issued the first English translation of several works by Friedrich Nietzsche, which inspired a series of introductory essays on the philosopher's thought in the *Savoy*, and they advertised in that journal as well (see Chapter 3). Amongst other characteristic Fin-de-Siècle titles, they also published the novel *Vain Fortune* (1892) by George Moore, as well as a play by Rhymers' Club member John Todhunter, and employed Todhunter's fellow Rhymers' Club members Ernest Dowson, G. A. Greene and A. C. Hillier on the translation from the German of a multivolume art history by Richard Muther. By and large their list shows no sign of their coveting the bohemian chic of an avant-garde position. Open-minded as they were, Henry and Co. was a trade publisher, and we may well ask why they decided to do business with two men whose single foray into periodical management was the consistently loss-making *Dial*.

It is likely that the agreement of Joseph William Gleeson White to become the *Pageant*'s literary editor won over the publisher to the enterprise. Apart from being a respected and well-connected critic himself, Gleeson White was a skilled hand at making artistic periodicals solvent, having headed the popular American *Art Amateur* (1873–1903) and, more importantly, the *Studio* for the all-important first two years in which it made its reputation as the internationally leading *Illustrated Magazine of Fine and Applied Art*. The latter magazine was sympathetic to all the styles and design rationales featured in both academic art journals and the little magazines of the 1890s, but itself aimed at a broader readership than little magazines hitherto had done, according to Gerry Beegan, 'not of connoisseurs and collectors, but of practitioners, students and middle-class enthusiasts'.[9] By welcoming all kinds of advertisements without discriminating on the basis of artistic or ideological justification, and by keeping the production costs low, the *Studio* managed to charge only sixpence for a well-designed and materially sound monthly issue filled to the brim with illustrations. The *Studio* and the *Dial* were also exact opposites in another way. Whereas the *Dial*, as discussed, after its first issue made a point of printing its illustrations directly from the stone or the wood to make a stand against new photographic image reproduction techniques, the *Studio* decided to print *only* photographic reproductions of images. Although the (*Century Guild*) *Hobby Horse* had some of these too, it was no doubt the *Studio* that gave Lane the idea to also use photographic line blocks for reproducing the dark and sinuous drawings of artists like Beardsley in the *Yellow Book*, and halftone photographs for paintings, instead of having engravers copy them manually. This made printing less laborious and costly, facilitated the inclusion of more illustrations, and allowed the magazine to buy reproductions of work by famous artists with no direct affiliation to the magazine's producers. While much effort still went into the design of the *Studio*, following its example, periodicals like the *Yellow Book* and *Savoy* abandoned artisanal production methods that were important to earlier little magazines.

As said above, an important part of the *Dial*'s mission had been to reinstate the art of original engraving, or, in the words of Gleeson White in the *Pageant*, 'to preach anew a truth out of favour at present'.[10] The colophon of the 1897 *Pageant* draws attention to the printing of the images by the Swan Electric Engraving Company 'to ensure the greatest possible delicacy of effect'.[11] Like with the *Studio* and other periodicals of the time, its editors valued photographic techniques for image reproduction largely because they did away with the inevitable compromising of the original image during the twofold transposition from original image to wood block, and from wood block to printed page. However, that does not mean that engravings and woodcuts are denigrated in the *Pageant*. As Gleeson White suggested in the spirit of compromise, wood-cutting was being 'restricted to the highest employment only from the commercial rivalry of process block'.[12] The implication is that periodicals like the *Studio* indirectly stimulated the development of original (as opposed to 'reproductive') engraving as an art form, because engravers were getting fewer and fewer assignments for copying works by other artists in different media. By its being superseded as a means of reproduction, engraving, then, was being fully emancipated as an artistic medium for original work in its own right. Counterintuitively perhaps, the new technique could be seen as the ally of the old. While this makes perfect sense, it is an argument that is nowhere to be found in the *Dial*, where the new techniques were altogether unmentionable.

Yielding the front stage to Shannon and Gleeson White allowed for some vintage Victorian puffery of Ricketts, who formed the topic of a ringing appreciation by Gleeson White that opens the *Pageant*'s first number. 'Cloth-binding, but lately a thing of horror, has suddenly become illuminated with intelligence: and for this no second name need be coupled with that of Mr. Ricketts',[13] conveniently drawing attention to the fact that Ricketts had been entrusted with the cloth bindings of the *Pageant*. Gleeson White's article also contains reproductions of several of Ricketts's illustrations from the *Dial*. Likewise, the predominance of friends of Shannon's and Ricketts's in the *Pageant* implies that they viewed it as an opportunity for publicity wholly different from that offered by the older periodical. In his article 'A Note on Original Wood Engraving' (No. 2), Ricketts indirectly seconds Gleeson White's point on the emancipatory effects of photographic reproduction in the first number by praising 'those few master craftsmen who were designers and engravers at once' in earlier ages, and spends some time on recent examples of such practitioners of original engraving. Significantly, he mentions several of the Vale coterie. Reginald Savage's *Dial* woodcut 'The Palace Burns and Behemoth' (No. 2), originally the frontispiece to the second number of the *Dial*, is printed as an example (Figure 10), and Savage, Thomas Sturge Moore and Lucien Pissarro are also the only living engravers working in Britain who are named. Nearly all other *Dial* contributors appear in the *Pageant* as well: John Gray, 'Michael Field', Laurence Housman and even the elusive Walter Delaplaine Scull all have material in at least one volume, and Pissarro also assisted with the paratext by designing the *Pageant*'s endpapers.

There is a distinct overlap in the interests of the two journals as well. Many reproduced artists are familiar from the older magazine, for instance the French Symbolist painters Puvis and Moureau (both No. 2), and the Pre-Raphaelites' legacy is notable celebrated in the persons of D. G. Rossetti, J. E. Millais and Edward Burne-Jones (all three in both issues). On at least one occasion, a textual ornament from the *Dial* (No. 1) was tacitly reused in the *Pageant* (No. 1).[14] Like the *Dial* with Verhaeren (No. 5), the *Pageant* has untranslated poems in French by Maeterlinck and Verlaine in its first issue. Furthermore, both issues of the *Pageant* include a play by Maeterlinck, albeit rendered into English by his friend and first translator, the upcoming playwright Alfred Sutro.

Next to these familiar contributors, with Yeats (No. 1), Ernest Dowson, Lionel Johnson and Victor Plarr (all No. 2) the *Pageant* also attracted some of the rising stars of the Rhymers' Club, who as we have seen had a connection to the publisher. Respected critics appear in No. 2, such as Edmund Gosse, on the French writer Barbey d'Aurevilly, and *The Spectator*'s (1828–) D. S. MacColl, seconding Ricketts on engraving with an appreciation of the Renaissance artist Giulio Campagnola; and there are several poets like the future poet laureate Robert Bridges, the anti-Decadent W. E. Henley, and a by now clubbable Swinburne (all No. 1), who had all three never contributed to little magazines. In so doing, the *Pageant* provides a cross-section of British art and literature in the 1890s. Obviously, all of these people, and all of these artistic or literary tendencies, could be found in other publications as well, but the numerous overlaps between the *Pageant* and the *Dial* indicate that one purpose of the new annual was to promote the members and creeds of the Vale coterie. David Corbett judges that '[o]nce again, the predominant tone is derived from Symbolist models, but given a characteristically British twist of medievalising codswallop'.[15] Granted, the occasional cod is walloped, but to reduce the *Pageant* to this is certainly not fair. Among the reproductions, we notably find next to the usual Pre-Raphaelites and French Symbolists a number of artists, like Rothenstein (No. 1) and Conder (No. 2), representing Impressionism and specifically the New English Art Club, who stylistically have as little in common with the PRB as with French Symbolism.

Importantly, a notable number of the reproductions are not recent; for instance, several paintings and sketches by Millais and D. G. Rossetti that are featured in both issues go back as far as the 1850s. These reproductions are definitely not meant for connoisseurs: in the 1890s, nobody seriously occupied with art would have been excited about a halftone of J. E. Millais's *Sir Isumbras at the*

Ford (1857) or Whistler's *Symphony in White, No. 3* (1867) from his series of paintings featuring the so-called 'white girls', as they will have seen these in the original or in earlier reproductions several times before. The choice of these specific works from outside of the Vale coterie can probably best be explained by reference to the contemporaneous category of the *juste milieu* ('golden mean'), a term originally from French politics that found its way into art criticism to denote work that resisted academic conventions but still was accessible enough to appeal to a wide audience, overlapping avant-garde and mainstream. As Robert Jensen points out, in late-nineteenth-century France, this term was often ironically applied by critics to those Impressionists who resisted the increasing abstraction of their movement and instead remained invested in figurative representation with 'the accessibility, the narrative and pictorial coherence of the academic tradition', and he sees it as applicable to Whistler and his followers.[16] Arguably, the Pre-Raphaelites after the initial shock of the 1850s came to be in a similar situation, when they were being patronised by wealthy admirers who were keen on showing off their artistic progressiveness but still wanted to understand what they were looking at. It is characteristic of the *Pageant*'s programme of giving a taste of Aestheticism that would be appreciated by the general public, that it offers initially controversial, but subsequently aesthetically and morally rehabilitated examples of a previous generation, in combination with the also accessible work of younger artists; the lay reader might buy the volume for the Rossetti plate and discover Reginald Savage, or find Conder by way of Whistler. It made sense to reproduce paintings by these artists of the previous generation from a purely practical point of view as well, as process blocks of their work were readily available from photography pioneers like Frederick Hollyer, who is credited in the *Pageant*'s colophon as the supplier of several plates. It is no coincidence that paintings by artists such as Rossetti, Millais, Watts and Burne-Jones that had been photographed by Hollyer were present in the *Pageant* and reproduced abundantly in other British periodicals of the time.[17]

The publishers of the *Pageant* told readers how they want it to be perceived when they advertised it as 'a stately and sumptuous gift-book',[18] but in fact the above discrepancies between the *Pageant* and the *Dial* alone could already have told us that it was taking inspiration from this publication genre in order to avoid the self-imposed isolationism of the little magazine. Gift books, now an obsolete genre, were a catch-all term for publications issued in November and marketed as Christmas presents. Many of these were simply illustrated books such as poetry collections, but the term was also applied to periodicals known specifically as 'Christmas annuals', whose yearly frequency makes them less obviously 'periodical', but that were organised along the same lines as magazines, and indeed, sometimes connected to these as they were often issued as supplemental seasonal numbers. Lorraine Janzen Kooistra finds that the

> principal criterion for a Christmas Book was not seasonal content but rather the material features of ornamental binding and wood-engraved illustration. In brilliant reds, blues and greens picked out with gilt, the packaging of these books announced their exchange value as gifts to be presented and then displaced: aesthetic objects combining instruction, entertainment, decoration, cultivation, and conspicuous consumption.[19]

Saccharine alternative names for the genre such as 'keepsakes' and 'forget-me-nots', after the titles of successful early instances, may sufficiently prove that gift books did not bank on critical prestige, let alone on being associated with artistic and literary innovation. For the strong emphasis on the visual in these ornate volumes, detractors would denigrate them as display items rather than books to be read. Their main appeal was the 'sumptuous' design of the bindings cited by the *Pageant* advert, and high-quality printing. Secondarily, they were valued by holiday shoppers for the literary contributions by well-paid famous authors (and badly paid obscurer ones) and the copious art plates of original illustrations as well as reproductions of paintings.[20] Gift-book editors realised that the included pictures were a major part of their appeal, and therefore subordinated all other contents to these, for instance commissioning ekphrastic poetry on specific reproductions to add an additional poetic veneer to the illustration, drawing attention to the visual yet again by means of the poem. Perversely, for these manifestly commercial reasons, they were thereby aiding the Pre-Raphaelite and later Arts and Crafts campaign to emancipate illustration from its subjection to literature in the book arts.

The *Pageant* may have had higher standards than most publications of its kind, but a review in the *Guardian* at least sounded a familiar note in criticism of gift books when it called the second *Pageant*, 'like its predecessor of 1896, [. . .] an attractive medley of excellent reproductions of good pictures by eminent artists, intermingled amid letterpress of various degrees of merit'.[21] The aforementioned poem by Verlaine, for instance, is an interesting case study for the subservience of literature to pictorial art in such publications, which admittedly is avoided for the most part in the *Pageant*. It is a purely ekphrastic commentary on Rossetti's painting *Monna Rosa* (1867), duly reproduced with this poem, although as is typical for halftones, in black and white (Figure 35). Verlaine's poem describes the female figure in the painting, 'en bandeaux d'or liquide, / En robe d'or fluide / Sur fond blanc dans le soir / Teinté d'or vert et noir' (ll. 2–5), and describes the background with a 'pot bleu japonise' (l. 6) and the 'plumage bleuté' of the peacock feathers. However, none of these colours can actually be seen in the greyscale plate.[22] More importantly, there is nothing 'bluish' (*bleuté*) about the peacock feathers in the painting at all, as in the original these are red in a hue that meaningfully resembles that of the model's hair. Verlaine had probably never seen the actual painting, which was in a private collection, and we know that this poem was especially commissioned by way of his main British contact Rothenstein, who had sent him the print.[23] Rothenstein's instructions have not been preserved, but one wonders if it contains (erroneous) notes on the colours of the original. Also, Verlaine in his poem cites exactly those elements of the painting that since its completion in the late 1860s had become clichés of Aestheticism: Japanese porcelain pots, peacock feathers standing for earthly beauty, roses standing for transcendental beauty, 'l'atmosphère exquise' (l. 9), and so on. Verlaine was at the time the most famous living French poet among a British readership, and had undertaken a lecture tour in Britain a few years before, with which several *Pageant* contributors and other figures associated with Aestheticism had been involved. His hardly memorable poem serves mainly as a celebrity contribution, common in gift books, and to further fetishise the reproduced painting, ensuring that readers would pick up on the appropriate details. Great poets, especially while in penury as Verlaine was at the time, will condescend to potboilers too. A more imaginative poem by Sturge Moore commenting on a printed reproduction of Botticelli's *Pallas and the Centaur* (1482) is the only other case of such an ekphrastic poem in the *Pageant*, and this was topical for once, as this painting had only been rediscovered in the Pitti Palace the year before.[24]

The upfront commercialism and usual imbalance between literary and pictorial content of gift books such as Christmas annuals would seem to place them at variance with all that the little magazines of the 1890s stood for. On closer inspection, however, some similarities appear that Aestheticist editors and designers could adapt to their purpose. A first advantage of the gift book genre is that it was perceived to be of more enduring value than the ephemeral magazine. As we have seen, this hint of lasting relevance was what the *Yellow Book* and the *Evergreen*, with its boarded covers and issue titles as 'The Book of Winter', hoped to appropriate from the book form. Secondly, both gift books and Aestheticist little magazines were commonly evaluated on their material characteristics and design. Gift books tended to have quality bindings and paper, and when the first examples appeared during the lean years of Victorian book design they had been rare instances of meticulous typography. The *Pageant*'s quarto volumes, with their dark-pink (strangely advertised as 'chocolate' colour) cloth covers with gilded ornaments, share these traits with Aestheticist book design, but are not fundamentally different from regular gift books. The broad page margins of the *Pageant* of course fit the page design canons of the Revival of Fine Printing, but these had been present in many older gift books, in which having less text on the page than in a regular trade book was meant to convey a sense of luxury, as not covering a large surface of the page as in standard printing went against the utilitarian logic of saving paper.

Unlike those of the previously discussed little magazines, advertisements for the *Pageant* always emphasised its accessible character, in both the intellectual and the financial senses. For instance, it was described as 'designed with a view to provide, at a price within everybody's means, a valuable and enduring Gift-Book for that increasing section of the public which can no longer derive any artistic enjoyment from the ordinary illustrated Christmas number'.[25] The adverts for the second number sometimes contained extracts from reviews of the first, but no disparaging comments were quoted, as the *Yellow Book* and the *Savoy* did do to highlight their avant-garde position. In adverts for the second *Pageant*, for instance, we find an excerpt from the *Review of Reviews* (1890–1936), calling the first *Pageant* 'the best gift-book for the ordinary reader'. It is quite surprising that it would be identified as being for a general readership, as the content in themes and styles was very similar to that of contemporaneous little magazines, whose content was frowned upon. The fact that it was possible to market this type of content as accessible at all is testimony to the effect that vulgarising periodicals such as the *Studio*, the *Yellow Book* and the *Savoy* must have had in familiarising critics and 'ordinary readers' alike with art and literature previously appreciated by a limited audience. One literary example of this familiarity is the *Pageant*'s essay 'Be It Cosiness' by Max Beerbohm, discussed in the Introduction to this book as the author's leave-taking of the ideals of 'those more decadent days of my childhood'.[26] Beerbohm, as ever, meant to be satirical, but by including this disavowal of doctrinal Aestheticism in a periodical marketed towards the uninitiated, his editors are signalling to their readers that they do not have to worry about the moral message of the *Pageant*'s content. Beerbohm states that he 'belong[s] to the Beardsley period', but that period is past with that artist's ostracism from the public stage, and so the themes that characterised it have lost their sting.[27] Beardsley was still alive at that point, but, as stated in Chapter 4, Beerbohm publishes this statement in the final month of the *Savoy*, apparently reckoning the failure of that magazine as an indication that a particular type of Aestheticism had had its day.

Still, while controversy is not courted in these two volumes as it was in other some earlier Fin-de-Siècle periodicals, it is not strenuously avoided either. Gleeson White's article on Ricketts in the first number does not overlook the artist's illustrations for Wilde's *A House of Pomegranates* (1891) and *The Sphinx* (1894). Of course, Wilde had been in prison for a year and half by then, and in comparison with the year before, the subject of literary and artistic Decadence hardly made the papers. Nevertheless, the public appeal that the *Pageant* clearly sought could have been jeopardised by even a faint association with Decadence, given the presence of several former contributors to the *Yellow Book* and the *Savoy*. The *Pageant* also featured several contributors who had previously either cryptically or openly featured same-sex attraction as themes in their work. A contribution by to the first *Pageant*, 'Death and the Bather', refers unmistakably to a commonplace of 1890s male queer art in its portrayal of nude bathing men, full-frontal in no fewer than four instances (Figure 36). Laurel Brake singles out this item as the most explicitly homoerotic in the two volumes, and of course the artist's well-known homosexuality substantiates such a reading.[28] Nevertheless, even here a distinct ambiguity in this in no way pleasant scene allowed late-Victorian readers to construe it as a warning against homosexuality, and at any rate it is not a straightforward celebration. The hermaphrodite figure in the foreground enticing the viewer to join the nude men can only be identified as the titular 'Death', and the 'Bather' would be the drowned figure trampled underfoot, while the other bathers are staring at the scene in horror. The reflection of the man standing nearest to the water's edge recalls the contemporaneous designation of 'sexual inversion' for homosexuality and its association with narcissism, and additionally places him forebodingly in the same situation as the present victim. Possibly, the tension between these two contradictory interpretations can be resolved if Housman's drawing is interpreted as a troubling representation of the risks faced by homosexual men in the wake of the Wilde trial, more poignant than an unambiguous representation would have been because its purport could be denied if necessary.

The *Pageant*'s advertisements also justly point out the accessibility of its modest price. For the mid-1890s, 6 shillings may not have been cheap, but it was a common price for a novel, only a shilling over the equally market-oriented and materially less impressive *Yellow Book*, and a lot cheaper than the *Dial*, which charged over twice as much for far less content. The *Pageant* is also cheaper than many gift books, which could cost as much as a guinea (£1 1s.). This is in fact the price of the *Pageant*'s limited edition of 150 deluxe large-paper copies, through which H. Henry, like other publishers in the 1890s, appealed to collectors. For additional revenue, the *Pageant* carried a small advertisement section, bound in after the body text, and paginated differently. The first issue contains an advert for its publisher, advertising mainly art books, the aforementioned editions of Nietzsche and a number of novels, but also a one-page advert for the Swan Electric Engraving Company. In the second issue, next to adverts for again H. Henry & Co. and Swan, and for publisher Marcus Ward announcing mainly seasonal titles, Messrs. Hacon and Ricketts – better known to us as the Vale Press – have a one-page advert too. This is possibly the only advert they ever had in a periodical other than their house periodical the *Dial*, confirming again the secondary role of the *Pageant* as a means of publicising the work of the Vale coterie.

The first item advertised in H. Henry's column in the *Pageant*'s 1897 number is arguably the most compelling of all featured. The *Parade* was another gift book issued by this publisher, also edited by Gleeson White, and clearly intended to be a companion piece for the similarly titled *Pageant*. Although only one issue would appear, it seems probable that it was intended to have an annual frequency like its older sibling, and indeed it is treated as a periodical in the few sources that notice it at all. Also like the *Pageant*, it is a visually and materially exceptional volume, with cloth bindings, designed endpapers, and a high density of photographically reproduced images. The *Parade*'s most distinguishing feature is one that sets it apart from not only the *Pageant*, but at once from all other publications discussed in this book: it was advertised as a 'Gift-Book for the Young', and declares itself intended 'for Boys and Girls' on its title page. Aestheticism, of course, has a long history of engaging with children and addressing childhood as a theme. Some of this is uncontroversial, such as the persistently popular illustrations by Kate Greenaway, but other cases, such as the ubiquitous late-Victorian appropriations of fairy-tale motifs, have made critics uneasy since their first appearance, for one thing because it is often difficult to determine their target audience. A reviewer for the *Pall Mall Gazette* wondered of Wilde's *A House of Pomegranates* (1891) whether it 'was intended for a child's book', as '[t]he ultra-aestheticism of the pictures seems unsuitable for children – as also the rather "fleshly" style of Mr. Wilde's writing', thereby dusting off the old epithet levelled at the allegedly immoral poetry of D. G. Rossetti and Swinburne twenty years before.[29] The author did not clear up the matter when he replied tartly that it had in fact not been intended for anybody at all.[30]

Through its list of contributors at least, the *Parade* might have been vulnerable to similar misgivings. As with the *Pageant* before, several names come with hardly pedagogic credentials. The title page, with audacious daringness, was designed by Aubrey Beardsley, who, however, restricts himself to a clean design that is similar to his mainly decorative work for the Bodley Head 'Keynotes Series' (Figure 37). Also here are Laurence Housman (again), Max Beerbohm (again), Richard Le Gallienne, Edgar Jepson and Mrs Percy Dearmer [Mabel Dearmer née White], who too had been in the *Yellow Book*, the *Savoy* or both. Sir Richard Burton, although he was a respected figure because as a famed explorer and writer of Oriental tales he exemplified British Imperial ideology, was also known as the translator of the first unexpurgated *Book of the Thousand Nights and a Night* (1885) and – though this was of course not publicised – he wrote for an underground pornography ring lead by the *Savoy*'s publisher Leonard Smithers.[31]

Like the *Pageant*, delivered by producers with links to the avant-garde and fulfilling a secondary purpose of promoting a specific coterie, the *Parade* also has some outsiders to balance the scale. Barry Pain, a journalist and short story writer for a number of successful magazines, had recently taken over from Jerome K. Jerome the editorship of the weekly *To-day* (1893–1905), which has recently been categorised as part of 'an emergent but undefined culture that only gained proper definition in the 1920s as "middlebrow"'.[32] He had previously also contributed to the aforementioned satirical magazine *Butterfly*, itself an excellent candidate for the middlebrow label for its combination of accessible humour, Whistlerian page design, and regular contributions by British Impressionist and Aestheticist illustrators. Pain's contribution, however, is all the more remarkable because he had written an exceptionally fierce dismissal of the first number of the *Yellow Book*, recommending the Napoleonic remedy of 'a whiff of grapeshot' against Beerbohm for writing 'A Defence of Cosmetics'.[33] In the *Parade*, not three years later, Pain and Beerbohm find themselves contributing to the same publication. Most of the now lesser-known letterpress contributors had recently appeared on Henry's publisher's list, such as Jepson, later Dublin Abbey Theatre director F. Norreys Connell, and Mary E. Mann, a since forgotten novelist of rural fiction. Like the *Pageant*, the *Parade* therefore does have a secondary function as a means of promotion for its publisher.

Also like the *Pageant*, the *Parade* follows the custom of some little magazines of listing letterpress and art separately in the table of contents. On the artistic side, there are a number of young artists who are not primarily associated with Aestheticism, such as the cartoonist Starr Wood, and Leonard Leslie Brooke who at the time was gaining prominence as an illustrator of famous children's books. Children's books were one of many topics that editor Gleeson White had opinions about, which he published a year after the *Parade* (which in the same way as the second *Pageant* was also published in November 1896 but postdated 1897) in a special issue on 'Children's Books and Their Illustrators' for the *Studio* (Winter 1897–8). Several artistic contributors to the Parade were singled out as promising in this article, and it is itself also explicitly mentioned twice, for instance when we are told that Leslie Brooke's 'very charming frontispiece and title to John Oliver Hobbes' [Pearl Craigie] "Prince Toto" [. . .] must not be forgotten' (Figure 40).[34] Another young artist singled out for praise, who was only just making a name for himself, is Paul Woodroffe, who by furnishing the *Parade*'s endpapers (Figure 38), half-title and several illustrations is one of the most prominent contributors and likely closely involved with the overall design concept of the entire volume. As Simon Houfe has noted, it is this repeated presence of Woodroffe's work and his consistent use of motifs throughout the *Parade* that brings the volume conceptually together, and stylistically he also straddles both the medievalist and the Greenaway-inspired current modes represented in the volume, in keeping with the integration demanded by the Total Art concept of the Book Beautiful.[35] Further conceptual coherence is arguably added, as Houfe further remarks, by a number of artist-authors who provide both text and illustration in the *Parade*.[36]

The *Parade* was obviously a primarily commercial enterprise, but it uses such Aestheticist tactics to sell itself. As is so often the case in the 1890s, the *Parade*'s visual and material presentation provides the key to its guiding principles. In the second number of the *Pageant*, which appeared in the same month, a causerie by the unidentified

Edward Purcell (perhaps a pseudonym) 'Of Purple Jars' emphasised children's instinctive and innocent appreciation of beautiful objects, unaffected as they are by the financial value or opportunity at conspicuous consumption discerned therein by their elders. Children would therefore be born aesthetes.[37] While the purple jar coveted by the child is a device borrowed from an old moral tale by Maria Edgeworth, there is an obvious connection to the dark-pink boards of the publication. The child's urge for acquiring this object in the face of the objections of her 'admirable Mama' is defended in the same breath as moral tales are decried that teach children to value 'the Useful' over 'the Beautiful'.[38] Ironically, there is one obvious use for youth's natural sensitivity to beauty: clever marketeers can make money out of it. Aestheticism had long been a form of sophisticated consumerism, but now it was being paired with the Christmas season, which in the late nineteenth century was already big business, and in a time when Christmas was increasingly centred around children. As Tara Moore notes, after the huge public interest in the spiritual and social significance of the holiday evinced throughout mid-Victorian print culture, by the 1890s, emotional engagement with the Christmas spirit increasingly came to be associated with children, and reviews of Christmas books and seasonal numbers of periodicals 'privileged the vibrant displays of books over the textual content'.[39] Additionally, Christmas annuals had of course been marketed towards younger (female) readers for decades. Aestheticist book design canons by 1897 were firmly associated with good taste, and it was therefore a safe gamble on publisher H. Henry's part that a version of his Aesthetic annual the *Pageant* for children would be well received. Kate Greenaway had been steadily publishing Aestheticism-inflected Christmas annuals since the 1880s, and they could also take advantage of the success of the recent forays into children's books by another trade publisher adept at making money out of Aestheticism: the Bodley Head. Over the past two Christmas seasons (1895–7), John Lane had republished Walter Crane's series of *Toy Books* that originally appeared with Routledge in the late 1860s and early 1870s; these volumes of classic fairy tales were celebrated for introducing Pre-Raphaelite illustration and design principles into children's books and, as Kooistra notes, had already upon their first appearance 'schooled the consumer as a collector of art in commodified form'.[40] Republishing these helped to create a context for Lane's publications of new children's books by Crane and others, so it was left for Henry to take the association of Aestheticism with children's literature to the next step by introducing those formal aspects of the genre of the 1890s little magazine to the annual gift book that could be adapted to commercially accessible Fine Printing.

The pre-eminence of beauty over usefulness in children's books is in line with Gleeson White's views expressed in the aforementioned *Studio* essay. There, he welcomes the fact that in recent years children's literature has left behind the 'dull moralising' of the past,

> when people professed to believe that you could admonish children to a state of perfection which, in their didactic addresses to the small folk, they professed to obey themselves. It was, not to put too fine a point on it, an age of solemn hypocrisy [. . .] Probably the honest sympathy now shown to childish ideals is not likely to be misinterpreted, for children are often shrewd judges, and can detect the false from the true, in morals if not in art.[41]

This point had already been emphasised by Gleeson White in his preface to the *Parade*. Here he starts by picking apart the patronising stance he found in his own children's gift books when he himself was a boy, when the juvenile readers would only indirectly be addressed by way of their parents, '[f]or boys and girls are not, I think, quite so silly as prefaces usually regard them'. Instead, he vindicates the ability of children to be themselves judges of their reading material, and like Purcell in the *Pageant*, appeals to their innate sensibilities:

> if any one of them finds any particular item [. . .] very, VERY stupid – I shall think that he (or she) is most likely right. For if one is not quite an infallible critic before one has left one's 'teens, when is there any hope of being so?[42]

The young reader is accordingly entrusted with three kinds of textual content and fitting illustrations: (1) a deliberately unmoralistic version of the type of content that was more commonly found in boys' and girls' periodicals at the time, (2) moderately Aesthetic content that appeals to the implied child-connoisseur reader, and (3) abridged classics. Among the first, more numerous items, we find stirring but unmemorable reads such as a Stevensonian story of sea voyages and cowboys and 'Indians', and several naughty accounts of mischief at school. Whereas these may be exceptional in the sense that they cater to a harmless boyish sensationalism rather than convey a clear moral lesson, they would not have surprised readers familiar with then highly successful children's periodicals such as *Our Young Folks* (1871–79) or even the *Boy's Own Paper* (1879–1967) in its less instructive moments. Addressing both boys and girls, the *Parade* does not maintain the strict gendering of content that was still typical of children's periodicals at the time, but it seems probable that the songs and fairy tales in this publication, with inevitably less realistic illustrations and more woodcut ornaments on the page, were mainly included to cater to young female readers who had less of an interest in gun-spinning and swashbuckling. Several of these fairy tales have densely integrated page designs that make the most of recent printing technologies to integrate text and image on the page (Figure 40). These tales fall in the *Parade*'s arguable second content category, which in their illustrations are often closer to the styles of the little magazines of the 1890s. Thirdly, perhaps the only genuinely educational aspect of the magazine is its abridged retellings of classic stories, including a tale from the *Pentamerone* translated by Burton, Irving's 'Rip Van Winkle' (1819) and Friedrich de la Motte Fouqué's German Romantic novella *Undine* (1811), the latter having been an Aestheticist favourite for decades.

In some instances, as said above, both illustrations and tale were from the same hand, as in the cases of the rising illustrator Alfred Garth Jones and Laurence Housman. Although Housman had by this point published several fairy tales, including some that were explicitly marketed towards children, he had in recent years contributed to several little magazines, including the morally suspect *Dial* and *Yellow Book*. Even in his work ostensibly for children he regularly referenced visual motifs that had become linked to Decadence, and in the *Parade* does not efface this signature style to the same extent as Beardsley does for its title page. His tale 'The Enchanted Princess' is the only item that appears to have been singled out in criticism of the *Parade* as unsuitable for children. The conservative weekly *The Spectator*, whose most authoritative critic MacColl in the same month contributed to the *Pageant*, found that

> this is not the proper place – if there is a proper place at all – for Mr. Housman's erotics; we hope that he would be ashamed to read p. 3 aloud to any of the 'boys and girls' for whom the volume is intended. The illustrations are mostly in the newest style. In this matter, too, we like the old fashion.[43]

In Housman's bewildering story, a boy receives from a race of flame-consuming creatures that literally eat him out of hearth and home a magic ring called 'the Sweetener' that heightens his sensory enjoyments, after which he sets off on travels and eventually rescues a princess from spell-induced lethargy. It is not entirely clear why the reviewer specifically objected to the third page of the story. The illustration (Figure 39) that appears in the same opening may be the key, especially as Housman is one of the artists in the *Parade* working 'in the newest style', meaning no doubt the style recently popularised through Aestheticist journals and books and therefore tainted with Decadence. It is important to note here that for the Victorians, the term 'erotics' did not have to mean coition, but usually referred to any literary composition in the amatory mode, although it is probable that this reviewer interpreted the feeding frenzy of the Fire-Eaters 'lapping up flames with their tongues' as a metaphor for insatiable sensualism.[44] The use of 'newest' in a pejorative sense is significant, and may reflect the association with cultural degeneration that newness had for morally conservative commentators. New Journalism, New Women, and the 'New Chivalry' coined by Charles Kains Jackson in 1894 as a euphemism for male homosexuality, are all examples of recent innovations that posed a threat to social orthodoxy.

If the (in every sense) too graphic representation of sensualism is indeed what was objected to, it is odd that no critic found fault with the *Parade*'s musical setting of Robert Herrick's characteristically explicit song 'I Call and I Call':

> I call, I call: who do ye call?
> The maids who catch this cowslip ball.
> But since these cowslips fading be,
> Troth leave the flowers & maids take me.
> Yet, if that neither you will do,
> Speak but the word and I'll take you.[45]

This song refers to a traditional custom in which a ball woven of cowslips was cast around by maidens during divination games, whereby names of potential future husbands would be recited, the last name said before the ball falls to the ground being that of the one. As in other poems of his *Hesperides* (1648), Herrick makes explicit the implicit sexuality of this rural custom with its nod at old spring fertility rites, which suits as ill Victorian sexual mores, let alone those that inform children's publications, as those of the seventeenth-century Puritans whom the Cavalier poet had sought to provoke. Herrick maybe fits in with the *Parade*'s plan to take its young readers seriously and to cultivate their tastes in literature and art by offering them valuable examples, already shown in its retold classics. Like the *Pageant* for adult readers, the *Parade* in its content for children generally shows a disregard for social convention rather than a desire for confrontation.

The *Dome* and the late-Victorian art press

Although the *Dome* starts and ends sooner than the *Page* and is therefore not literally the youngest journal in the roster, this final case study is for various reasons often considered the last true little magazine of the Nineties or, in the imprecise but helpful terms of Cornelius Darcy, a 'final attempt' after the *Yellow Book* and the *Savoy* 'to create a worthwhile review'.[46] The *Dome* (1897–1900) shares several contributors with its predecessors, picking up from them several salient themes, styles and schools, and itself helped to launch the careers of some rising artists and authors who would grow into authorities during the coming Edwardian and modernist eras. It also, however, has some traits that do not come across as typical of the little magazine genre, or rather, it demonstrates more openly some tendencies that are present but hidden in earlier journals of its kind. Like the *Yellow Book* and the *Savoy*, it courted a more central market position among artistic-literary periodicals than was available to more uncompromising little magazines such as the *Dial* or the *Quest*, and it was willing to nuance its avant-garde sensibilities, but it did so less coyly than its peers. Ian Fletcher believes that '[c]onfrontation having disastrously failed' after the Wilde affair and the recent failure of the two most afflicted little magazines, in the *Dome* 'genial compromise was deployed, and with some success'.[47]

The genially compromising editor of the *Dome* and its most frequent contributor was Ernest J. Oldmeadow, owner of the Unicorn Press that also issued the magazine, a small player among the spate of recently founded trade publishers seeking to apply Fine Printing principles to lucrative publications. According to book historian Paul Wells, the Unicorn Press published 'works which, if they were not important or memorable, were at least exquisite and original' in appearance, and he furthermore believes they were inspired by the famous work done at Kelmscott.[48] The tidily designed Unicorn books do show an adherence to Fine Printing, yet considering the absence of medievalism or other deliberately nostalgic features, a comparison to trade publishers such as Heinemann or the Bodley Head makes more sense. With these firms, the Unicorn shares its dedication to cost-effective production methods in order to keep its books within reach of a wide audience, and it too appealed to collectors through pricier limited deluxe editions for some of its publications. The newly expanded readership was addressed by means of the 'Artist's Library' series of introductory monographs on famous artists, edited by former *Hobby Horse* contributor Laurence Binyon. These cheap books (2s. 6d) were copiously illustrated with photographic reproductions, and written by (upcoming) scholar-artists who often appeared in little magazines, such as Herbert Horne and William Rothenstein, and the young Roger Fry, later grey eminence of the Bloomsbury Group. Outside of this series, the Press issued original literary, artistic and critical work that as a rule did not leave a lasting impression, but there are some notable low-key publications on its list, such as the first book-length study on *Aubrey Beardsley* (1898) by Arthur Symons, and the *Page*'s Edward Gordon Craig's *A Book of Woodcuts* in the same year. Oldmeadow published pseudonymous work by himself, including fiction and drama such as the Wagnerite parody *Lady Lohengrin* (1896) under the name 'J. A. Wooldmeald', and pastiche poetry as 'Louis Barsac'. All of the above-mentioned names, including the alter egos used by Oldmeadow, are also found in the *Dome*, the latter not unlike William Sharp's masquerade in the *Pagan Review* (see Chapter 3).

One other indicator that the Unicorn Press should not be categorised among small presses such as Kelmscott is its rare degree of activity as a publisher in the periodical press. Whereas the small presses of the 1890s would at best have one flagship little magazine – for example, the Vale Press had its *Dial* and the Birmingham Guild of Handicraft issued the *Quest* under the likely spin-off firm of G. Napier – the Unicorn Press attempted three periodical ventures in a short space of time, not all of them artistic or literary. Alongside the *Dome*, the Unicorn Press also published the monthly current affairs periodical the *New Century Review* (January 1897–December 1900), which is remarkable in its genre for its low price of sixpence, and appears to have been managed by a non-doctrinal but broadly progressive agenda. Hardly any scholarship on this periodical has appeared, but it was occasionally quoted in newspapers and appears to have been valued for its commentary. The Unicorn's short-lived music magazine the *Chord* (May 1899–September 1900) shared most of its contributors with the *Dome*, and only survived for five quarterly issues.

In total, twenty-six numbers of the *Dome* were issued: five quarterly from March 1897 to May 1898, followed by a 'New Series' of twenty-one monthly numbers from October 1898 to July 1900, the latter also available bound in seven quarterly 'volumes'. During the four-month interval between these two series, the firm moved premises, but more interesting is the change in frequency. As we have seen, its initial quarterly frequency was common among little magazines of the 1890s because readers and critics associated this frequency with the prestigious genre of the review periodical, and its abandonment in favour of the more typical monthly magazine frequency may indicate an abandonment of the little magazine's continuous cultivation of an aura of exclusivity. The *Dome* is also, with the unillustrated and slimmer *Pagan Review*, the least expensive periodical included in this study. Throughout the run it was sold for 1 shilling, making it remarkably cheap for an illustrated literary-artistic periodical, and at least in price accessible to a wide readership. A 'Memorandum for Collectors' in the first number tells us that a bound '*Édition de luxe*' on hand-made paper is available at the still low price of 5 shillings – the same as a regular issue of the *Yellow Book* – in a tantalisingly limited edition of 100 copies.[49]

The *Dome* is nothing if not eclectic, already attesting to the width of its scope in its subtitle, *A Quarterly Containing Examples of All the Arts*, which was changed to *Illustrated Magazine and Review of Literature, Music, Architecture and the Graphic Arts* after it became a monthly. The mentions of 'quarterly' and 'review' once more evoke the prestigious high-end criticism of review periodicals, as referenced by several other little magazines before. Both subtitles once again also attest to a belief in the unity of the arts, even though, as we shall see, this is developed less ambitiously than in some earlier little magazines. To highlight the diversity of the contents, each number of the *Dome* is divided into sections per art with a separate title page announcing successively 'Architecture' (from No. 2: 'Architecture and Sculpture'), 'Literature', 'Drawing, Painting and Engraving', and 'Music'. All sections contained both articles *on*, and specimens *of* the particular art in question.

For 'Architecture and Sculpture', drawings of the work are provided, and in one case a photograph, accompanying an article on chryselephantine sculpture by Olivier Destrée in No. 3 (September 1897), the textures and dimensions of which could of course not be conveyed in any other way. While the *CGHH* too had featured photographs of such arts in which the materiality is indispensable to an understanding of the work, this openness to new technological procedures recalls the more recent *Studio*, and the *Dome* may be said to be a modest attempt to occupy the same niche as this by then highly successful periodical, but with the added selling points of including literary contributions and of supposedly being closer to the avant-garde. The *Dome*'s pictorial art section naturally contains reproductions of painting, always produced as halftones; drawings, printed from the also photographic line blocks; as well as original engravings, printed straight from the wood. 'Music' contains sheet music and song lyrics. Most musical contributions are original work, including one early song by Elgar in No. 4 (January 1898). While the endorsement in its pages of this current by vocal partisans such as Yeats and Symons has made some critics claim the *Dome* for Symbolism,[50] no one school actually predominates, and no one artistic or literary coterie or association is more present than another. Instead, the magazine offers a wide range of recent literature, and subscribes to the same art-historical traditions that played a part in previous little magazines. The Pre-Raphaelite tradition is present through reproductions of D. G. Rossetti and Burne-Jones; and with articles on and work by Hokusai and Hiroshige, the periodical also addresses then fashionable Japanese art, a passion of the Unicorn Press reader and author Binyon. Because it is not limited to specific creeds, it has more of an opportunity than most little magazines to cover the whole of art history, and, like the publisher's 'Artist's Library' series, could apply itself to the formation of a pantheon of great art consisting of a more diverse range of hallowed artists. The typical Italian Renaissance painters and German woodcut artists are featured, but there is also a marked interest in Dutch seventeenth-century landscape painters like Meindert Hobbema, and Baroque painters such as Murillo.

Binyon's biographer John Hatcher feels that 'the slim volumes of the *Dome* [. . .] epitomise Binyon's most congenial milieu at the turn of the century and beyond: wide-ranging, non-partisan, mildly avant-garde, symbolist but emphatically post-Decadent'.[51] In fact, like the *Pageant* before it, the *Dome* was 'post-' several aspects commonly associated with Fin-de-Siècle little magazines. British Aestheticism never was devoid of a sense of humour, but some regular *Dome* contributors seem to have been especially aware of the relativity of their claims. The tone in its critical pieces veers between self-conscious irony and sincerity, especially in the frequent contributions of the editor. As we have seen, the *Yellow Book* had included a review of its own first issue in the second number, written by the established critic Hamerton in order to assertively counter negative assessments in the press (see Chapter 4). The *Dome* takes this clever scheme one step further, and has an anonymous mock-review of its first number, likely written by editor Oldmeadow, already included *in* that first number. This inventively serves as an ironic preface for the new magazine.

> As there are already quite twice as many magazines in existence as there ought to be, we are a little sorry that the Editor of this latest addition to their numbers has not condescended to spare half-a-dozen pages for

> an account of his Aims. He probably imagines that the very unwieldy sub-title tells the public quite enough; and indeed, it tells them too much, for while promising Examples of All the Arts, there is not so much as a reference to Sculpture, Poker-work, or Self-defence.[52]

The *Dome* would amend its ways so far as to cover sculpture in its future numbers, but pokers and the martial arts would regrettably remain conspicuous by their absence. It becomes clear as this 'review' goes on that the persona Oldmeadow takes up here is that of the philistine mainstream critic, who cannot grasp what 'superfine persons' (i.e. Aesthetes) look for in a magazine such as this. This critic warns that '[i]f the superfine person is at all costs to be coddled, we predict for the Dome a very short career'.[53] The point of this intentionally transparent joke is not to make fun of lay readers, who after all needed to be attracted to the *Dome* instead of antagonised. Rather, it shows such prospective readers that the standards of the magazine were not those of 'superfine' affectation, but that its principles would not be found in artistic periodicals of the mainstream, with which the supposed reviewer is meant to be identified. This is in accordance with an advertisement for the *Dome* printed in the advertisement section of the *Chord* (May 1899), in which it is stated more belligerently that 'in contents [the *Dome*] appeals only to men and women of taste'. To highlight the base preferences of the strawman/critic, he is made to lament that '[t]he letterpress strikes us most by its omissions. Has the Editor not yet heard of the Kailyard School?', whereby the *Dome* joins the controversy surrounding this contemporaneous trend of Scottish rural fiction (see Chapter 5). The *Dome*'s article by Gleeson White on Botticelli is said to be characterised by 'all the foppishness of the Culchawd Person',[54] mostly because he dares to address the problem of how the recently rediscovered painter had of late become trendy among poseurs, to the point of being undeservedly deemed unmentionable by those with a genuine passion for Renaissance painting.

The comments voiced in the mock-review are more than a disarming a priori refutation of anticipated unfavourable notices of the opening issue's contents. When we look into some of the other things the fictional critic harps on about, we come across an oblique justification of the magazine's formal features as well. There is an obvious nod to Revivalist page layout in the following remark: 'The pictures might in some instances be worse, though it is a great pity that more care has not been exercised, so as to get them exactly into the centre of the page.'[55] The margins of pages in Fine Printing publications are, of course, never equal so as to get the printed surface squarely in the centre; their relative size is usually calculated by means of a variant of the Golden Ratio to make sure that the inner margin is the narrowest, then the head, then the outer and finally the tail margin as largest. Unsurprisingly, Revivalist printers referred for this to the day of Gutenberg and Jenson. This approach was consistently kept up throughout the run of the *Dome*, as was the case in the other little magazines of the Nineties, for both letterpress and illustration, but was not observed in many cheaper magazines at the time, which increased the printed surface of the page to save paper. Related to this is another comment:

> The illustrations [. . .] are all placed together in one section – no doubt to meet the case of the superfine persons who profess to be shocked at finding 'repro' at the bottom of one page, and then, after four pages of title, picture, and blanks, 'duction' at the top of what ought to be the next. Of the superfine person, however, – although he (or more probably, she) will certainly faint at the coarseness of our parable – we should like to inquire whether suet should permeate a pudding, or lurk lumpwise in the middle, like an apple in a dumpling.[56]

In the first number of the *Dome*, as is explained with such a homely simile, all pictorial items that bear no relation to the 'Architecture' section (though in this number too consisting of drawings of buildings without textual comment) are bundled together in their own 'Drawing, Painting and Engraving' section, a practice that was already abandoned in the second issue. The problem referred to in the quote above was probably sometimes seen in sloppily printed older periodicals when letterpress and woodblocks were printed on pages of the same sheet, which often made for such unattractive solutions as described above, but no longer in literary-artistic magazines in the late-Victorian age, where the mutual boons of improved technology (among them the new photographic methods of image reproduction) and increased care had made sure that this could be avoided. Once again, the fictional critic shows off his lack of expertise, and editor Oldmeadow, comfortable behind his mask, can indirectly highlight the expertise behind the design and printing of this new periodical. As in some other little magazines, all illustrations get a separate page of their own, with the title announced on a previous page. Apart from this, the design of the *Dome* is very sober, although its typography is in itself exquisite. Titles are simply set in capitals and there are no decorated initials or other ornamental devices. As with some previously discussed magazines, some illustrations are loosely inserted plates that function as gift supplements; unfortunately, these can be difficult to retrieve because they are usually missing from library and antiquarian copies, and are often not mentioned in the tables of contents. Such plates occasionally illustrate one of the longer articles inside the issue, as is the case with a reproduction after Dutch master Hobbema in the February 1899 issue, linked to the article 'Nature and Landscape Painting' by Charles Holmes.

The *Dome*'s lack of misgivings about its commercial aspect shows from the advertisements. These advertisements appear in an unpaginated separate section at the back of the issue, which is not mentioned in the table of contents, and is usually preceded by a page simply reading 'Advertisements'; so far, this is in accordance with what we find in the more awkwardly commercialist *Yellow Book*, for instance. Among the magazine's front matter, and on both sides of the back cover, there occasionally are adverts as well; these sections are usually reserved for the magazine itself and its publisher. Like all the other little magazines, the *Dome* never places advertisements among its body text. As with all periodicals, the adverts reveals a lot about the ambitions of the magazine and the market position it coveted, and how its success or potential were assessed at the time. Recurrent adverts for the *Dome* abundantly quote reviews in international publications, from the *Guardian* (1821–) to the South African *Cape Argus* (1857–), and from Continental periodicals such as the acclaimed French magazine with Symbolist connections *Mercure de France* (1890–) and the Flemish art journal *De Vlaamse School* (1855–1901), respectively cited in the original French and Dutch. This corroborates our earlier characterisation of the *Dome* as inspired by the *Studio*, which had special columns for international correspondents and licensed successful American and French editions, and thereby could more rightfully lay claim to the title of being an internationally focused publication.

These adverts also inform the reader that 'proofs' of some plates, most likely high-quality India proofs of the loose gift supplements, are for sale from the publisher at the price of 1 guinea – as with the luxury limited editions of the magazine itself, a way to draw the attention of collectors. As is usually the case, the magazine's own publisher takes up the most advert space, publicising several pages of titles from its list. However, there are many external advertisers as well, and these are very diverse. There are, for instance, adverts for the *Artist and Journal of Home Culture*, which after all hoped to address the same readership and also competed with the *Studio*, although it had never before advertised in little magazines. We find the usual external publishers' lists as well, for instance from Chatto & Windus, but these are not as numerous as in some of our other case studies, where external publishers were the primary advertisers. As in other little magazines, some advertisements have an interesting link to the production of the *Dome*. For instance, there are regular appearances by the Strand Engraving Company, Frederick Hollyer and the Autotype Company, all three companies having been contracted by the periodical for their services pertaining to image printing. Among the readership there would also be some (aspiring) authors and artistic practitioners, and therefore it is also not surprising to see adverts here for typewriters and art supplies. One more exceptional find is an advertisement for 'Calvert's Carbolic Disinfectants', including 'soaps, ointments, toothpowder and toothpaste', strikingly even printed in plain sight on the back cover of the magazine. Printing such an advert would have been unthinkable in earlier, purportedly more purist little magazines. Oldmeadow was less fazed by the supposedly corrupting influence of the mundane outside world and did not conceptualise the *Dome* as an unassailable fortress to keep it out.

Silly as the example of the toothpowder advert may seem, its presence is symptomatic of a larger issue with major implications for aesthetic theory in the periodical press. The *Dome* contains a few statements on the Total Work of Art ideal that implicitly say a lot about the temporarily waning importance of this principle at the end of the 1890s. The diversity of the art forms and their explicit mention suggests that the magazine subscribed to the belief in the Unity of Art that we first saw explicitly defended in the *CGHH*, and their equal coverage invited cross-medial collaborations, but apart from short stories illustrated by their own artist-authors, such as again Laurence Housman, these are rare, and not intrinsically different from those in earlier magazines. In the second number, however, there is an odd aphorism by the unidentified C. H. Enston (perhaps again Oldmeadow) entitled '"Frozen Music": Fifty Words' in the 'Architecture' section that comments ambiguously on the supposed similarity between music and architecture, and by extension different art forms in general. It refers to a *bon mot* that exists in several variants attributed to Goethe and Schopenhauer, always in support of intrinsic links between the arts:

> It is true that under these Northern skies of ours her stones are nearly always icy cold; but this poor one is the only reason for naming Architecture 'Frozen Music.' It were as good, or rather as barren, a saying, that Music is Architecture false to her vow of silence.[57]

While it bears no immediate relation to the image on the opposite page, a drawing of 'Monnow Bridge' in the Welsh town of Monmouth, its inclusion in the 'Architecture' section rather than among the 'Literature' suggests that the editor wanted readers to reflect on the statement within this immediate context (Figure 41). By stating that there is no sense in likening architecture to music, the aphorism already early on in its run goes against the current of interartistic comparatism that had been typical of Aestheticism since the earliest days in the 1850s, and which it simultaneously carries out and cancels. This fragment seems a curious pastiche of Pater's essay on 'The School of Giorgione' in his *Renaissance*, which too starts with a dismissal of the misassumption that 'all the various products of art [. . .] are but translation into different languages of one and the same fixed quantity of imaginative thought', but goes on to nuance this claim in an argument that does confirm the connection between the arts and its aesthetic potential, stating that 'it is noticeable that, in its special mode of handling its given material, each art may be observed to pass into the condition of some other art, by what German critics term an *Anders-streben*'.[58] The often-cited example Pater gives is that '[a]ll art constantly aspires to the condition of music'.[59] While it would appear that the magazine wants to house the different arts under the same roof or 'dome', including both architecture and music, this contribution at least suggests that a facile equation between them compromises our understanding of each.

In fact, the title of the periodical already appeared to be a reference to a desired conceptual unity of form and content, which is problematised in later contributions as well. The architectural dome is a complex structure that crowns such places of worship as cathedrals, which in turn are a common metaphor for the potential unity of the arts. Cathedrals combine several forms of fine and applied art in their physical construction and decoration – for example, construction, sculpture and painting – and are furthermore intended to provide suitable surroundings for highly aestheticised liturgical proceedings that among others include music and the ritual choreography of the service. They are common metaphors for Total Art projects, for instance in the aforementioned description by Burne-Jones of the Kelmscott *Chaucer* as a 'pocket cathedral' (see Chapter 2). The *Dome*'s title also suggests some link with the ideas of Wagner, by way of the dome in the scenery of *Parsifal* (1882), from which springs the divine light illuminating the Grail in the final scene, when order is restored to the universe. Verlaine lets his eponymous 1886 sonnet-summary of this music drama, translated during the 1890s by Arthur Symons and John Gray, reach its climax on the ecstatic verse: 'Et, ô ces voix d'enfants chantant dans la *coupole*'. In the first number of the 'New Series' (or the sixth in the entire run of the magazine), this is further explored in the two opening items, which can be read as providing a form of rationale for this unofficial relaunch of the periodical. Oldmeadow had recently converted to Roman Catholicism, later going on to become a fervent contributor to the Catholic weekly the *Tablet* (1840–),[60] and chose to start this series of the *Dome* with a short poem named 'Introit', for the hymn beginning a Catholic mass:

> Help us, O Great Architect,
> Sure foundations here to lay,
> Though before thy Shrine we slay
> Not one ox with garlands deck'd.
> As we carve for Thee a throne,
> Guide the chisel o'er the stone,
> Guide it, O Great Architect.[61]

God, who is Art personified, is here hailed as the 'Great Architect' whose design has shaped the world. In the context of this prayer, the 'laying of foundations' mentioned is no doubt the establishment of aesthetic principles for the contents of the coming numbers, and, considered at its broadest, perhaps even for art in general. The magazine will not, however, lapse into the idolatry of debunked principles represented by the 'ox with garlands deck'd', but instead pay immediate homage to divine art.

The following item, one of the most important in the magazine, is a prose poem entitled 'The Master-Builder', named for a persona that Oldmeadow invented for himself in his capacity as editor and assumes every once in a while in a tone of mock-solemnity, which was ultimately inspired by Ibsen's play *The Master Builder* (1892). The protagonist of the play believes that he is ordained by God to become the greatest architect of all time, which dream is eventually tragically shattered. In this particular item, the *Dome*'s 'Master-Builder', though represented with the magazine's characteristic irony, similarly is an artist who claims to heed the call of the gods, and he too fails to live up to divine expectations:

> One night a certain man fell into a deep sleep. And in this sleep the gods granted him to behold a vision, strange and very glorious. And in his vision he saw a rosy sunrise; and against the sunrise a temple, rearing its proud *dome* up into the brightening sky.[62]

'The dreamer' entered the temple, which was revealed to be a glorious wonder of combined artistry. Every component of its architecture was distinguished while harmonising with its surroundings; it was decorated with exquisite paintings depicting scenes mythical and natural, and with the most beautiful sculptural ornaments. After he awakened, he decided to recreate in the real world the ideal vision which he beheld in his dream. Yet,

> because of the scantiness of his own strength, and the clumsiness of his hands, and the number and heaviness of works to be done, he sought out a hundred men, skilful with the chisel, the plumb-line, the brush, the harp, and diverse tools and instruments.[63]

This artistic labour can only be an allegory for producing the periodical work of art like the *Dome*, as editors assemble around themselves a team of contributors, designers and printers to cover an array of indispensable activities, unable to perform every task by themselves. It is important to note here, that in the spirit of the Wagnerite and Arts and Crafts versions of the Total Work of Art, this is supposed to be a communal project, where the combined efforts of every individual artist and writer, though each deserving of praise in their own right, create something which is decidedly more valuable than the sum of its parts.

Unfortunately, dream visions, for temples and magazines alike, are not lightly achieved. The setbacks that are listed here are suggestive of problems that beset the avant-garde during the Fin de Siècle. The Master-Builder found that not all artisans and artists who had agreed to contribute turned up for the promised labour. Some were 'departed into far countries, and some were busy with other building',[64] like the divided avant-garde in the 1890s that was spread across rivalling movements and coteries. Some did not understand his vision, as 'the poet had written a song of women and wine' – a debauched Decadent; 'and the musician a dirge, very lamentable' – a grim Naturalist; 'and one who should have carved a keystone into a certain great angel, showed with pride a corbel shaped into a grinning devil'[65] – perhaps an illustrator of what *Punch* called the 'Daubaway Weirdsley' school. How is it possible to work harmoniously together towards one collective end result, when you have to deal with all of these human faults and all of this incongruence?

The Master-Builder was disillusioned, but decided to make do anyway:

> Yet because he knew that nearly all the workmen had laboured heartily and with good intent, and that much people [sic] would gather on the day appointed, he commanded that certain of the stones and timber that had been wrought should nevertheless be piled and joined together.[66]

The end result, of course, did not measure up to the ideal that was presented to him in the vision, and as 'he saw [. . .] his work against a forlorn sunset, thrusting its mean dome up into the darkening sky',[67] he was at first greatly disappointed. However, he soon realised that he should find comfort in two wise lessons. The first is that '[t]o accomplish a little, as well as to dream much, was surely good'.[68] Secondly, all the criticism and divergent opinions on his imperfect life's work should be weighed against the conditions with which he had to contend: 'of the multitudes that had poured through the temple (each man declaring how he himself would have built it), there were a few of whom the dreams were less fair than his own accomplishment'.[69] That night, after the Master-Builder finally fell into a deep sleep, he once again had an audience with the gods. After he pleaded long with them to pardon him his failure, they at last smiled benevolently upon him. He woke up, looked again at the temple, and now was able for the first time to recognise in his actual achievement 'the temple of his dream'.[70]

The moral of the story is not difficult to work out. The Total Work of Art, as an untainted and fully integrated ideal work, can never be achieved. Even though it is the highest artistic ideal imaginable, we can only aspire to get as close as we possibly can, realising our artistic potential but also our inevitable shortcomings, and allow for the small ruptures that are impossible to avoid. At the end of the decade, like Beerbohm who in his facetious *Pageant* essay questioned the feasibility of the Total Work of Art and of Aestheticist creeds in general, the *Dome* humanised the myths that had informed the little magazine genre for the entire late-Victorian period. The little magazine and its connection to Total Art had a bright future ahead of it, but its role as the ideal medium of Aestheticism was coming to an end, now that the diverse artists and authors of Aestheticism were gradually letting go of their former avant-garde position.

Notes

1. Poggioli, *Theory of the Avant-Garde*, p. 226.
2. Bürger, *Theory of the Avant-Garde*, p. 27.
3. Ibid., pp. 27, 49.
4. See Eburne and Felski, 'Introduction', *passim*.
5. Maltz, *British Aestheticism and the Urban Working Classes*, p. 206.
6. Diedrick, 'Dark Blue', p. 161.
7. See Brake, '"Gay Discourse"', *passim*.
8. Rothenstein, *Men and Memories*, p. 226.
9. Beegan, '*Studio*', p. 48.

10. Gleeson White, 'Work of Charles Ricketts', p. 86.
11. 'Foreword', n.p.
12. Gleeson White, 'Work of Charles Ricketts', p. 92.
13. Ibid., p. 85.
14. Watry, *Vale Press*, p. 99.
15. Corbett, 'Symbolism in British "Little Magazines"', p. 110.
16. Jensen, *Marketing Modernism in Fin-de-Siècle Europe*, p. 139.
17. Barnes, 'Hollyer, Frederick', p. 711 .
18. 'Some Illustrated Gift-books for Children and Others Published by Messr. H. Henry and Co., Ltd.', n.p.
19. Kooistra, *Poetry, Pictures, and Popular Publishing*, p. 2.
20. Ledbetter, *Tennyson and Victorian Periodicals*, pp. 7–8.
21. 'Notices', p. 233.
22. 'in bands of liquid gold, / In a dress of fluid gold / On a white base in the evening / Tainted with green gold and with black'; 'blue Japanese jar'; 'bluish plumage' (Verlaine, 'Monna Rosa', pp. 14–16).
23. Le Dantec, 'Notes et Variantes', p. 1038.
24. Horne, *Alessandro Filipepi*, p. 158.
25. 'Messrs. Henry's Announcements', p. 12.
26. Beerbohm, 'Be It Cosiness', p. 230.
27. Ibid., p. 235.
28. Brake, '"Gay Discourse"', p. 290 n. 25.
29. 'A House of Pomegranates', p. 3.
30. Quoted in Beckson, *Oscar Wilde*, p. 125.
31. Nelson, *Publisher to the Decadents*, p. 34.
32. Kane, '*To-day* Has Never Been "Highbrow"', p. 58.
33. Quoted in Waller, *Writers, Readers and Reputations*, p. 562.
34. Gleeson White, *Children's Books and Their Illustrators*, p. 47.
35. Houfe, *Illustrators of the Nineties*, p. 150.
36. Ibid., p. 152.
37. Sumpter, *Victorian Press and the Fairy Tale*, p. 151.
38. Purcell, 'Of Purple Jars', pp. 199–200.
39. Moore, *Victorian Christmas in Print*, p. 118.
40. Kooistra, *Poetry, Pictures, and Popular Publishing*, p. 245.
41. Gleeson White, *Children's Books and Their Illustrators*, p. 14.
42. G. W. [Gleeson White], 'Preface', n.p.
43. 'Two Children's Books', p. 9.
44. Housman, 'Enchanted Princess', p. 66.
45. Herrick, 'I Call, I Call', pp. 62–3.
46. Darcy, '*Dome*', p. 116.
47. Fletcher, 'Decadence and the Little Magazines', p. 201.
48. Quoted in Stetz, 'Pre-Raphaelitism's Farewell Tour', p. 172.
49. 'A Memorandum for Collectors', p. 88.
50. See Corbett, 'Symbolism in British "Little Magazines"'; Hatcher, *Laurence Binyon*.

51. Hatcher, *Laurence Binyon*, p. 58.
52. [Oldmeadow, Ernest J.], 'Review: *The Dome*', p. 101.
53. Ibid., p. 102.
54. Ibid., p. 102.
55. Ibid., p. 102.
56. Ibid., pp. 101–2.
57. Enston [Oldmeadow?], '"Frozen Music"', p. 20.
58. Pater, 'School of Giorgione', pp. 130, 133–4.
59. Ibid., p. 135.
60. Hatcher, *Laurence Binyon*, p. 57.
61. [Oldmeadow], 'Introit', n.p.
62. [Oldmeadow], 'Master-Builder', p. 2. My emphasis.
63. Ibid., p. 2.
64. Ibid., p. 3.
65. Ibid., p. 3.
66. Ibid., p. 3.
67. Ibid., p. 4.
68. Ibid., p. 4.
69. Ibid., p. 4.
70. Ibid., p. 4.

Inconclusions

Fifty years and thirteen periodicals later, a narrative has emerged for the early history of the little magazine genre, which has revealed itself to have developed alongside the diverse but overlapping schools of aesthetic theory, literary writing and artistic practice that are now commonly designated as Aestheticism. The *Germ* of Aestheticism was also that of the little magazine in Britain, and arguably even of the avant-garde position on which both (initially) relied. The Pre-Raphaelite Brotherhood established their periodical organ in order to circulate their art and opinions without having to defer to the authority of external editors, and to sidestep the demands of a market intent on the short-term profit that they neither could nor wished to guarantee. In doing so, they established a basic format for such low-circulation periodicals issued by groups of heterodox self-declared artistic and literary dissidents, or the avant-garde, in their challenge to a perceived alliance of commercial, aesthetic and ideological orthodoxy, jumbled together in the equally vague category of the mainstream. This dualism was applied opportunistically, but it underpinned the rhetoric of all avant-garde output, periodical or otherwise.

Aestheticism, as said in the Introduction to this book, is an umbrella term covering a host of divergent opinions, but one shared doctrine is that the sphere of art is potentially expansive and should be made to cover as many aspects of individual and social life as possible. Already in the context of *The Germ*, the individual contribution was presented as potentially autonomous but not meant to function only on its own; the magazine as carrier of the content was designed so as to add coherence to the text and a combined meaning and aesthetic value that is greater than the sum of its parts: a first step towards the ideal of the Total Work of Art. When adopting *The Germ*'s early little magazine model, subsequent groups would integrate into their periodical projects ever more aspects of its publication context and surroundings, going beyond the integration of content into a common ideological and artistic system soon after, when the *Oxford and Cambridge Magazine* added a political dimension to this still fundamentally artistic concept. This stimulated the incorporation of the magazine's production methods into the artistic process in later little magazines. The *Century Guild Hobby Horse* saw the different skills going into its production as forms of applied art on a par with the fine arts and literature of the contents, an outlook that fitted in with the ongoing Revival of Fine Printing. The Revivalists believed a printed text should be a fully integrated design endeavour, and now the choice of materials became 'aestheticised' as well. Later journals would function as meticulously coordinated portfolios for close-knit coteries (the *Dial*) or even individuals (the *Pagan Review* and the *Page*) to circulate samples of their talents, and to practise their skills in applied, fine or literary art. Politicised artistic associations such as the Arts and Crafts Movement (of the *Quest*) and the Celtic Revival (the *Evergreen*) likewise saw the potential of the little magazine as a collective, ostensibly uncompromising Total Work of Art that could carry their message and exemplify their beliefs. Along the way, businesses that were not run by art practitioners or authors themselves saw potential in the little magazines as commodities, and appropriated the genre to expand it towards the mainstream market. In the *Yellow Book* and already less so the *Savoy*, this happened with a disingenuous show of commercial disinterestedness that was belied by their marketing strategies, but both retained the basic function of the little magazine as a means of disseminating the work of (among others) authors and artists identifying as avant-garde, and the dedication to an impeccable visual and material presentation. Finally, at the end of the decade, due to the cumbersome associations with the Wilde affair and a changed situation in the periodical press, it was no longer deemed opportune to even claim an exclusive avant-garde position for Aestheticism, and three divergent but principally similar publications (the *Pageant*, the *Parade* and the *Dome*) gave up the alleged purism of the genre in order to adopt features from other periodical formats that were openly commercial.

Thus concludes the story of the little magazine of the late-Victorian era. However, we have had occasion to note before that history does not start afresh at the end of decades, centuries or reigns of monarchs who give their names to historical eras. While this is all too obvious, the always debatable demarcation of eras is a genuine problem for cultural historians who need to make sense of the fact that any period that they suggest will contain traces of the preceding one, and the spores of the next. Both the little magazine and the Aestheticist legacy are such phenomena that overstay their historical welcome and refused to go away at the *fin* of the Fin de Siècle. Arnold Bennett, best-selling novelist and celebrity omelette namesake of the early twentieth century, had started his career modestly in the 1890s, and before his first book came out had a story in the sixth number of the *Yellow Book* of July 1895. According to Peter McDonald, 'the publication of **his** tale in **that** periodical radically altered his sense of his position, or potential position, in the literary field', because it showed him that there were alternative media out there that would publish the style of literature that he himself admired, instead of the potboilers pitched to no-risk mainstream periodicals and publishers who still complied with the moralism of Mudie's Library.[1] A few years into the next century, Bennett's combined commercial and critical success had made him an authority on all matters authorial, and apart from books on how to get published, he also furnished a column on 'Books and Persons' to the left-wing and avant-garde-leaning weekly the *New Age* (1907–22). In the instalment of 8 September 1910, he gives advice to the editors of an unidentified new 'purely literary paper' that had recently been announced: 'The aim of the paper will be to print, and to sell, imaginative writing of the highest character. Its purpose is artistic, and neither political nor moral. Dangers and difficulties lie before an enterprise of this kind.'[2] This sounds familiar. Bennett warns the prospective editors that the primary difficulty is to maintain a level of consistent quality for the contents, as 'the whole mass of really high-class stuff produced is relatively small':[3]

> There are dozens and scores of men who can write stuff which has all the mannerisms and external characteristics of high-class stuff, but which is not high-class. Extinct exotic periodicals, such as the Yellow Book, the Savoy, the Dial, the Anglo-Saxon, and such publications as the Neolith, richly prove this. What was and is the matter with all of them is literary priggishness, and dullness. One used to read them more as a duty than as a pleasure. A great danger is the inevitable tendency to disdain the public, and to appeal only to artists. Artists, like washer-women, cannot live on one another.[4]

The *Anglo-Saxon Review* (1898–1901), though published by John Lane, was not a little magazine, but an Imperialist quarterly that was edited by Lady Randolph Churchill, and that offered a mixture of highbrow literature and casually racist articles on the state of the Empire, each number issued in a replica of old, gilt-tooled leather Renaissance bindings that are always explicated in an opening essay. The *Neolith* (1907–8) was a literary and artistic journal issued by E[dith] Nesbit that is notable for having been almost completely hand-lettered, and printed by means of lithography. Both publications, as can already be inferred from how Bennett discusses them, are examples of materially overambitious periodicals for which the combined insistence on formal opulence and elitist content made it impossible to attract a sufficiently large readership.

Though Bennett himself no longer had any need for periodicals of a clearly avant-garde disposition and may by then have been embarrassed about the company he had kept in the 1890s, he seems not to be primarily disparaging the contents of these magazines, which due to the significance to himself of the most famous one mentioned would be rather transparently hypocritical. Rather, he finds fault with how these *presented* themselves to the public. His description of the avant-garde position as catering only for its peers is strikingly similar to Bourdieu's notion of the field of restricted production in which cultural wares are in the first place produced for other producers (see Chapter 1). The 'priggishness' and 'dullness' that they exude are related to their material presentation and marketing strategies, both relatable to the magazine as a Total Work of Art because they involve the internal cohesion and outward aspect of the journals in question. By indicating that the setbacks of the *Yellow Book* were perceived as paradigmatic and still threatening examples at the end of the Edwardian era, he furthermore points out a lasting legacy, and at exactly the time that modernism studies usually situates the first instances of the little magazines that supposedly had started to 'Make It New'.

With *The Little Magazine: A History and a Bibliography* (1947), Hoffmann et al. have bequeathed us a very useful study that has informed a growing body of scholarship on this genre. They would, however, have been very surprised to have seen publications from the 1850s in this book on the early history of the little magazine genre. Indeed, for several decades virtually all work done on the little magazine happened within the institutional limits of modernism studies, which long took at their word the master critics of its own institutionalised canon, whose critical writings were often riddled with a near-Oedipal disdain for the preceding generation. For many of these, even the Fin de Siècle might as well have been the dark ages, and we have had to wait for the publication of the three volumes of the admirable multivolume *Oxford Critical and Cultural History of Modernist Magazines* (2009–13) for a number of nineteenth-century examples to be reinstated as belonging to the same genre as a high-modernist journal such as *BLAST* (1914–15). Yet, there too, the '*[m]odernist*' perspective of the series put the covered Victorian little magazines in a teleological framework that made the Victorian journals seem valid only as precursors to the supposed real thing of the twentieth century. More recently, an otherwise brilliant book by Robert Scholes and Clifford Wulfman appears to have situated the socio-economic and technological developments necessary for the emergence of modernism (and by implication of the little magazine as they see the two as intimately connected) only in the 1890s, which, as argued, is a few decades too late.[5]

If scholars of early-twentieth-century literature and art until fairly recently sometimes made the mistake of thinking that the switch to experimental art and literature happened only when Virginia Woolf's half-serious essay allowed it to, the little magazines of the Edwardian/Georgian and modernist periods were clearly still informed by their Victorian forebears. Chapter 6 ended on a discussion of the *Dome*, because it obligingly engages with the dissolution of the doctrines of Aestheticism and pretensions of avant-garde elitism, and conveniently does this at the end of the 1890s, but it was not the last journal to be at least informed by the principles of Aestheticist little magazines.

The *Venture* (1903–4), for instance, was another annual between hard boards like the *Pageant* and the *Parade*. Its first of two issues was edited by Laurence Housman and a young W. Somerset Maugham, and it also in other ways exemplifies the long moment of transition of the period between the death of Victoria and the outbreak of the First World War. According to his biographer Rodney Engen, Housman accepted the job because of the relative commercial success of the *Dome*, to which he had been a frequent contributor, and it is true that the *Venture* too delivers a cross-section of recent art with only a minimum of shock value or doctrinal zealotry.[6] It includes several familiar names from the 1890s, such as virtually the entire Vale coterie familiar from the *Dial* and the *Pageant* and Arthur Symons, but also contributors who are nowadays rather associated with the early twentieth century, such as G. K. Chesterton, John Masefield, James Joyce (who still thought he wanted to be a poet instead of a novelist) and the regenerate Thomas Hardy (who had only recently realised that he actually wanted to be a poet instead of a novelist). Housman stepped down for the second issue and left Somerset Maugham to his own devices, but his designs for the first number contain references that we nowadays think of as quintessentially Aestheticist, such as vaguely menacing peacocks on the endpapers, and a *japoniste* frontispiece.

Housman would later recall that '[his] one experiment in editing was not a success, though I think it deserved to be'.[7] A reviewer thought that even the second number resembled '"the Hobby Horse"' and the '"Yellow Book" of ten years ago', which is an interesting remark because it suggests that these were already then starting to be seen as respected but superseded relics of a bygone age.[8] The *Venture* clearly ran into similar problems as the little magazines of the 1890s as well. Contributors were not paid in advance, but had agreed to a share of the profits – if any – and nobody got any money in the end. Housman believed that 'the whole thing was, of course, too highbrow to be popular: perhaps if it had been published at a guinea instead of five shillings, it would have done better', wryly alluding to the practice of publishing houses like the Bodley Head, and others in its wake, of suggesting rarity and intrinsic value for their periodicals by means of a high price and luxurious collector's editions.[9] Somerset Maugham also did not make a lot of money from editing the *Venture* instantly, but in the best little magazine tradition, he did receive some exposure for his own writing, and he managed to expand his professional network.[10] As before, there are advertisements in the *Venture* that prominently feature publications by, or galleries and art schools associated with, contributing authors and artists, all serving the old purpose of the little magazine as a means of publicity. Recent research by Leah Budke has suggested that the annual anthology of female poets *Wheels* (1916–21), very similar in concept and design to the *Venture* and its 1890s predecessors, consciously 'used the tradition of aestheticism and Decadence as their chosen weapon' in the battle against a mainstream that they perceived as inherently misogynist.[11]

Despite the ironic distancing that many actual contributors would later maintain towards the *Yellow Book*, when little magazine editors of the early twentieth century referred to any precursors at all, this controversial periodical was usually their point of reference. This was no doubt due to the impact it had made by combining content that challenged moral and artistic orthodoxy with a thought-out and initially successful marketing strategy. When John Middleton Murry set up his *Rhythm* (1911–13), he wanted it to be 'the *Yellow Book* for the modern movement',[12] and when his magazine reinvented itself under the title of the *Blue Review* for its final three issues, regular contributor Rupert Brooke tried to entice engraver Gwen Raverat by telling her that the new journal would be 'better than the *Yellow Book* or the Pre-Raphaelites or any other body', affirming a perceived continuous tradition from this early-modernist journal all the way back to *The Germ*.[13] Faith Binckes has suggested that what

Murry found appealing in the *Yellow Book* was John Lane's strategy of 'ensuring the connection between literary talent', to which we might add artistic talent, 'and commercial viability while simultaneously disowning it'.[14] Wyndham Lewis shouted in *BLAST* (1914–15), the loudest little magazine of the modernist age, that one of the supposedly obsolete cultural phenomena to be blasted was the inheritance of the 1890s, 'that debile and sinister race of diabolical dandies and erotically bloated diablesses and their attendant abortions', and singled out the *Yellow Book* as its representative.[15] However, his magazine was published by John Lane, who, as he had done twenty years before, smelled an opportunity to cash in on polemical avant-gardists who would clamour for attention until the mainstream market was forced to take note, and thereby consolidate the reputation of the publisher as connected to the latest new literary and artistic crazes. In an advertisement for *BLAST*'s first number included in the second issue, which contained Lewis's denunciation of the little magazines of the 1890s, Lane included a press excerpt from a review in the *Sunday Times* explicitly stating that '[w]hat the Yellow Book did for the artistic movement of its decade, BLAST aims at doing for the arts and literature of to-day'.[16] In fact, the advertisement section for BLAST's first number itself had publicised the 'Complete Set of Thirteen Volumes' of the *Yellow Book*, and advertised work by several other authors and artists who would be castigated in the second. There is nothing new under the sun.

As late as 1917, *BLAST* contributor Ezra Pound wrote to Margaret Anderson of the American *Little Review* (1914–29), for whom he scouted for copy in London, that old veteran of the 1890s little magazines Arthur Symons hoped to get a new play published and 'would rather have it in us and not get paid than to have me send it elsewhere and get paid'.[17] Anderson herself, though a wily and daring businesswoman, acknowledged journals of the 1890s as representative of the genre to which her own periodical belonged. In her memoirs, she recalls that friends warned her about the chances of success:

> Look at the 'Yellow Book.' It had the backing of John Lane and everyone on its staff, even Henry James. And it couldn't keep alive a year. [sic] Well yes, said I, look at the 'Yellow Book.' You can look at it on the library shelves of almost any book lover, richly bound, and rated among his more precious possessions.[18]

Of course, the *Yellow Book* 'kept alive' for three years instead of one, but Anderson's friends were certainly right about the commercial challenge of keeping a journal alive on new principles against which the ever-fickle public can turn, or that they can simply tire of, at any moment. Her courageous reply that she acknowledged this, but that she admired it as an artistic object with lasting value, is testimony to the enduring legacy of Aestheticist little magazines.

Explicit references to Victorian little magazines continue to appear throughout the twentieth century, and with the recent resurgence of the *Evergreen* as discussed in Chapter 5, can be found in our own century as well. We, however, have to halt our history somewhere. At least now we know where it should begin.

Notes

1. McDonald, *British Literary Culture and Publishing Practice*, p. 70. Emphases original.
2. Bennett, 'Literary Periodical', p. 242.
3. Ibid., p. 243.
4. Ibid., p. 243.
5. Scholes and Wulfman, *Modernism in the Magazines*, p. 27.
6. Engen, *Laurence Housman*, p. 95.
7. Housman, *Unexpected Years*, p. 202.
8. 'Christmas Books. Final Notice', p. 5.
9. Housman, *Unexpected Years*, p. 202.
10. Hastings, *Secret Lives of Somerset Maugham*, p. 88.
11. Budke, 'Reading Edith Sitwell's Annual Poetry Anthology Wheels', *passim*.
12. Quoted in Binckes, *Modernism, Magazines and the British Avant-Garde*, p. 47.
13. Quoted in ibid., p. 166.
14. Ibid., p. 38.
15. Lewis, 'Art of the Great Race', p. 70.
16. 'Some Press Notices', n.p.
17. Quoted in Bishop, 'Re:Covering Modernism', p. 307.
18. Anderson, *My Thirty Years' War*, p. 42.

Appendix: Illustrations

Unless indicated otherwise, all images were supplied by the Mark Samuels Lasner Collection, University of Delaware Library.

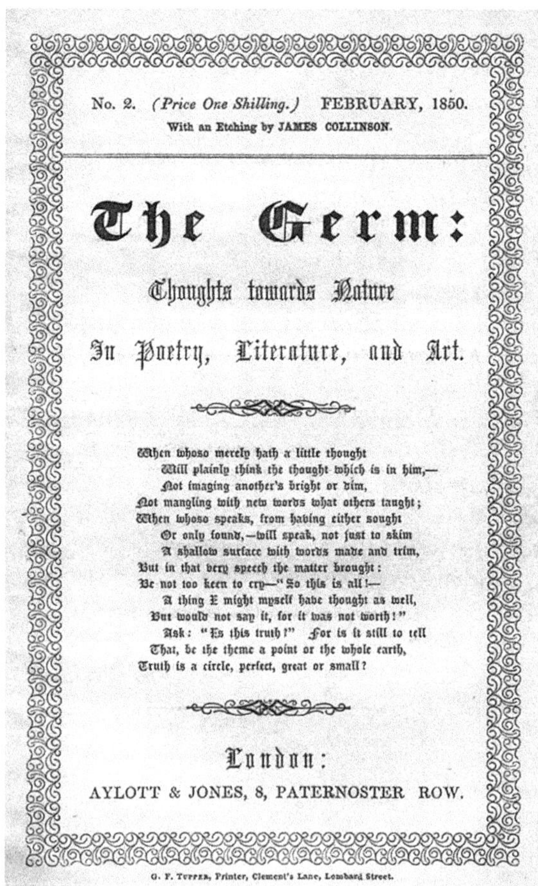

No. 2. *(Price One Shilling.)* FEBRUARY, 1850.
With an Etching by JAMES COLLINSON.

The Germ:

Thoughts towards Nature

In Poetry, Literature, and Art.

When whoso merely hath a little thought
Will plainly think the thought which is in him,—
Not imaging another's bright or dim,
Not mangling with new words what others taught;
When whoso speaks, from having either sought
Or only found,—will speak, not just to skim
A shallow surface with words made and trim,
But in that very speech the matter brought:
Be not too keen to cry—"So this is all!—
A thing I might myself have thought as well,
But would not say it, for it was not worth!"
Ask: "Is this truth?" For is it still to tell
That, be the theme a point or the whole earth,
Truth is a circle, perfect, great or small?

London:

AYLOTT & JONES, 8, PATERNOSTER ROW.

G. F. Tupper, Printer, Clement's Lane, Lombard Street.

Figure 1 Title page, *The Germ* 2 (February 1850).

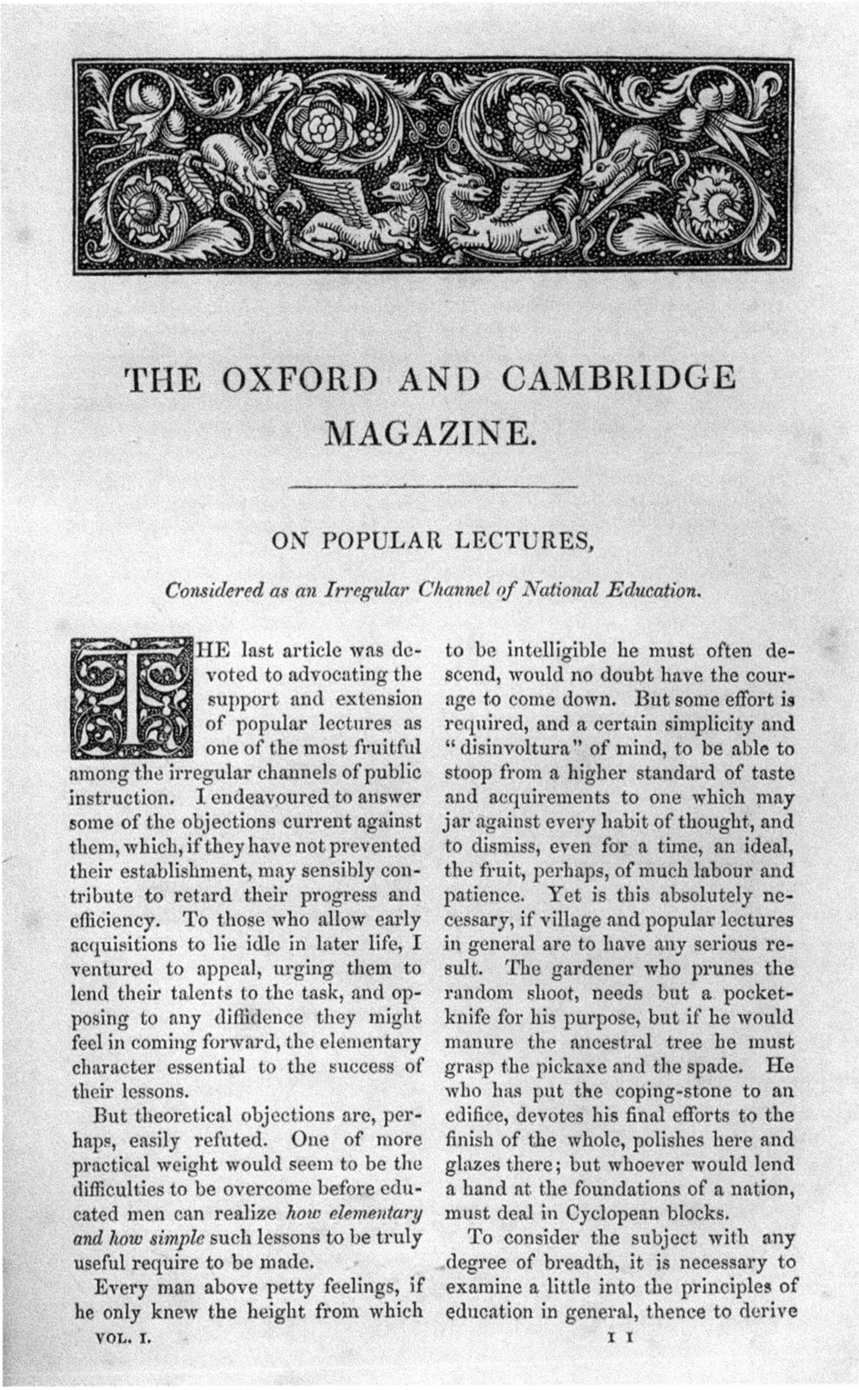

THE OXFORD AND CAMBRIDGE MAGAZINE.

ON POPULAR LECTURES,

Considered as an Irregular Channel of National Education.

THE last article was devoted to advocating the support and extension of popular lectures as one of the most fruitful among the irregular channels of public instruction. I endeavoured to answer some of the objections current against them, which, if they have not prevented their establishment, may sensibly contribute to retard their progress and efficiency. To those who allow early acquisitions to lie idle in later life, I ventured to appeal, urging them to lend their talents to the task, and opposing to any diffidence they might feel in coming forward, the elementary character essential to the success of their lessons.

But theoretical objections are, perhaps, easily refuted. One of more practical weight would seem to be the difficulties to be overcome before educated men can realize *how elementary and how simple* such lessons to be truly useful require to be made.

Every man above petty feelings, if he only knew the height from which to be intelligible he must often descend, would no doubt have the courage to come down. But some effort is required, and a certain simplicity and "disinvoltura" of mind, to be able to stoop from a higher standard of taste and acquirements to one which may jar against every habit of thought, and to dismiss, even for a time, an ideal, the fruit, perhaps, of much labour and patience. Yet is this absolutely necessary, if village and popular lectures in general are to have any serious result. The gardener who prunes the random shoot, needs but a pocket-knife for his purpose, but if he would manure the ancestral tree he must grasp the pickaxe and the spade. He who has put the coping-stone to an edifice, devotes his final efforts to the finish of the whole, polishes here and glazes there; but whoever would lend a hand at the foundations of a nation, must deal in Cyclopean blocks.

To consider the subject with any degree of breadth, it is necessary to examine a little into the principles of education in general, thence to derive

VOL. I. I I

Figure 2 *Oxford and Cambridge Magazine* 8 (August 1856), p. 11.

145

Viola and Olivia.

When Viola, a servant of the Duke,
Of him she loved the page, went, sent by him,
To tell Olivia that great love which shook
His breast and stopt his tongue; was it a whim,
Or jealousy or fear that she must look
Upon the face of that Olivia?

'Tis hard to say if it were whim or fear
Or jealousy, but it was natural,
As natural as what came next, the near
Intelligence of hearts: Olivia
Loveth, her eye abused by a thin wall
Of custom, but her spirit's eyes were clear.

Clear? we have oft been curious to know
The after-fortunes of those lovers dear;
Having a steady faith some deed must show
That they were married souls—unmarried here—
Having an inward faith that love, called so
In verity, is of the spirit, clear
Of earth and dress and sex—it may be near
What Viola returned Olivia?

K

Figure 3 *Art and Poetry/The Germ* 4 (April 1850), pp. 144–5.

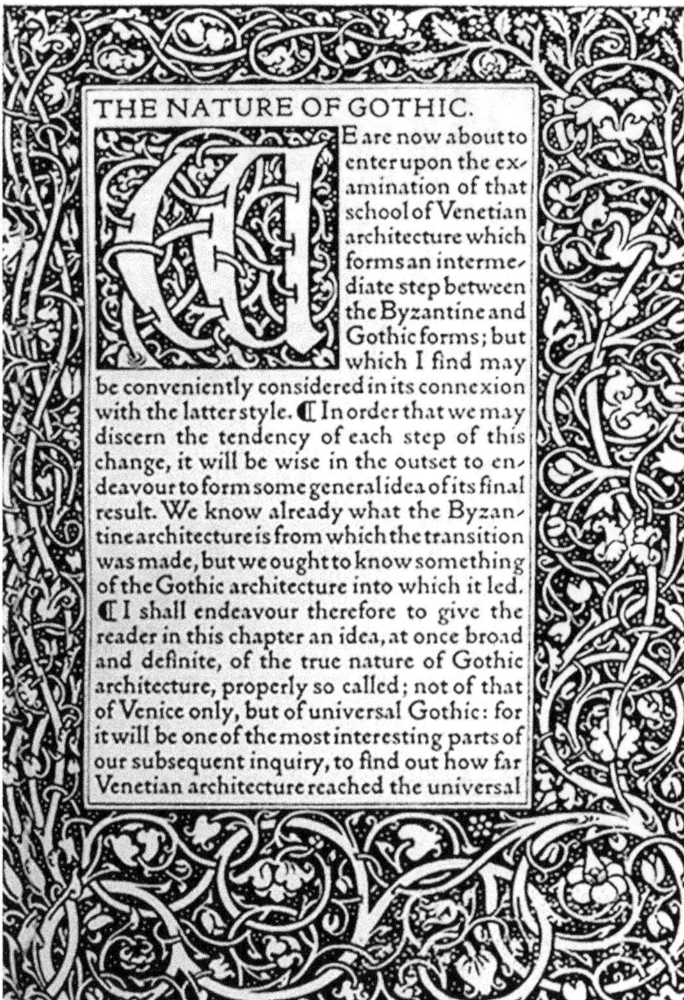

THE NATURE OF GOTHIC.

WE are now about to enter upon the examination of that school of Venetian architecture which forms an intermediate step between the Byzantine and Gothic forms; but which I find may be conveniently considered in its connexion with the latter style. ¶ In order that we may discern the tendency of each step of this change, it will be wise in the outset to endeavour to form some general idea of its final result. We know already what the Byzantine architecture is from which the transition was made, but we ought to know something of the Gothic architecture into which it led. ¶ I shall endeavour therefore to give the reader in this chapter an idea, at once broad and definite, of the true nature of Gothic architecture, properly so called; not of that of Venice only, but of universal Gothic: for it will be one of the most interesting parts of our subsequent inquiry, to find out how far Venetian architecture reached the universal

Figure 4 *The Nature of Gothic* (London: Kelmscott Press, 1892), p. 1.

Figure 5 Front cover, *Century Guild Hobby Horse* 12 (October 1888).

Figure 6 Front cover, *Hobby Horse* 3 (October 1894).

ON SOME OLD TITLE-PAGES, WITH A SKETCH OF THEIR ORIGIN, AND SOME SUGGESTIONS FOR THE IMPROVEMENT OF MODERN ONES.

In the year 1650 was born John Bagford. His father apprenticed him to a shoemaker, but Nature had intended him to be the minister and scourge of bookmen, and to this end it was necessary for him to leave his last and seek his living as a caterer for the libraries of great men. He served his patrons honestly and well. His most embittered biographers do justice to the untiring zeal which made him take walking tours through Holland and Germany in search of bargains, and so little profit did he make from his business that it was only a nomination to the Charterhouse that saved his old age from penury. He was one of the resuscitators of the Society of Antiquaries; he made a famous collection of old ballads; and his contemporaries, when he died in 1716, paid elaborate compliments to his memory. Yet that memory has ever since been execrated, and the justice of the execration is indisputable. When the name of John Bagford is mentioned book-lovers hiss through their teeth the word Biblioclast, and in that mysterious expression lies the secret of his misdoing. "He spent his life," says his latest biographer with terrible judiciality, "in collecting materials for a history of printing which he was quite incompetent to write." His materials were title-pages, and it is probably a moderate estimate which places the number of them at about five-and-twenty thousand. About ten thousand of these are pasted into nine large folio volumes which now belong to the Department of Printed Books in the British Museum; the rest form part of the one hundred and ninety-eight volumes of his Remains in the Harleian Collection in the Department of Manuscripts of the same institution. Specimens of Chinese paper, fragments of rare bindings, engravings, initial letters, publishers' marks, literary correspondence, lives of the early English printers in Bagford's manuscript, make up the other volumes of this melancholy, yet profoundly interesting, collection; and if there be any reader of this paper possessed of a little learned leisure, it

57 I

Figure 7 *Century Guild Hobby Horse* 10 (April 1888), p. 57.

CONTENTS OF NO. VII.

The Initial Letters and Tailpieces in this Number are designed by Selwyn Image, and cut by C. M. Padday.

Figure 8 Detail contents page *Century Guild Hobby Horse* 7 (July 1887).

Figure 9 Frontispiece *Dial* 1 (1898).

Figure 10 Frontispiece *Dial* 2 (1892).

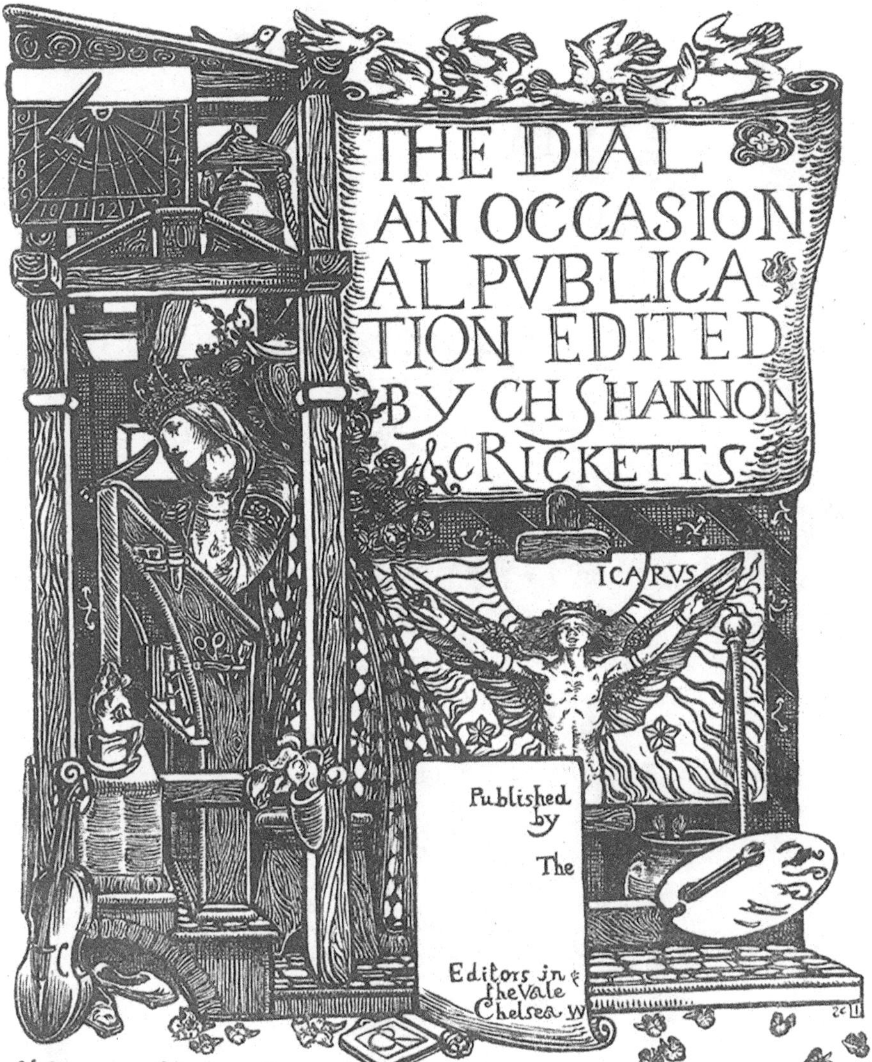

Figure 11 Front cover *Dial* 2 (1892).

N° 1.
August 15, 1892.

THE
PAGAN REVIEW

. . . . Foreword.
W. S. Fanshawe: The Black Madonna.
Geo. Gascoigne: The Coming of Love.
Willand Dreeme: The Pagans: a Romance.
Lionel Wingrave: An Untold Story.
James Marazion: The Rape of the Sabines.
Charles Verlayne: The Oread.
Wm. Windover: Dionysos in India.
Contemporary Record.
Editorial.

Sic Transit Gloria Grundi.
One Shilling.

Figure 12 Front cover *Pagan Review* (1892).

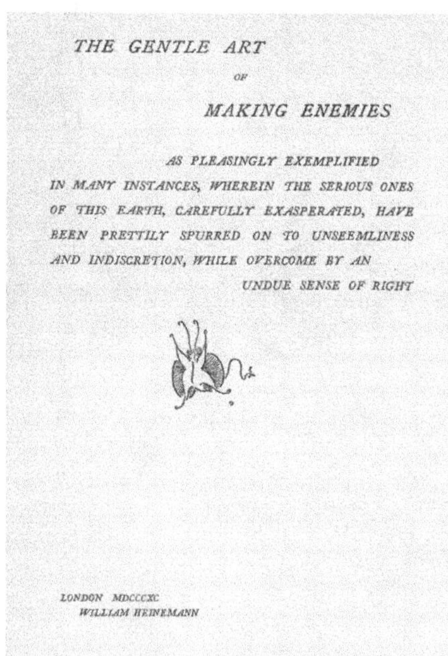

THE GENTLE ART
OF
MAKING ENEMIES

AS PLEASINGLY EXEMPLIFIED
IN MANY INSTANCES, WHEREIN THE SERIOUS ONES
OF THIS EARTH, CAREFULLY EXASPERATED, HAVE
BEEN PRETTILY SPURRED ON TO UNSEEMLINESS
AND INDISCRETION, WHILE OVERCOME BY AN
UNDUE SENSE OF RIGHT

LONDON MDCCCXC
WILLIAM HEINEMANN

Figure 13 Title page J. M. Whistler, *The Gentle Art of Making Enemies* (London: Heinemann, 1890).

Figure 14 *Page* 2.2 (February 1899), n.p. © British Library.

Figure 15 *Page* 1.2 (February 1898), supplement. © British Library.

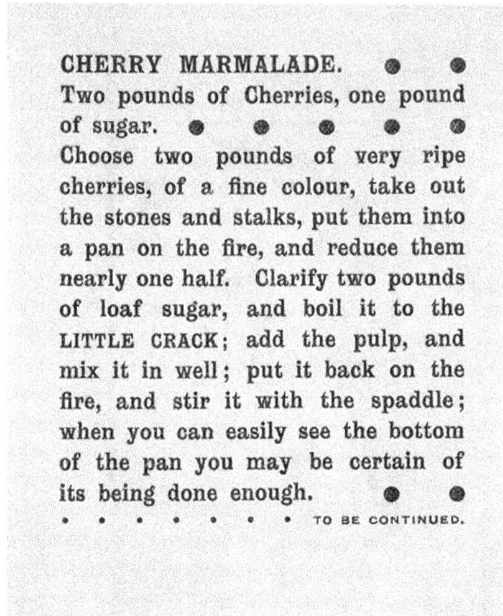

CHERRY MARMALADE. ● ●
Two pounds of Cherries, one pound of sugar. ● ● ● ● ●
Choose two pounds of very ripe cherries, of a fine colour, take out the stones and stalks, put them into a pan on the fire, and reduce them nearly one half. Clarify two pounds of loaf sugar, and boil it to the LITTLE CRACK; add the pulp, and mix it in well; put it back on the fire, and stir it with the spaddle; when you can easily see the bottom of the pan you may be certain of its being done enough. ● ●
• • • • • • • TO BE CONTINUED.

Figure 16 *Page* 1.8 (August 1898), n.p. © British Library.

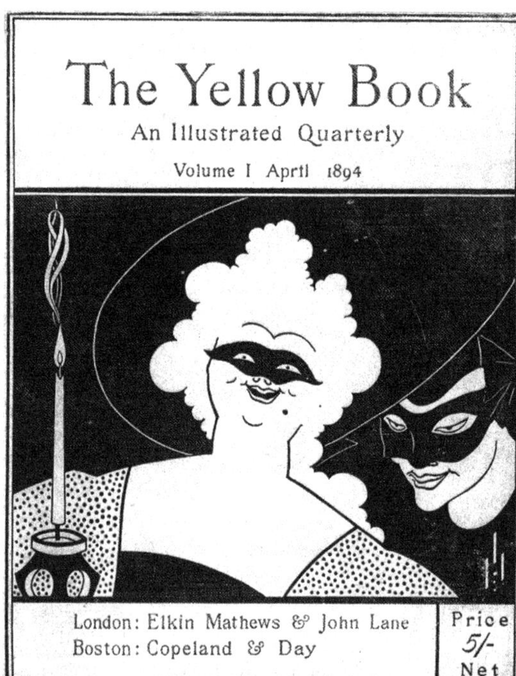

Figure 17 Front cover *Yellow Book* 1 (April 1894).

Figure 18 *Yellow Book* 1 (April 1894), p. 217.

Figure 19 *Yellow Book* 4 (January 1895), supplement.

Figure 20 *Punch* (2 February 1895), p. 58.

Figure 21 Promotional poster *Yellow Book* (1894).

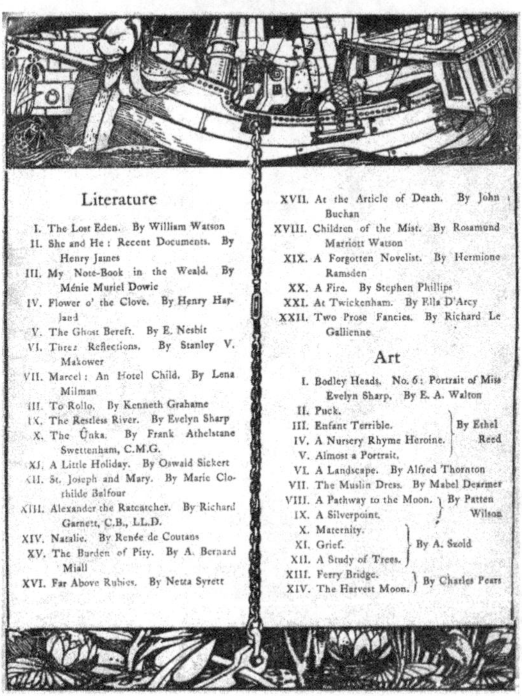

Figure 22 Back cover *Yellow Book* 12 (January 1897).

Figure 23 *Yellow Book* 6 (July 1895), p. 117.

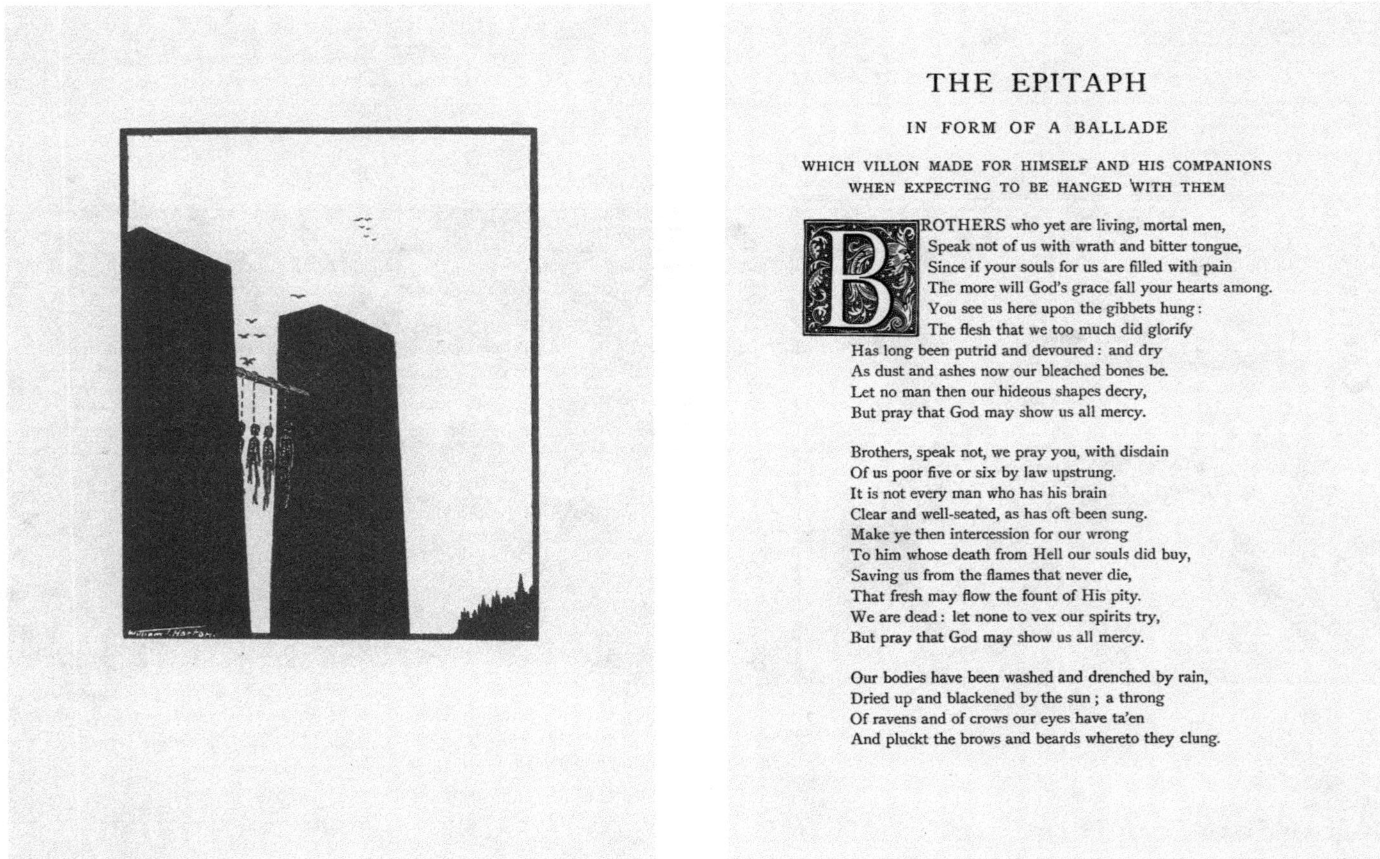

THE EPITAPH

IN FORM OF A BALLADE

WHICH VILLON MADE FOR HIMSELF AND HIS COMPANIONS
WHEN EXPECTING TO BE HANGED WITH THEM

BROTHERS who yet are living, mortal men,
Speak not of us with wrath and bitter tongue,
Since if your souls for us are filled with pain
The more will God's grace fall your hearts among.
You see us here upon the gibbets hung:
The flesh that we too much did glorify
Has long been putrid and devoured: and dry
As dust and ashes now our bleached bones be.
Let no man then our hideous shapes decry,
But pray that God may show us all mercy.

Brothers, speak not, we pray you, with disdain
Of us poor five or six by law upstrung.
It is not every man who has his brain
Clear and well-seated, as has oft been sung.
Make ye then intercession for our wrong
To him whose death from Hell our souls did buy,
Saving us from the flames that never die,
That fresh may flow the fount of His pity.
We are dead: let none to vex our spirits try,
But pray that God may show us all mercy.

Our bodies have been washed and drenched by rain,
Dried up and blackened by the sun; a throng
Of ravens and of crows our eyes have ta'en
And pluckt the brows and beards whereto they clung.

Figure 24 *Savoy* 6 (October 1896), pp. 60–1.

Figure 25 *Savoy* 1 (January 1896), n.p.

Figure 26 Detail *Savoy* 1 (January 1896), supplement.

Figure 27 Front cover *Quest* 1 (November 1894).

work without any conscious moral purpose. Yet if his work is really great, it will exercise a moral influence; for it will be the product of a great and serious mind. Such an artist resembles those constructors of cathedrals of whom Emerson said "They builded better than they knew."

E. A. Sonnenschein.

The writer desires to acknowledge obligations in the latter part of his paper to Bosanquet's History of Aesthetic.

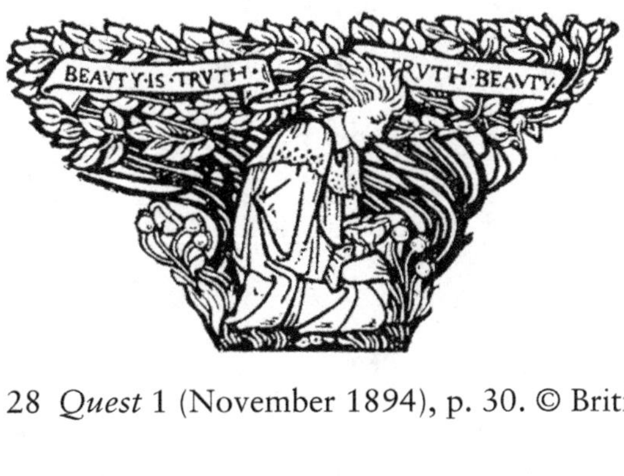

Figure 28 *Quest* 1 (November 1894), p. 30. © British Library.

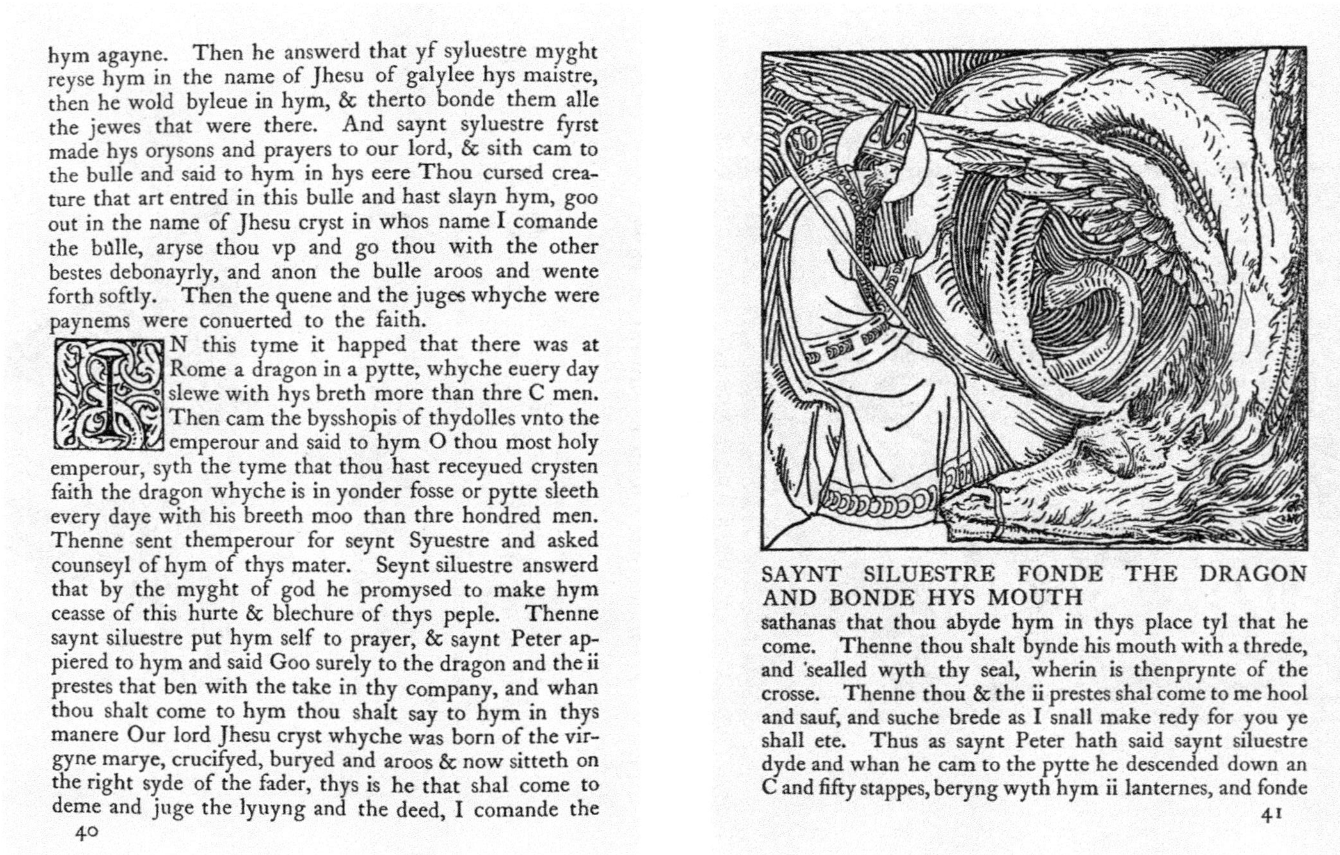

hym agayne. Then he answerd that yf syluestre myght reyse hym in the name of Jhesu of galylee hys maistre, then he wold byleue in hym, & therto bonde them alle the jewes that were there. And saynt syluestre fyrst made hys orysons and prayers to our lord, & sith cam to the bulle and said to hym in hys eere Thou cursed creature that art entred in this bulle and hast slayn hym, goo out in the name of Jhesu cryst in whos name I comande the bulle, aryse thou vp and go thou with the other bestes debonayrly, and anon the bulle aroos and wente forth softly. Then the quene and the juges whyche were paynems were conuerted to the faith.

IN this tyme it happed that there was at Rome a dragon in a pytte, whyche euery day slewe with hys breth more than thre C men. Then cam the bysshopis of thydolles vnto the emperour and said to hym O thou most holy emperour, syth the tyme that thou hast receyued crysten faith the dragon whyche is in yonder fosse or pytte sleeth every daye with his breeth moo than thre hondred men. Thenne sent themperour for seynt Syuestre and asked counseyl of hym of thys mater. Seynt siluestre answerd that by the myght of god he promysed to make hym ceasse of this hurte & blechure of thys peple. Thenne saynt siluestre put hym self to prayer, & saynt Peter appiered to hym and said Goo surely to the dragon and the ii prestes that ben with the take in thy company, and whan thou shalt come to hym thou shalt say to hym in thys manere Our lord Jhesu cryst whyche was born of the virgyne marye, crucifyed, buryed and aroos & now sitteth on the right syde of the fader, thys is he that shal come to deme and juge the lyuyng and the deed, I comande the

40

SAYNT SILUESTRE FONDE THE DRAGON AND BONDE HYS MOUTH

sathanas that thou abyde hym in thys place tyl that he come. Thenne thou shalt bynde his mouth with a threde, and 'sealled wyth thy seal, wherin is thenprynte of the crosse. Thenne thou & the ii prestes shal come to me hool and sauf, and suche brede as I snall make redy for you ye shall ete. Thus as saynt Peter hath said saynt siluestre dyde and whan he cam to the pytte he descended down an C and fifty stappes, beryng wyth hym ii lanternes, and fonde

41

Figure 29 *Quest* 1 (November 1894), pp. 40–1. © British Library.

Figure 30 Frontispiece *Quest* 1 (November 1894), n.p. © British Library.

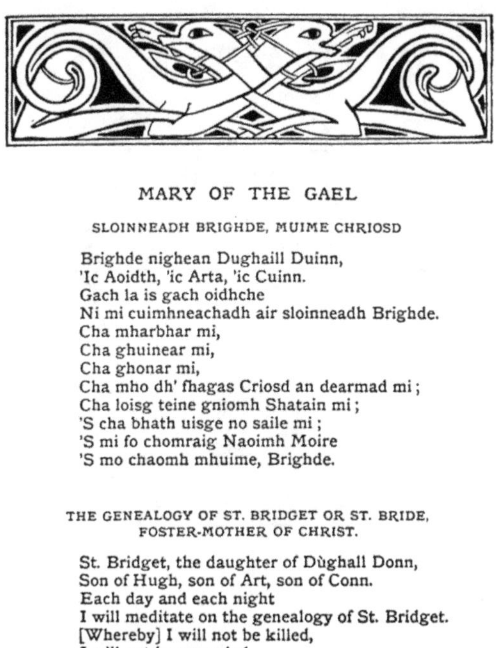

MARY OF THE GAEL

SLOINNEADH BRIGHDE, MUIME CHRIOSD

Brighde nighean Dughaill Duinn,
'Ic Aoidth, 'ic Arta, 'ic Cuinn.
Gach la is gach oidhche
Ni mi cuimhneachadh air sloinneadh Brighde.
Cha mharbhar mi,
Cha ghuinear mi,
Cha ghonar mi,
Cha mho dh' fhagas Criosd an dearmad mi;
Cha loisg teine gniomh Shatain mi;
'S cha bhath uisge no saile mi;
'S mi fo chomraig Naoimh Moire
'S mo chaomh mhuime, Brighde.

THE GENEALOGY OF ST. BRIDGET OR ST. BRIDE,
FOSTER-MOTHER OF CHRIST.

St. Bridget, the daughter of Dùghall Donn,
Son of Hugh, son of Art, son of Conn.
Each day and each night
I will meditate on the genealogy of St. Bridget.
[Whereby] I will not be killed,
I will not be wounded,

Figure 31 *Evergreen* 2 (autumn 1895), p. 123.

Figure 32 *Evergreen* 1 (spring 1895), p. 27.

WHAT IF
THE CITY
FAILS
TO WORK

ALI
MILLAR

41

Figure 33 *Evergreen: A New Season in the North* 2 (2015), p. 41. © Word Bank.

Figure 34 Front cover *Pageant* 2 (1897).

Figure 35 *Pageant* 1 (1896), p. 17.

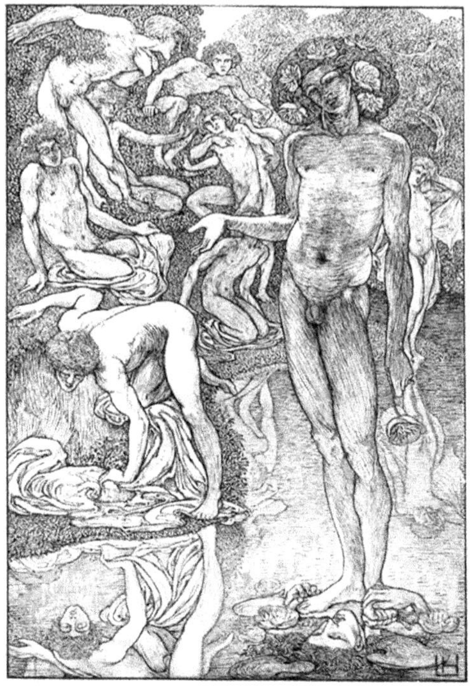

Figure 36 *Pageant* 1 (1896), p. 199.

THE PARADE
AN ILLUSTRATED
GIFT BOOK FOR
BOYS AND GIRLS
1897

LONDON H. HENRY AND CO. LTD.
93 ST. MARTIN'S LANE W.C. 1897

Figure 37 Title page *Parade* (1897).

Figure 38 Endpapers *Parade* (1897).

Figure 39 *Parade* (1897), p. 67.

ALL HER OWN COURT . . . SHRIEKED WITH LAUGHTER AT HER QUEER FACE AND DID NOT KNOW HER

PRINCE·TOTO

To My Little Son. By John Oliver Hobbes.

THIS is the story of Prince Toto, who thought everything hideous and everybody ugly. If any one said to him, 'Look at the sun sparkling on the sea,' he would say, 'Don't be silly'; and when his mother, the Queen, would say, 'Come and sit with me under this beautiful rose-bush,' he would get irritable, and reply, 'I would as soon see a radish as a rose!' It was impossible to please him. This was a great sorrow to his parents, the King and Queen of the fairies, because there were few fairies left on the earth, and they did not wish the last of them to seem so disagreeable. The King and whole court wondered what they could do to cure Prince Toto.

Copyright in the United States of America, 1896, by Pearl Mary Craigie. 3

Figure 40 *Parade* (1897), pp. 2–3.

Of Frozen Music

It is true that under these Northern skies of ours her stones are nearly always icy cold; but this poor one is the only reason for naming Architecture "Frozen Music." It were as good, or rather as barren, a saying, that Music is Architecture false to her vow of silence.

C. H. Enston.

Figure 41 *Dome* 2 (June 1897), pp. 20–1.

Bibliography

Primary sources

'A House of Pomegranates', *Pall Mall Gazette* (30 November 1891), p. 3.

'A Memorandum for Collectors', *Dome* 1 (1897), p. 88.

'Art and Poetry', *Guardian* (28 August 1850), p. 623.

'Books of the Week', *The Times* (Thursday, 30 January 1896), p. 8.

'Book-Song', *The Library: Transactions of the Bibliographical Society* 1 (1894), p. 117.

'Christmas Books. Final Notice', *Guardian* (Saturday, 3 December 1904), p. 5.

'Dullness in Yellow', *National Observer* (18 August 1894), p. 359.

'Editorial Note', *Savoy* 1 (January 1896), n.p.

'Foreword', *Pageant* 2 (1897), n.p.

'Interview: Gertrude Hammond', *Woman's Herald* (10 January 1891), pp. 177–8.

'Messrs. G. Napier and Company', *Quest* 3 (July 1895), n.p.

'Messrs. Henry's Announcements', *The Times* (Thursday, 3 December 1896), p. 12.

'Notices', *Guardian* (10 February 1897), pp. 232–4.

'Notions', *Pick-Me-Up* (1 February 1896), p. 13.

'Prospectus: *The Yellow Book* 1 (Apr. 1894)', Mark Samuels Lasner Collection, on loan to the University of Delaware Library, Newark, *The Yellow Nineties Online*, ed. Dennis Denisoff and Lorraine Janzen Kooistra (Ryerson University, 2011), <http://www.1890s.ca/HTML.aspx?s=YBV1_prospectus.html> (last accessed 28 June 2017).

'Some Illustrated Books', *Quest* 1 (November 1894), pp. 42–52.

'Some Illustrated Gift-books for Children and Others Published by Messr. H. Henry and Co., Ltd.', *Parade* (1897), n.p.

'Some Press Notices', *BLAST* 2 (1915), n.p.

'The Birmingham Guild of Handicraft', *Quest* 1 (November 1894), p. iii.

'The Century Guild of Artists', *Century Guild Hobby Horse* 1.1 (January 1886), n.p.

'The Century Guild Work', *Century Guild Hobby Horse* 1 (April 1884), n.p.

'The Chronicle of Art: December 1889', *Magazine of Art* (January 1890), pp. x–xv.

'The Yellow Book, An Illustrated Quarterly', *The Times* (Friday, 20 April 1894), p. 3.

'Two Children's Books', *Spectator* (5 December 1896), pp. 8–9.

'Yellow Book', *Westminster Gazette* (18 April 1894), p. 3.

[Allen, Grant?], 'The Century Guild Hobby Horse', *Bibliographer* 6.2 (July 1884), pp. 51–2.

Anderson, Margaret, *My Thirty Years' War* (London: Alfred Knopf, 1930).

Authors of 'The Evolution of Sex', the [Patrick Geddes and John Arthur Thomson], 'The Moral Evolution of Sex', *Evergreen* 3 (Summer 1896), pp. 73–88.

Baring, Maurice, 'The Nineties', *Lost Lectures* (Leipzig: Tauchnitz, 1931).

Beerbohm, Max, 'A Defence of Cosmetics', *Yellow Book* 1 (April 1894), pp. 65–82.

Beerbohm, Max, 'Be It Cosiness', *Pageant* 2 (1897), pp. 230–5.

Beerbohm, Max, 'Letter to the Editor', *Yellow Book* 2 (July 1894), pp. 281–4.

Bennett, Arnold, 'The Literary Periodical', in *Books and Persons: Being Comments on a Past Epoch 1908–1911* (London: Chatto & Windus, 1917), pp. 242–8.

Branford, Victor and Patrick Geddes, 'Prefatory Note', *Evergreen* 2 (Autumn 1895), pp. 8–9.

Branford, Victor, 'A Series of Remarks', *New Evergreen* (December 1894), p. 33.

Brooks, W. H. [William Sharp], 'Forecast', *Pagan Review* (August 1892), pp. 63–4.

Brooks, W. H. [William Sharp], 'Foreword', *Pagan Review* (August 1892), pp. 1–4.

[Burne-Jones, Edward], 'Essay on *The Newcomes*', *Oxford and Cambridge Magazine* 1 (January 1856), pp. 50–61.

[Burne-Jones, Edward and William Morris?], 'Ruskin and the Quarterly', *Oxford and Cambridge Magazine* 6 (June 1856), pp. 353–61.

Burne-Jones, Georgiana, *Memorials of Edward Burne-Jones* (London: Lund Humphries, 1993).

Christie, Nimmo, 'Between the Ages', *Evergreen* 4 (Winter 1896), pp. 61–2.

Corbeille, L. A. [Ernest J. Oldmeadow], 'Utrecht Cathedral', *Dome* 2 (June 1897), pp. 13–16.

Crackanthorpe, Hubert, 'Reticence in Literature: Some Roundabout Remarks', *Yellow Book* 2 (July 1894), pp. 259–74.

Craig, Edward Gordon, 'Foreword', *Nothing or the Bookplate* (London: Chatto & Windus, 1925), n.p.

Crane, Walter, *Of the Decorative Illustration of Books Old and New* (London: George Bell, 1905).

Dixon, Arthur, 'Manufacture and Handicraft, with Some Account of the Guild of Handicraft in Birmingham', *Quest* 2 (March 1895), pp. 25–30.

Dreeme, Willand [William Sharp], 'The Pagans: A Memory', *Pagan Review* (August 1892), pp. 20–8.
Dyer, Louis, 'A New Fount of Greek Types', *Hobby Horse* 3 (July 1893), pp. 83–96.
Enston, C. H. [Ernest Oldmeadow?], '"Frozen Music": Fifty Words', *Dome* 2 (June 1897), p. 20.
G. W. [J. W. Gleeson White], 'Preface', *Parade* (1897), n.p.
G. W. [J. W. Gleeson White], 'To Richard Le Gallienne', in J. W. Gleeson White (ed.), *Book-Song* (London: Elliot Stock, 1893), n.p.
Galton, Arthur, 'Some Letters of Matthew Arnold', *Century Guild Hobby Horse* (April 1890), pp. 47–55.
Gascoigne, Geo. [William Sharp], 'The Coming of Love', *Pagan Review* (August 1892), p. 19.
Geddes, Patrick, *Cities in Evolution: An Introduction to the Town Planning Movement and to the Study of Civics* (New York: Harper & Row, 1968).
Geddes, Patrick, 'Flower of the Grass', *Evergreen* 3 (Summer 1896), pp. 43–67.
Geddes, Patrick, 'Life and Its Science', *Evergreen* 1 (Spring 1895), pp. 29–38.
Geddes, Patrick, 'The Scots Renascence', *Evergreen* 1 (Spring 1895), pp. 131–40.
Geddes, Patrick, 'The Sociology of Autumn', *Evergreen* 2 (Autumn 1895), pp. 27–38.
Geddes, Patrick and William Macdonald, 'Envoy', *Evergreen* 4 (Winter 1896), pp. 155–6.
Geddes, Patrick and John Arthur Thomson, *The Evolution of Sex* (London: Walter Scott, 1889).
Gleeson White [Joseph Gleeson White], 'At the Sign of the Dial: Mr. Ricketts as a Book-Builder', *Magazine of Art* (January 1897), pp. 304–9.
Gleeson White, J. W., *Children's Books and Their Illustrators*, *Studio*, special issue (Winter 1897–8).
Gleeson White, J. W., 'The Work of Charles Ricketts', *Pageant* 1 (1896), pp. 79–93.
Hamerton, P. G., 'Picture Buying', in *Thoughts About Art* (London: Macmillan, 1873), pp. 125–43.
Hamerton, P. G., 'The Yellow Book: A Criticism of Volume I', *Yellow Book* 2 (July 1894), pp. 179–94.
Herrick, Robert, 'I Call, I Call', *Parade* (1897), pp. 62–3.
Holme, Charles, 'Reviews and Notices: The *Page*', *Dome* New Series 2.3 (March 1899), pp. 167–70.
Horne, Herbert P., 'A Preface', *Century Guild Hobby Horse* (January 1889), pp. 1–8.
[Horne, Herbert?], 'Contemporary Notes', *Century Guild Hobby Horse* (October 1889), pp. 176–8.
Horne, Herbert P., 'Some Considerations on the Nature of Fine Art', *Century Guild Hobby Horse* (July 1891), pp. 83–92.

Horne, Herbert, 'The Century Guild', *Art Journal* (September 1887), pp. 297–300.

Housman, Laurence, 'The Enchanted Princess', *Parade* (1897), pp. 64–93.

Housman, Laurence, *The Unexpected Years* (London: Jonathan Cape, 1937).

Image, Selwyn, 'A Lecture on Art: Delivered in London in December 1882', *Century Guild Hobby Horse* (April 1884), pp. 34–70.

Image, Selwyn, 'A Ternary of Reflections', *Hobby Horse* 2 (April 1893), pp. 40–5.

Image, Selwyn, 'From a Secondhand Bookstall', *Century Guild Hobby Horse* (October 1889), pp. 122–5.

Image, Selwyn, 'Of Criticism and the Critic', *Savoy* 1 (January 1896), pp. 141–5.

Image, Selwyn, 'On the Unity of Art', *Century Guild Hobby Horse* (January 1887), pp. 2–8.

Image, Selwyn, 'Three Notes on Art: II. On the Theory that Art Should Represent the Surrounding Life', *Century Guild Hobby Horse* (January 1886), pp. 13–16.

Image, Selwyn, 'Three Notes on Art: III. On Nature and Art', *Century Guild Hobby Horse* (January 1886), pp. 16–18.

James, Henry, 'London', in *English Hours* (London: Heinemann, 1905), pp. 1–43.

James, Henry, 'The Death of the Lion', *Yellow Book* 1 (April 1894), pp. 7–56.

Jepson, Edgar, *Memoirs of a Victorian*, vol. 1 (London: Gollancz, 1933).

Klein, Félix (Abbé), 'La Dilèttantisme', *Evergreen* 2 (Autumn 1895), pp. 83–8.

[Lane, John], *Aubrey Beardsley and the Yellow Book* (London: Bodley Head, 1903).

Le Gallienne, Richard, 'Confessio Amantis, A Sonnet', in *Limited Editions, A Prose Fancy* (London: The Bodley Head, 1893), n.p.

Le Gallienne, Richard, *The Romantic '90s* (New York: Doubleday, Page, 1925).

Lethaby, William, 'Arts and the Function of Guilds', *Quest* 6 (July 1896), pp. 98–105.

Lewis, Wyndham, 'The Art of the Great Race', *BLAST* 2 (1915), pp. 70–2.

Macdonald, William and John Arthur Thomson, 'Proem', *Evergreen* 1 (Spring 1895), pp. 9–16.

Mackmurdo, A. H, 'Forenoon Echoes of Love's Evensong', *Century Guild Hobby Horse* (April 1884), pp. 71–94.

Mackmurdo, Arthur, 'Century Guild Notes', *Century Guild Hobby Horse* (April 1884), pp. 99–104.

Macleod, Fiona [William Sharp], 'Day and Night', *Evergreen* 1 (Spring 1895), pp. 47–8.

Mallarmé, Stéphane, 'Quant au Livre: Le Livre, Instrument Spirituel', in *Œuvres complètes*, ed. Georges Jean-Aubry and Henri Mondor (Paris: Gallimard, 1945), pp. 369–82.

MCG [Arthur Mackmurdo], 'The Guild's Flag Unfurling', *Century Guild Hobby Horse* (April 1884), pp. 2–13.

Moréas, Jean, 'Le Symbolisme', *Figaro*, 'Supplément littéraire' (18 September 1886), pp. 1–2.

[Morris, William], 'The Story of the Unknown Church', *Oxford and Cambridge Magazine* 1 (January 1856), pp. 28–33.

Morris, William, *An Address Delivered by William Morris at the Distribution of Prizes to Students of the Birmingham Municipal School of Art on February 21, 1984* (London: Longmans, 1898).

Morris, William, 'Preface', in John Ruskin, *The Nature of Gothic* (London: Kelmscott Press, 1892), pp. i–v.

Morris, William, 'The Ideal Book', in *The Ideal Book: Essays and Lectures on the Arts of the Book*, ed. William Peterson (Berkeley: University of California Press, 1982), pp. 67–73.

Morris, William, 'The Influence of Building Materials upon Architecture', *Century Guild Hobby Horse* (January 1892), pp. 1–14.

Morris, William, 'The Revival of Handicraft', *Fortnightly Review* 44.2 (November 1888), pp. 603–10.

Napier-Clavering, Claude, 'Fine Feathers and Fine Birds', *Quest* 2 (March 1895), pp. 48–53.

Nordau, Max, *Degeneration* (New York: Appleton, 1895).

[Oldmeadow, Ernest J.], 'Introit', *Dome* 1 New Series (December 1898), n.p.

[Oldmeadow, Ernest J.], 'The Master-Builder', *Dome* 1 New Series (October 1898), pp. 1–4.

[Oldmeadow, Ernest J.], 'Review: *The Dome*', *Dome* 1 (March 1897), pp. 101–3.

Pater, Walter, 'The School of Giorgione', in *Studies in the History of the Renaissance* (London: Macmillan, 1900), pp. 130–54.

Purcell, Edward, 'Of Purple Jars', *Pageant* 2 (1897), pp. 198–221.

Radford, Dollie [Caroline Maitland], 'A Song', *Yellow Book* 6 (July 1895), pp. 121–2.

[Ricketts, Charles?], 'Apology', *Dial* 1 (1889), p. 36.

[Ricketts, Charles?], 'The Unwritten Book', *Dial* 2 (1892), pp. 25–8.

Ricketts, Charles, *A Bibliography of Books Issued by Hacon and Ricketts* (London: Vale Press, 1904).

Ricketts, Charles, 'A Note on Original Wood Engraving', *Pageant* 2 (1897), pp. 253–66.

[Rossetti, Dante Gabriel], 'Hand and Soul', *Germ* 1 (January 1850), pp. 23–33.

Rossetti, Dante Gabriel, 'I. St. Luke the Painter', in *Collected Poems and Prose*, ed. Jerome McGann (New Haven: Yale University Press, 2003), p. 160.

Rossetti, Dante Gabriel, 'Sonnet on the Sonnet', in *Collected Poems and Prose*, ed. Jerome McGann (New Haven: Yale University Press, 2003), p. 127.

Rossetti, William Michael, *Life of John Keats* (London: Walter Scott, 1887).

Ruskin, John, *The Nature of Gothic* (London: Kelmscott Press, 1892).

Salt, Cecil E., 'University Hall', *British Medical Journal* (28 April 1894), pp. 942–3.

Saroléa, Charles, 'La Littérature Nouvelle en France', *Evergreen* 1 (Spring 1895), pp. 92–7.

Sharp, William, 'Dedicatory Note', in *Romantic Ballads and Poems of Phantasy* (London: Walter Scott, 1888), pp. i–xiii.

[Sharp, William], 'Forecast', *Pagan Review* (August 1892), pp. 63–4.

Sharp, William, 'Section IX. Life: July–December, 1892', *The William Sharp 'Fiona Macleod' Archive*, ed. William F. Halloran, <http://www.ies.sas.ac.uk/sites/default/files/files/Research%20Projects/Fiona%20McLeod%20Archive/1892b.pdf> (last accessed 27 June 2017).

Shaw, Bernard, *The Perfect Wagnerite: A Commentary on the Ring of the Niblungs* (London: Grant Richards, 1898).

Shaw, G. Bernard, 'On Going to Church', *Savoy* 1 (January 1896), pp. 13–28.

Sleigh, Bernard, 'Memoirs of Bernard Sleigh', in Maureen Watry, *The Vale Press: Charles Ricketts, a Publisher in Earnest* (London: British Library, 2004), pp. 247–50.

Sonnenschein, E. A., 'The Platonic Theory of Art', *Quest* 1 (November 1894), pp. 26–30.

[Symons, Arthur], 'Editorial Note', *Savoy* 7 (November 1896), n.p.

Symons, Arthur, 'Causerie: By Way of Epilogue', *Savoy* 8 (December 1896), pp. 91–2.

Symons, Arthur, 'In the Vale of Llangollen', *London Nights* (London: Leonard Smithers, 1896), pp. 29–30.

Symons, Arthur, 'The Decadent Movement in Literature', *Harper's New Monthly Magazine* 87 (November 1893), pp. 858–69.

Thomson, John Arthur, 'Germinal, Florial, Prairial', *Evergreen* 1 (Spring 1895), pp. 21–7.

Thomson, John Arthur, 'The Biology of Autumn', *Evergreen* 2 (Autumn 1894), pp. 9–20.

Verlaine, Paul, 'Monna Rosa', *Pageant* 1 (1896), pp. 14–16.

Waugh, Arthur, 'Reticence in Literature', *Yellow Book* 1 (April 1894), pp. 201–23.

Wells, H. G., 'Bio-Optimism', in *Early Writings in Science and Science-Fiction*, ed. Robert M. Philmus and David Y. Hughes (Berkeley: University of California Press, 1975), pp. 206–10.

Wilde, Oscar, *The Picture of Dorian Gray*, ed. Joseph Bristow (Oxford: Oxford University Press, 2008).

Wells, H. G., 'Zoological Retrogression', *Gentleman's Magazine* 271.9 (September 1891), pp. 246–53.

Williams, Raymond, *Marxism and Literature* (Oxford: Oxford University Press, 1985).

Woolf, Virginia, *Mr. Bennett and Mrs. Brown* (London: Hogarth Press, 1924).

Wordsworth, John, 'John Wordsworth on Pater's Philosophy', in R. M. Seiler (ed.), *Walter Pater: The Critical Heritage* (London: Routledge, 1995), pp. 61–3.

Yeats, William Butler, 'The Lake Isle of Innisfree', in *The Countess Kathleen and Various Legends and Lyrics* (London: Roberts Bros, 1892), p. 121.
Yeats, William Butler, 'The Trembling of the Veil', in *Autobiographies* (London: Macmillan, 1956), pp. 109–286.
Zangwill, Israel, 'Edinburgh', in *Without Prejudice* (London: T. Fisher Unwin, 1896), pp. 289–94.

Secondary sources

Adamson, Walter L., *Embattled Avant-Gardes: Modernism's Resistance to Commodity Culture in Europe* (Berkeley: University of California Press, 2007).
Adorno, Theodor, *Aesthetic Theory*, trans. Robert Hullot-Kentor (London: Continuum, 1997).
Adorno, Theodor and Max Horkheimer, *Dialectic of Enlightenment*, trans. John Cumming (New York: Herder & Herder, 1972).
Alaya, Flavia, *William Sharp – 'Fiona Macleod': 1855–1905* (Cambridge, MA: Harvard University Press, 1970).
Arnar, Anna Sigrídur, *The Book as Instrument: Stéphane Mallarmé, The Artist's Book, and the Transformation of Print Culture* (Chicago: University of Chicago Press, 2011).
Carter, John and Nicolas Barker, *ABC for Book Collectors* (New Castle, DE/London: Oak Knoll Press/British Library, 2004).
Barnes, Martin, 'Hollyer, Frederick', in John Hannavay (ed.), *Encyclopedia of Nineteenth-Century Photography* (London: Routledge, 2008), pp. 710–12.
Beckson, Karl, *Arthur Symons: A Life* (Oxford: Oxford University Press, 1987).
Beckson, Karl (ed.), *Oscar Wilde: The Critical Heritage* (London: Routledge, 2005).
Beegan, Gerry, 'The *Studio*: Photomechanical Reproduction and the Changing Status of Design', *Design Issues* 23.4 (Autumn 2007), pp. 46–64.
Beetham, Margaret, 'Magazines', in Laurel Brake and Marysa Demoor (eds), *Dictionary of Nineteenth-Century Journalism in Great Britain and Ireland* (London/Ghent: British Library/Academia Press, 2009), pp. 391–2.
Berman, Avis, 'Whistler and the Printed Page: The Artist as Book Designer', *American Art* 9.2 (Summer 1995), pp. 63–87.
Binckes, Faith, *Modernism, Magazines and the British Avant-Garde: Reading Rhythm, 1910–1914* (Oxford: Oxford University Press, 2010).
Bishop, Edward, 'Re:Covering Modernism – Format and Function in the Little Magazines', in Ian Willison, Warwick Gould and Warren Chernaik (eds), *Modernist Writers and the Marketplace* (Houndmills: Macmillan, 1996), pp. 287–319.
Blaikie-Murdoch, W. G., *The Renaissance of the Nineties* (London: De La More Press, 1911).

Boos, Florence S., '"A Holy Warfare against the Age": Essays and Tales of the *Oxford and Cambridge Magazine*', *Victorian Periodicals Review* 47.3 (Autumn 2014), pp. 344–468.

Booth, Michael R., 'Terry, Ellen', in H. C. G. Matthew and Brian Harrison (eds), *Oxford Dictionary of National Biography* (Oxford: Oxford University Press, 2004). Online edn, ed. David Cannadine (May 2011), <http://www.oxforddnb.com/view/article/36460> (last accessed 28 June 2017).

Bourdieu, Pierre, *The Field of Cultural Production*, ed. and trans. Randal Johnson (Cambridge: Polity Press, 1993).

Boyiopoulos, Kostas, *The Decadent Image: The Poetry of Wilde, Symons and Dowson* (Edinburgh: Edinburgh University Press, 2015).

Boyiopoulos, Kostas, Yoonjoung Choi and Matthew Brinton Tildesley (eds), *The Decadent Short Story: An Annotated Anthology* (Edinburgh: Edinburgh University Press, 2014).

Boyiopoulos, Kostas and Mark Sandy, 'Introduction: Decadent Romantics, Romantic Decadents', in Kostas Boyiopoulos and Mark Sandy (eds), *Decadent Romanticism: 1780–1914* (London: Routledge, 2015), pp. 1–14.

Bradley, Sean, 'Introduction', *The Evergreen: A New Season in the North* 1 (2014), pp. 7–10.

Brake, Laurel, 'Endgames: The Politics of the *Yellow Book*, or, Decadence, Gender and the New Journalism', in Laurel Brake (ed.), *The Ending of Epochs* (Cambridge: D. S. Brewer, 1995), pp. 65–88.

Brake, Laurel, '"Gay Discourse" and the *Artist and Journal of Home Culture*', in Laurel Brake, Bill Bell and David Finkelstein (eds), *Nineteenth-Century Media and the Construction of Identities* (Basingstoke: Palgrave Macmillan, 2000), pp. 271–94.

Brake, Laurel, 'Marketing Notoriety: Advertising the *Savoy*', in *Print in Transition: Studies in Media and Book History* (London: Palgrave Macmillan, 2001), pp. 171–80.

Brake, Laurel, 'Pater, Symons and the Culture of the Fin de Siècle in Britain', in *Print in Transition: Studies in Media and Book History* (London: Palgrave Macmillan, 2001), pp. 268–82.

Briggs, Asa, *Victorian Cities* (Harmondsworth: Penguin, 1970).

Brooker, Peter and Andrew Thacker (eds), *The Oxford Critical and Cultural History of Modernist Magazines*, 3 vols (Oxford: Oxford University Press, 2009–13).

Budke, Leah, 'Reading Edith Sitwell's Annual Poetry Anthology *Wheels* Through the Lens of Female Aestheticism', *English Literature in Transition 1880–1920* 61.2 (2018), pp. 232–49.

Bürger, Peter, *Theory of the Avant-Garde*, trans. Michael Shaw (Minneapolis: University of Minnesota Press, 1984).

Carruthers, Anne, *The Arts and Crafts Movement in Scotland: A History* (New Haven: Yale University Press, 2013).

Chan, Winnie, *The Economy of the Short Story in British Periodicals of the 1890s* (Abingdon: Routledge, 2007).

Claes, Koenraad, 'Supplements and Paratext: The Rhetoric of Space', *Victorian Periodicals Review* 43.2 (Summer 2010), pp. 196–210.

Codell, Julie, '*The Century Guild Hobby Horse*: 1884–1894', *Victorian Periodicals Review* 16.2 (Summer 1983), pp. 43–53.

Cohen, Philip K., 'Richard Le Gallienne's *The Book-Bills of Narcissus*: An Account Rendered', in Jonathan Allison (ed.), *Bound for the 1890s: Essays and Writing and Publishing in Honor of James G. Nelson* (High Wycombe: Rivendale Press, 2006), pp. 89–118.

Coleman, B. I., *The Idea of the City in Nineteenth-Century Britain* (London: Routledge & Kegan Paul, 1973).

Corbett, David Peters, 'Symbolism in British "Little Magazines": *The Dial* (1889–97), *The Pageant* (1896–7), and *The Dome* (1897–1900)', in Peter Brooker and Andrew Thacker (eds), *The Oxford Critical and Cultural History of Modernist Magazines. Volume 1: Britain and Ireland 1880–1955* (Oxford: Oxford University Press, 2009), pp. 101–19.

Crackanthorpe, David, *Hubert Crackanthorpe and English Realism in the 1890s* (Columbia: University of Missouri Press, 1977).

Craig, Edward, *Gordon Craig: The Story of His Life* (London: Gollancz, 1968).

Crawford, Alan, 'The Birmingham Setting', in Alan Crawford (ed.), *By Hammer and Hand: The Arts and Crafts Movement in Birmingham* (Birmingham: Birmingham Museums and Art Gallery, 1984), pp. 27–40.

Cumming, Elizabeth, *Hand, Heart and Soul: The Arts and Crafts Movement in Scotland* (Edinburgh: Birlinn, 2013).

Darcy, Cornelius P., 'The *Dome*', in Alvin Sullivan (ed.), *British Literary Magazines: The Victorian and Edwardian Age, 1837–1913* (Westport: Greenwood Press, 1984), pp. 116–19.

de Gourmont, Remy, *Les Petites Revues: Essai de Bibliographie* (Paris: Librairie du Mercure de France, 1900).

Delaney, Paul, *Charles Ricketts: A Biography* (Oxford: Clarendon Press, 1990).

Demoor, Marysa, 'In the Beginning, There Was *The Germ*: Pre-Raphaelites and the "Little Magazine"', in Peter Brooker and Andrew Thacker (eds), *The Oxford Critical and Cultural History of Modernist Magazines. Volume 1: Britain and Ireland 1880–1955* (Oxford: Oxford University Press, 2009), pp. 51–68.

Denisoff, Dennis, 'The Dissipating Nature of Decadent Paganism from Pater to Yeats', *Modernism/Modernity* 15.3 (2008), pp. 431–46.

Derrida, Jacques, *The Truth in Painting*, trans. Geoff Bennington and Ian McLeod (Chicago: University of Chicago Press, 1987).

Diedrick, James Keith, 'Dark Blue', in Laurel Brake and Marysa Demoor (eds), *Dictionary of Nineteenth Century Journalism* (London/Ghent: British Library/Academia Press, 2009), p. 161.

Dowling, Linda, 'Letterpress and Picture in the Literary Periodicals of the 1890s', *The Yearbook of English Studies 16* (1986), pp. 117–31.

Dowling, Linda, *The Vulgarization of Art: The Victorians and Aesthetic Democracy* (Charlottesville: University of Virginia Press, 1996).

Eburne, Jonathan P. and Rita Felski, 'Introduction', *What Is an Avant-Garde?*, special issue, *New Literary History* 41.4 (Autumn 2010), pp. v–xv.

Elliot, Elizabeth, 'Old-World Verse & Scottish Renascence: Flourishing Evergreen', *The Evergreen: A New Season in the North* 1 (2014), pp. 149–56.

Engen, Rodney, *Laurence Housman* (Stroud: Catalpa Press, 1983).

Felstiner, John, *The Lies of Art: Max Beerbohm's Parody and Caricature* (London: Gollancz, 1973).

Fleming, P. C., 'Oxford and Cambridge Magazine', *Rossetti Archive*, <http://www.rossettiarchive.org/docs/ap4.o93.raw.html> (last accessed 21 June 2017).

Fletcher, Ian, 'Decadence and the Little Magazines', in Ian Fletcher (ed.), *Decadence and the 1890s* (London: Edward Arnold, 1979), pp. 172–202.

Fletcher, Ian, *Rediscovering Herbert Horne: Poet, Architect, Typographer, Art Historian* (Greensboro: ELT Press, 1990).

Fletcher, Ian, 'Some Aspects of Aestheticism', in O. M. Brack (ed.), *Twilight of Dawn: Studies in English Literature in Transition* (Tucson: University of Arizona Press, 1987), pp. 1–33.

Frankel, Nicholas, 'James McNeill Whistler and the Politics of the Page', in *Masking the Text: Essays on Literature and Mediation in the 1890s* (High Wycombe: Rivendale Press, 2009), pp. 223–47.

Franklin, Colin, *Fond of Printing: Gordon Craig as Typographer & Illustrator* (London: Hurtwood Publications, 1980).

Freedman, Jonathan, *Professions of Taste: Henry James, British Aestheticism, and Commodity Culture* (Stanford: Stanford University Press, 1993).

Freeman, Nicholas, *Conceiving the City: London, Literature and Art 1870–1914* (Oxford: Oxford University Press, 2007).

Furbank, Philip Nicholas, *Mallarmé on Fashion: A Translation of the Fashion Magazine La Dernière Mode with Commentary* (Oxford: Berg, 2004).

Gagnier, Regenia, *The Insatiability of Human Wants: Economics and Aesthetics in Market Society* (Chicago: University of Chicago Press, 2000).

Gagnier, Regenia, 'Twenty-First-Century and Victorian Ecosystems: Nature and Culture in the Developmental Niche', *Victorian Review* 36.2 (Fall 2010), pp. 15–20.

Garbáty, Thomas Jay, 'The French Coterie of the *Savoy* 1896', *PMLA* 75.5 (December 1960), pp. 609–15.

Genette, Gérard, *Paratexts: Thresholds of Interpretation*, trans. Jane Lewin (Cambridge: Cambridge University Press, 1997).

Grainger, Hilary J., 'Mackmurdo, Arthur Heygate', in Joanna Banham (ed.), *Encyclopedia of Interior Design. Volume 2: M–Z* (Chicago: Fitzroy Dearborn, 1997), pp. 763–4.

Grilli, Elisa, 'Funding, Publishing, and the Making of Culture: The Case of the *Evergreen* (1895–1897)', *Journal of European Periodical Studies* 1.2

(2016), pp. 19–44, <http://dx.doi.org/10.21825/jeps.v1i2.2638> (last accessed 1 July 2017).

Groys, Boris, *The Total Art of Stalinism: Avant-garde, Aesthetic Dictatorship, and Beyond*, trans. Charles Rougle (Princeton: Princeton University Press, 1992).

Gwynn, Frederick L., *Sturge Moore and the Life of Art* (Lawrence: University of Kansas Press, 1951).

Hadjiafxendi, Kyriaki and John Plunkett, 'The Pre-history of the "Little Magazine"', in Peter Brooker and Andrew Thacker (eds), *The Oxford Critical and Cultural History of Modernist Magazines. Volume 1: Britain and Ireland 1880–1955* (Oxford: Oxford University Press, 2009), pp. 33–50.

Hastings, Selina, *The Secret Lives of Somerset Maugham* (London: John Murray, 2009).

Hatcher, John, *Laurence Binyon: Poet, Scholar of East and West* (Oxford: Oxford University Press, 1996).

Hoffman, Frederick J., Charles Allen and Carolyn F. Ulrich, *The Little Magazine: A History and a Bibliography* (Princeton: Princeton University Press, 1947).

Holmes, C. J., *Self & Partners (Mostly Self)* (London: Constable, 1936).

Horne, Herbert, *Alessandro Filipepi, Commonly Called Sandro Botticelli, Painter of Florence* (London: G. Bell, 1908).

Hosmon, Robert Stahr, 'Hobby Horse, the', in Alvin Sullivan (ed.), *British Literary Magazines: The Victorian and Edwardian Age, 1837–1913* (Westport: Greenwood Press, 1984), pp. 163–7.

Hosmon, Robert Stahr, 'Oxford and Cambridge Magazine, the', in Alvin Sullivan (ed.), *British Literary Magazines: The Victorian and Edwardian Age, 1837–1913* (Westport: Greenwood Press, 1984), pp. 294–302.

Houfe, Simon, *The Illustrators of the Nineties* (London: Barrie & Jenkins, 1992).

Howsam, Leslie, *Kegan Paul: A Victorian Imprint, Publishers, Books and Cultural History* (London: Routledge, 1999).

Hughes, Linda, 'Women Poets and Contested Spaces in the *Yellow Book*', *Studies in English Literature, 1500–1900* 44.4 (Autumn 2004), pp. 849–72.

Innes, Christopher, *Edward Gordon Craig* (Cambridge: Cambridge University Press, 1983).

Jackson, Holbrook, *The Eighteen Nineties: A Review of Art and Ideas at the Close of the Nineteenth Century* (London: Grant Richards, 1922).

Jackson, Holbrook, *The Printing of Books* (London: Cassell, 1938).

Jacobi, Charles, *On the Making and Issuing of Books* (London: Bodley Head, 1891).

Jensen, Robert, *Marketing Modernism in Fin-de-Siècle Europe* (Princeton: Princeton University Press, 1994).

Jones, Peter, *Industrial Enlightenment: Science, Technology and Culture in Birmingham and the West Midlands, 1760–1820* (Manchester: Manchester University Press, 2008).

Kane, Louise, '*To-day* Has Never Been "Highbrow": Middlebrow, Modernism and the Many Faces of *To-day*', in Kate Macdonald and Christoph Singer (eds), *Transitions in Middlebrow Writing, 1880–1930* (Basingstoke: Palgrave Macmillan, 2015), pp. 57–76.

King, Andrew, *The London Journal, 1845–83: Periodicals, Production and Gender* (Aldershot: Ashgate, 2004).

Köhler, Joachim, *Wagner's Hitler: The Prophet and His Disciple*, trans. Ronald Taylor (Cambridge: Polity Press, 2000).

Kooistra, Lorraine Janzen, 'A Modern Illustrated Magazine: The *Yellow Book*'s Poetics of Format', in Luisa Calè and Patrizia Di Bello (eds), *Illustrations, Optics and Objects in Nineteenth-Century Literary and Visual Cultures* (London: Palgrave Macmillan, 2010), pp. 128–46.

Kooistra, Lorraine Janzen, *Poetry, Pictures, and Popular Publishing: The Illustrated Gift Book and Victorian Visual Culture, 1855–1875* (Athens: Ohio University Press, 2011).

Kooistra, Lorraine Janzen, *The Artist as Critic: Bitextuality in Fin-de-Siècle Illustrated Books* (Aldershot: Scolar Press, 1995).

Kooistra, Lorraine Janzen, 'The Politics of Ornament: Remediation and/in the *Evergreen*', *ESC: English Studies in Canada* 41.1 (March 2015), pp. 105–28.

Lambert, J. W., *The Bodley Head: 1887–1987* (London: The Bodley Head, 1987).

Le Dantec, Y.-G., 'Notes et Variantes: Poèmes divers: "Monna Rosa"', in Paul Verlaine, *Œuvres Complètes* (Paris: Gallimard, 1962), p. 1038.

Ledbetter, Kathryn, *Tennyson and Victorian Periodicals: Commodities in Context* (London: Routledge, 2007).

LeMire, Eugene, 'Introduction', in William Morris, *The Hollow Land and Other Contributions to the Oxford and Cambridge Magazine* (Bristol: Thoemmes Press, 1996), pp. i–xxx.

MacCarthy, Fiona, *The Last Pre-Raphaelite: Edward Burne-Jones and the Victorian Imagination* (Cambridge, MA: Harvard University Press, 2012).

McCormack, Jerusha H., *John Gray: Poet, Dandy, Priest* (Hanover, NH: Brandeis University Press, 1991).

Macdonald, Kate, 'Buchan and the *Yellow Book*', in Kate Macdonald and Elizabeth Foxwell (eds), *John Buchan: A Companion to the Mystery Fiction* (Jefferson: McFarland, 2009), pp. 48–9.

McDonald, Peter D., *British Literary Culture and Publishing Practice, 1880–1914* (Cambridge: Cambridge University Press, 1997).

McGann, Jerome, 'Herbert Horne's *Diversi Colores* (1891): Incarnating the Religion of Beauty', in Joseph Bristow (ed.), *The Fin-de-Siècle Poem: English Literary Culture and the 1890s* (Athens: Ohio University Press, 2005), pp. 158–77.

McGann, Jerome, *The Textual Condition* (Princeton: Princeton University Press, 1991).

Mackail, John William, *The Life of William Morris*, vol. 1 (London: Longman, 1899).

McLean, Ruari, *Victorian Book Design and Colour Printing* (London: Faber & Faber, 1963).

MacLeod, Kirsten, *Fictions of British Decadence: High Art, Popular Writing, and the Fin de Siècle* (Basingstoke: Palgrave Macmillan, 2006).

McLuhan, Marshall, *Understanding Media: The Extensions of Man* (New York: McGraw Hill, 1964).

Mahoney, Kristin, 'Work, Lack, and Longing: Rossetti's "The Blessed Damozel" and the Working Men's College', *Victorian Studies* 52.2 (Winter 2010), pp. 219–48.

Maidment, Brian, 'George Allen', in Patricia J. Anderson and Jonathan Rose (eds), *British Literary Publishing Houses, 1820–1880. Dictionary of Literary Biography, Volume 106* (London: Gale, 1991), pp. 6–8.

Maidment, Brian, 'Influence, Presence, Appropriation – Ruskinian Periodicals 1890–1910', in Keith Hanley and Brian Maidment (eds), *Persistent Ruskin: Studies in Influence, Assimilation and Effect* (London: Ashgate, 2013), pp. 67–80.

Mallett, Phillip, 'The City and the Self', in Michael Wheeler (ed.), *Ruskin and Environment: The Storm-Cloud of the Nineteenth Century* (Manchester: Manchester University Press, 1995), pp. 38–57.

Maltz, Diane, *British Aestheticism and the Urban Working Classes, 1870–1900: Beauty for the People* (London: Palgrave, 2006).

Marsh, Jan, *Dante Gabriel Rossetti: Painter and Poet* (London: Phoenix, 2005).

Mavor, James, *My Windows on the Street of the World*, vol. 1 (London: J. M. Dent, 1923).

Meller, Helen, *Patrick Geddes: Social Evolutionist and City Planner* (London: Routledge, 1993).

Mendelsohn, Michèle, *Henry James, Oscar Wilde and Aesthetic Culture* (Edinburgh: Edinburgh University Press, 2007).

Miller, Elizabeth Carolyn, *Slow Print: Literary Radicalism and Late Victorian Print Culture* (Stanford: Stanford University Press, 2013).

Mitchell, Rebecca, 'The Century Guild Hobby Horse: Crafting Generic Networks in Fin-de-Siècle England', *Papers of the Bibliographic Society of America* 112.1 (March 2018), pp. 75–104.

Mix, Katherine, *A Study in Yellow: The Yellow Book and Its Contributors* (London: Constable, 1960).

Moore, Tara, *Victorian Christmas in Print* (Basingstoke: Palgrave Macmillan, 2009).

Nash, Andrew, 'The Kailyard: Problem or Illusion?', in Thomas Owen Clancy and Murray G. Pittock (eds), *The Edinburgh History of Scottish Literature: Volume 2, Enlightenment, Britain and Empire (1707–1918)* (Edinburgh: Edinburgh University Press, 2007), pp. 317–23.

Nelson, James G., *Elkin Mathews: Publisher to Yeats, Joyce, Pound* (Madison: University of Wisconsin Press, 1989).

Nelson, James G., *Publisher to the Decadents: Leonard Smithers in the Careers of Beardsley, Wilde, Dowson* (University Park: Pennsylvania State University Press, 2000).

Nelson, James G., *The Early Nineties: A View from the Bodley Head* (Cambridge, MA: Harvard University Press, 1971).

Peterson, William S., *The Kelmscott Press: A History of William Morris's Typographical Adventure* (Oxford: Clarendon Press, 1991).

Pittock, Murray, *Spectrums of Decadence: The Literature of the 1890s* (Abingdon: Routledge, 1993).

Pittock, Murray and Isla Jack, 'Patrick Geddes and the Celtic Revival', in Thomas Owen Clancy and Murray G. Pittock (eds), *The Edinburgh History of Scottish Literature: Volume 2, Enlightenment, Britain and Empire (1707–1918)* (Edinburgh: Edinburgh University Press, 2007), pp. 338–46.

Poggioli, Renato, *The Theory of the Avant-Garde*, trans. Gerald Fitzgerald (Cambridge, MA: Belknap Press, 1968).

Reynolds, Siân, *Paris-Edinburgh: Cultural Connections in the Belle Époque* (Aldershot: Ashgate, 2007).

Ricketts, Charles, *Michael Field*, ed. Paul Delaney (Edinburgh: Tragara Press, 1976).

Roberts, David, *The Total Work of Art in European Modernism* (Ithaca: Signale, 2011).

Rossetti, William Michael, 'Introduction', in *The Germ: Thoughts towards Nature in Poetry, Literature and Art; Being a Facsimile of the Literary Organ of the Pre-Raphaelite Brotherhood, Published in 1850* (London: Elliot Stock, 1901), pp. 5–30.

Rothenstein, William, *Men and Memories, Volume 1: 1872–1900* (London: Faber & Faber, 1931).

Sambrook, James, 'Dixon, Richard Watson (1833–1900)', in H. C. G. Matthew and Brian Harrison (eds), *Oxford Dictionary of National Biography* (Oxford: Oxford University Press, 2004). Online edn, ed. David Cannadine (May 2011), <http://www.oxforddnb.com/view/article/7704> (last accessed 22 June 2017).

Scholes, Robert and Clifford Wulfman, *Modernism in the Magazines: An Introduction* (New Haven: Yale University Press, 2010).

Scholnick, Robert J., *Edmund Clarence Stedman* (Boston: Twayne, 1977).

Seiler, Robert, *The Book Beautiful: Walter Pater and the House of Macmillan* (London: Bloomsbury, 1999).

Sharp, Elizabeth, *William Sharp (Fiona Macleod), a Memoir* (New York: Trow Press, 1910).

Shaw, Michael, 'Aestheticism and Decadence in Patrick Geddes's Socioeconomics', in Wendy Parkins (ed.), *Victorian Sustainability in Literature and Culture* (London: Routledge, 2017), pp. 165–79.

Smith, Matthew Wilson, *The Total Work of Art: From Bayreuth to Cyberspace* (London: Routledge, 2007).

Spinozzi, Paola and Elisa Bizzotto, *The Germ: Origins and Progenies of Pre-Raphaelite Interart Aesthetics* (Berlin: Peter Lang, 2012).

Stetz, Margaret, 'Pre-Raphaelitism's Farewell Tour: "Israfel" [Gertrude Hudson] Goes to India', in Thomas J. Tobin (ed.), *Worldwide Pre-Raphaelitism: Critical Theory, Popular Culture, Audiovisual Media* (Albany: SUNY Press, 2005), pp. 171–84.

Stetz, Margaret D., 'Sex, Lies, and Printed Cloth: Bookselling at the Bodley Head in the Eighteen-Nineties', *Victorian Studies* 35.1 (Autumn 1919), pp. 71–86.

Stetz, Margaret D. and Mark Samuels Lasner, *England in the 1890s: Literary Publishing at the Bodley Head* (Washington D. C.: Georgetown University Press, 1990).

Stetz, Margaret D. and Mark Samuels Lasner, *The Yellow Book: A Centenary Exhibition* (Cambridge, MA: Houghton Library, 1994).

Sturge Moore, Thomas, 'Preface', in Michael Field [Katherine Bradley and Edith Cooper], *A Selection from the Poems of Michael Field* (London: The Poetry Bookshop, 1923), pp. 11–17.

Sumpter, Caroline, *The Victorian Press and the Fairy Tale* (Basingstoke: Palgrave Macmillan, 2008).

Sutton, Emma, *Aubrey Beardsley and British Wagnerism in the 1890s* (Oxford: Oxford University Press, 2002).

Symons, Arthur, 'Mallarmé', in *The Symbolist Movement in Literature* (New York: E. P. Dutton, 1919), pp. 180–203.

Szeemann, Harald, *Der Hang zum Gesamtkunstwerk* (Arau: Sauerländer, 1983).

Tarr, Rodger L., 'Editions', in Mark Cumming (ed.), *The Carlyle Encyclopedia* (Madison: Fairleigh Dickinson University Press, 2004), pp. 140–1.

Wagner, Richard, 'The Artwork of the Future', in *Prose Works*, vol. 1, trans. William Ashton Ellis (London: Kegan Paul, Trench, Trubner, 1895), pp. 69–214.

Wald, James, 'Periodicals and Periodicity', in Simon Eliot and Jonathan Rose (eds), *A Companion to the History of the Book* (Oxford: Blackwell, 2007), pp. 412–33.

Waller, Philip, *Writers, Readers and Reputations: Literary Life in Britain 1870–1918* (Oxford: Oxford University Press, 2006).

Waters, Bill, 'Book Illustration', in Alan Crawford (ed.), *By Hammer and Hand: The Arts and Crafts Movement in Birmingham* (Birmingham: Birmingham Museums and Art Gallery, 1984), pp. 85–96.

Watry, Maureen, *The Vale Press: Charles Ricketts, a Publisher in Earnest* (London: British Library, 2004).

Whitely, Jon, *Lucien Pissarro in England: The Eragny Press 1895–1914* (Oxford: Ashmolean Museum, 2011).

Wolfreys, Julian, *Writing London: The Trace of the Urban Text from Blake to Dickens* (Houndmills: Macmillan, 1998).

Index

Page numbers in *italics* refer to illustrations.

CPSIA information can be obtained
at www.ICGtesting.com
Printed in the USA
BVHW061554300620
582685BV00002B/11

9 781474 426220